EVERY PARENT'S
NIGHTMARE

EVERY PARENT'S NIGHTMARE

Jock Palfreeman and the true story
of his father's fight to save him
from a lifetime in a Bulgarian jail

BELINDA HAWKINS

Research assistance by Boryana Dzhambazova
Translations by Boryana Dzhambazova and Nadejda Collins

ALLEN&UNWIN
SYDNEY · MELBOURNE · AUCKLAND · LONDON

First published in 2013

Allen & Unwin
83 Alexander Street
Crows Nest NSW 2065
Australia
Phone: (61 2) 8425 0100
Email: info@allenandunwin.com
Web: www.allenandunwin.com

Cataloguing-in-Publication details are available
from the National Library of Australia
www.trove.nla.gov.au

ISBN 978 1 74237 985 2

Internal design by Lisa White
Maps by Ian Faulkner
Set in 11/16 pt Minion Pro by Bookhouse, Sydney
Printed and bound in Australia by Griffin Press

10 9 8 7 6 5 4 3 2 1

MIX
Paper from
responsible sources
FSC® C009448

The paper in this book is FSC® certified.
FSC® promotes environmentally responsible,
socially beneficial and economically viable
management of the world's forests.

CONTENTS

PART III   THE TRIAL

PART IV   THE FINAL VERDICT

In memory of my wonderful father,
Dr H Stuart Hawkins

MAP OF ST NEDELYA SQUARE CRIME SCENE

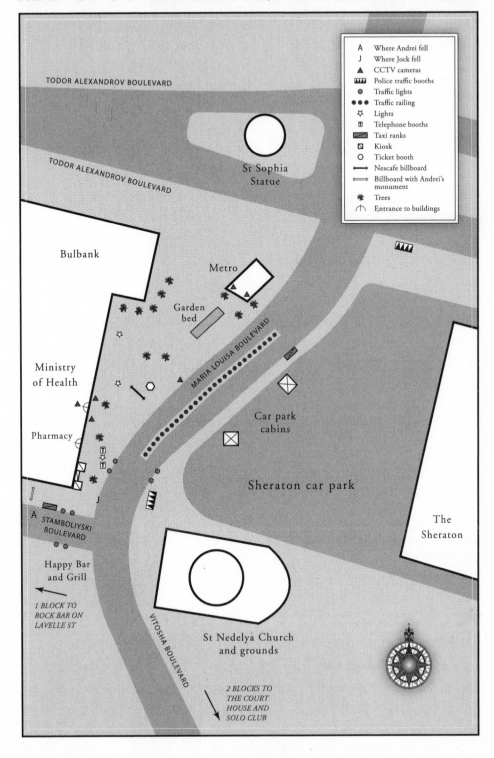

MAP OF BULGARIA

PROLOGUE

Jock's smiling face watches from a framed photograph as Dr Simon Palfreeman takes a new slide and peers down the microscope, searching for clues. The pathologist has been back in Australia for some time now and, at first glance, nothing about him has changed since he got the telephone call every parent dreads. Patient and methodical, he appears completely unflappable.

But away from the laboratory, Simon is living a nightmare. He is not alone. On the other side of the world there is a Bulgarian father named Hristo Monov, whose son, Andrei, was the same age as Jock. Despite the distance that separates them, both fathers are haunted by the same incident. Simon and Hristo have done well in their chosen professions. Their sons were popular and bright. Moreover, Jock and Andrei had every opportunity their parents could give them. Yet one late-December night their lives collided.

The year was 2007. Bulgaria had finally been accepted into the European Union after forty-five years behind the Iron Curtain and a difficult transition to a capitalist economy. Sitting at the gateway between east and west, the Balkan nation shares a border with Romania, Serbia, Macedonia, Greece and Turkey. Russia is not far away, across the Black Sea. Poor and corrupt, Bulgaria was a nation on probation.

Debate raged within the European Union about whether membership had been granted too hastily. Brussels waited to see if financial assistance and time would enable the Bulgarian government to improve public infrastructure and bring its law enforcement and justice system into line with European standards. Most Bulgarians knew they lived in a troubled country and were frustrated by the slow pace of change. But some regarded the EU's scrutiny as a slap in the face. Bulgarians are a proud people and they had already suffered generations of humiliation.

During its 1300-year-long history, Bulgaria had endured much foreign domination. When the Soviet-backed Communist Party resigned without bloodshed soon after the Berlin Wall came down in 1989, it seemed that Bulgaria could finally take pride in being an independent nation. Instead, things just got harder.

At football matches, in bars, on the trams and buses that carried commuters through the canyons of crumbling Soviet-style apartment blocks, people muttered that Bulgaria could be a great country if it could just get rid of its pestilences, which ranged from organised crime to Gypsy ghettos.

For some, the worst problems were holdovers from the Soviet era. The most common of these was cronyism. Getting admission to a university, a job, or justice, often depended as much on whom you knew as on your talent or the merits of your case. But Bulgaria's ills went far beyond influence peddling and rumour mongering.

Into the vacuum of authority had rushed mafia-style gangsters known as *mutri*, many of whom were sports figures who had moved into security businesses. Some were controlled by former Communist Party bosses and members of the state security apparatus who had become entrepreneurs and whose ventures ranged from racketeering to trafficking drugs, weapons and sex. All too often, taking care of business meant murdering rivals and anyone else who got in the way. People who wanted to get ahead joined in the corruption, among them judges and prosecutors. Shady figures haunted the streets in late-model Mercedes with black tinted windows. They were known by names such as the Godfather, the Doctor and the Beak.

For most people, the crooks were untouchable and cronyism was just part of life. It was much easier to blame outsiders. By 2001 public displays of extremist racism and nationalism were growing frequent. The chant was 'Bulgaria for Bulgarians'. Adolf Hitler's *Mein Kampf* was republished and sold like hot cakes, along with the writings of fascists and Holocaust deniers. In the 2005 election an extremist nationalist party called Ataka entered parliament.

Many turned their hatred upon Gypsies, whom they stereotyped as impoverished, dirty pickpockets, fringe dwellers who contributed nothing but trouble and strife. According to the 2007 census, Gypsies, also referred to as Roma, made up about one in twenty of Bulgaria's seven and a half million people. Unofficially it was estimated that the real figure was closer to ten per cent. They were, and continue to be, over-represented in prisons across the country.

In July 2007 the European Court of Human Rights chastised Bulgaria for failing to effectively pursue the alleged teenaged killers of a Gypsy. This was not the first time Bulgaria's human rights record had come under scrutiny, nor would it be the last. According to the Bulgarian Penal Code acts of racial or national intolerance are forbidden but the relevant article has seldom been applied.

The summer of 2007 was swelteringly hot. As temperatures rose across Bulgaria, so too did tempers. Although the country had entered the EU in January that year, the roads were still decrepit, the hospitals run-down, the courts too slow, the crooks at large. Bulgarian youth were especially restless. Something was going to snap.

In Sofia, there was an outbreak of violence between Gypsies and Bulgarian skinheads. The head of another extreme right-wing party called the Bulgarian National Union tried to form a citizens' militia to protect ethnic Bulgarians against Roma. After a night when skinheads brutally attacked Gypsies in a Roma quarter, one Gypsy was quoted as shouting 'Death to Bulgarians'.

On an oppressively hot August night, seventeen-year-old Asparuh Asenov was killed in the centre of Samokov, a town south of Sofia. Asenov was a Gypsy. That night, he and his friends had got into a fight with four young ethnic Bulgarians. In the melee, one of the Bulgarians had king-hit Asenov, who died from his injuries. This was not the first such death in recent years, and hundreds of Gypsies took to the streets of Samokov in protest.

Hristo Monov had followed the events that summer. The forty-nine-year-old psychology lecturer at Sofia University specialised in crises and disasters and had become the media's go-to man for comment on youth violence, particularly if it involved murder. Hristo wrote an opinion piece titled 'Gypsies versus Bulgarians: Two worlds on a knife edge', in which he referred to the death of Asparuh Asenov. According to him, the Samokov youths had been angry that Gypsies had ventured outside the town's Roma area. The psychologist had some sympathy for the ethnic Bulgarians, arguing that tragedies like that in Samokov were inevitable because young men working hard to get ahead were understandably sick of seeing Gypsies on welfare, driving their 'stinking horse-drawn carts on the streets of a European capital' where the Bulgarian youth hoped one day to drive 'nice cars'.

By December 2007, winter had set in and the violence subsided. But the underlying tensions remained. Walking through the centre of Sofia with his twenty-year-old son, Andrei, Hristo's mind was on Christmas shopping. But he was not looking at the goods on offer in shop windows; his eyes were glued to the footpath. You had to watch your step here to avoid the broken pavers, potholes, puddles and mud. Hristo did not know it, but his world was about to implode.

. . .

It was June 2008. Deep in concentration, I took a telephone call in one of ABC TV Melbourne's edit suites, where I was working on an episode of *Australian Story*. The editor and I were in a rush. We had a deadline to meet.

A young woman called Ash was on the line. She sounded anxious and upset. Her friend was in trouble in Bulgaria, she said. Was there any chance I could look into it?

'Maybe,' I said, distracted but intrigued. 'But who is the best person to speak to about what's happened?'

'His father,' she said. 'Dr Simon Palfreeman. But I doubt he'll talk to a journalist, and anyway I don't have his number.' All Ash could tell me was that Simon was a pathologist and that he had spent five months travelling back and forth to the Bulgarian capital, Sofia, trying to help his son Jock.

I hung up, thinking that was the last I would hear about the Palfreemans and Bulgaria.

But the call had stirred my curiosity. When I got home, I searched online for references to Jock Palfreeman. One news story after another flickered on my screen. The mystery surrounding Jock and Andrei snared me, and it wouldn't let go. I have children their age. This could have happened to them.

Generally, it takes me a couple of months at most to take a project from research to broadcast. After that, my notes go into a file and the cabinet drawer shuts. This case would be an exception. It has haunted me.

Over the next three years, I produced two documentaries for the ABC about the story. I then took a year off work to continue research in Australia, the United Kingdom and Bulgaria. I uncovered documents that had been suppressed or ignored, commissioned translations of court files and media reporting, and sifted through letters, CCTV recordings, television coverage and photographs, some of which were provided anonymously.

During the course of seven trips to Bulgaria and with help from a Sofia-based journalist, I tracked down and spoke with many people who had firsthand knowledge of the incident. They included those who were at the crime scene in the early hours of 28 December 2008, as well as those who played a role in the investigation and court proceedings that followed. I sat in on many of the court hearings. My reconstruction of dialogue which took place when I was not present is based on the recollections of at least one of those present at the time or on documentation in the court file. Quoted thoughts are also based on interviews. Descriptions of a subject's mannerisms and interaction are based on my observation of the subject. As much as possible, descriptions of locations are also from my own observation.

It is impossible to pin down exactly what happened on that late-December night in Sofia's St Nedelya Square. What happened over the next five years has been almost as chaotic. This story lays out what is known, and tries to piece together the facts about a tragedy that has shattered two families.

PART I
ST NEDELYA SQUARE

CHAPTER 1

December 2007
Sydney, Australia

Simon Palfreeman is tall and lightly built, straight-backed and fit. He has short fair hair and freckled skin that is slightly blotchy from the insidious sunspots of middle age. Every Christmas, Simon, his six siblings and their families gather at their mother's house in Mosman, a block away from the shore of Sydney Harbour. Simon's traditional job is to prepare the punch. It has to be child-friendly, with lots of fruit and no alcohol.

Christmas 2007 began in the usual way. Only three of the family were missing. Simon's sister Geri and her partner, Paul, lived in Bath, England. His eldest son, Jock, was travelling: this was the second Christmas he had missed.

Simon arrived with his two younger sons, his wife, Helen, and an armload of presents. A barrage of questions about Jock greeted them at the door.

'We think he might be with Geri this year,' Simon said as he moved through to the kitchen. 'He's got a week off training. He was even thinking of coming home.'

Simon's youngest son, Angus, looked a little wistful. At thirteen, Angus missed his big brother, who had been backpacking around Europe since he left school. Jock had turned twenty-one in November and was legendary in the extended family for sweeping in like a hot wind through an open door, gathering up young and old alike in the excitement of whatever fired him up at that moment. Big and strong, with a voice to match, he would fill the room with his laughter.

Barbara Palfreeman also missed Jock terribly. Her eldest grandchild had always been close to his paternal grandparents: his mother's parents had died before he got to know them. All Barbara wanted in life was to have her family together, safe and sound. Every year she made decorations out of photographs of the family members who could not make it for Christmas lunch. Jock's face now beamed among the twinkling lights on the Christmas tree.

'Signing up with the British Army,' said one of Simon's five sisters. 'I just cannot understand what possessed him to do that.'

Simon laughed. 'Who knows with Jock? But Geri says he is incredibly happy there, and I have to say for the first time we've actually been getting letters from him.'

Helen smiled. Four years younger than Simon, who was now fifty-two, she was a scientist and had met him at work. After Simon left Mary Jane, the mother of his children, the friendship between him and Helen had developed into a relationship. Several years later, they had married in a simple ceremony. Simon's three young sons had attended, dressed in suits. Soon after the wedding, Jock had moved in with the couple. He was fourteen, full of adolescent anger. His brothers continued living with Mary Jane but stayed with Simon on the weekends and at holidays.

Having no children of her own, Helen grew attached to her husband's. She enjoyed watching them grow up, especially Jock, who spent more time with Simon and her than the younger two. Helen had the invidious role of stepmother, neither in charge of Jock's upbringing nor unaffected by what happened to him. The teenager was a handful, and Helen hoped this trip away would mature and steady him. She could see why he wanted to be a soldier. He had loved the discipline and the hard work of rowing at school, even as he was rebelling against everything else there. And joining the British Army would let him stay longer in Europe.

'The main thing is Jock is settled and happy,' said Simon as he mixed the punch. 'Finally it actually looks like he might risk having a career other than wandering the world in search of another good time!' As the talk moved from Jock to plans for the rest of the Christmas holidays, Simon's mind wandered. He had nothing to worry about. His eldest was a survivor, streetwise. Wherever Jock was, he would be safe. For the first time in years, Simon felt quietly confident that Jock was on track. He could now turn his full attention to the younger boys.

A heat haze rose from the bitumen in the driveway. Along this middle-class street, other families were also ripping into wrapping paper and prawns, a ritual that signalled the start of yacht races, cricket tests and hot summer days.

Simon and Helen were looking forward to a much needed holiday. Two days later, they took Angus away with them for a short voyage on a friend's yacht.

. . .

Sofia, Bulgaria

A sprinkle of snow fell silently on St Nedelya Square as Viktor Georgiev rushed to work on Thursday 27 December. He had to get there in time to change into his navy-blue suit and black-and-navy tie. He often joked that the uniform made him look like a secret agent. But tonight Viktor was in no mood for frivolity. The church bells cut across the squabble of evening traffic that pushed its way along Maria Louisa Boulevard. The footpaths were slippery with slushy ice. Like most parts of Sofia the square was littered with broken and dislodged concrete pavers known as *plyueshti plochki* or *spitting stones* because when it rained or snowed they flicked water at anyone who walked on them. It was hard to get anywhere fast.

An elderly Gypsy man played a bittersweet melody on a violin at the entrance to the subway. As Viktor passed the kiosk that sold cigarettes and alcohol, he looked at his watch and picked up his pace. He was due at 8 p.m. and hated being late.

A young man in the square was selling *survachka*s, Bulgarian Christmas decorations made out of twigs from the cornel tree with wool and cotton fluff wound around their branches, forming a fan.

Viktor barely noticed the man. Instead he crossed the boulevard to the Sheraton hotel. Inside, he greeted his fellow security workers. For the second half of the night he would be stationed in the front car park.

The Sheraton sits right in the middle of Sofia, its neon sign blinking high above the streetlights. The hotel is modern and grand. The open-air car park is neither. In late 2007, guards sat in two makeshift cabins at the front of the car park that looked onto the boulevard and the square. Sheraton employees took money from drivers wanting to park. The job of security guards like Viktor was to ensure the safety of the hotel's property and its guests.

Behind the Sheraton sit Roman ruins and the fourth-century red-brick church of St George Rotunda, looking like crippled old women alongside the sleek hotel. On one side of the car park is St Nedelya Church, around which prostitutes ply their trade.

Viktor's companion on the bleak and bitterly cold 11 p.m. shift was the giant bronze-and-copper statue of St Sofia, after whom Bulgaria's capital is named. Holding the symbols of wisdom and fate, she faced the former headquarters of the Communist Party but kept watch over St Nedelya Square out of the corner of her eye.

Two months shy of twenty-one, Viktor was in the second year of an insurance degree and took his studies seriously. After eight months in this part-time job, he had had enough. It was boring. The hours dragged. The only point of interest was the late-night parade of revellers and drunks.

In Bulgaria, the period between Christmas and 6 January is known as *Mrusni Dai*, or Dirty Days. Viktor's mother and his grandmother had warned him to be extra careful. According to folklore, evil monsters and goblins come out at this time of the year to play tricks on people. As a Christian, Viktor knew he should dismiss such pagan nonsense. But he couldn't help wondering if the women in his family were onto something. *Whatever could go wrong*, Viktor thought, *will go wrong now.*

. . .

Jock Palfreeman was enjoying himself. Overall, it had been a great holiday, and he was glad he had decided to return to Bulgaria for Christmas with his British friends Grayham Saunders and Lindsay Welsh, rather than stay in the United Kingdom. The trio had been staying in Grayham's house in Madjare, a mountain village sixty kilometres from Sofia. But on the morning of 27 December, Jock had been tired and irritable. He had been to see his Bulgarian mates in Samokov and walked ten kilometres to get home again. It was bitterly cold. Jock had been sopping wet from the snow and, to top it off, a pack of dogs had attacked him. Once back in Madjare, he had just wanted to stay put.

When Grayham suggested they go to the capital, Jock had been dead against it. All that he loved about Bulgaria was here in the mountains, including his close friends. He had no desire to go anywhere else on this trip. Cities meant hassles, and Jock had seen enough violence in Bulgaria to want to steer clear of potential trouble spots. He had learnt the hard way to carry pepper spray if he thought he was going anywhere risky. In the past Jock had been able to buy it easily but this time he had not seen any in the shops around here.

But Grayham wanted Lindsay to have a night out in Sofia for her send-off celebration. Reluctantly, Jock agreed to go. Just as the three friends got in Grayham's rented Renault Clio, Jock remembered he had left his identification behind and ran back inside to get it. In this country, authorities had the right to demand proof of identity anywhere, anytime. Jock's Army ID card was sitting on the kitchen table next to Grayham's pocket knife; his passport was somewhere upstairs. The Army card would do.

On the drive to Sofia, they passed through villages of crumbling houses with their red-tiled roofs covered in snow. For a while Jock stared out the window. As always, Grayham was at the wheel. Jock did not have a licence, so he was no help on that front. He started to remove some of the badges he had pinned onto his black jacket, so as not to attract any unwanted attention. The first to go was the swastika with a cross through it. But he left in place the badge of a Celtic folk punk band called Flogging Molly and one of the Communist red star. He also left the large white one pinned across his back that he had bought in Sydney as a fifteen-year-old, when he helped a protestor who was being beaten by police at a Sydney May Day rally. On it were the words 'Capitalism or die' and a picture of police beating someone. The jacket itself had a story to tell. A Bulgarian skinhead had left it lying on the ground after Jock intervened to stop an attack on a young Roma man near Madjare the year before.

When they got to Sofia, Grayham took Jock and Lindsay to the Rock Bar, a small, dark place on a street that ran behind the courthouse. It was a five-minute walk from the hostel where they would stay overnight. They played good music there, heavy metal, not the Balkan–Turkish fusion called Chalga that was popular in Bulgaria. Jock encouraged the barman to put on AC/DC's 'Thunderstruck'. He was not homesick, but at the familiar sound of the repetitive guitar riff, he smiled and started singing.

Jock later estimated that he had five or six beers and a shot of tequila over the long evening. Lindsay drank a fair bit more.

At one stage he went down the spiral metal staircase to the restroom, which consisted of a toilet and a sink. An older man came out of the toilet and held a pistol to Jock's head, laughing menacingly. Jock looked at him but said nothing, and the man disappeared up the stairwell. Jock did not tell his friends what had happened, as he did not want to scare Lindsay, who was always a bit nervy. In any event, they were having a good time with some Bulgarians they had met in the bar. *Why wreck the atmosphere*, he thought.

Lindsay cut a striking figure, with her spiky, peroxide-blonde hair, multiple piercings and fluffy white jacket. She and Grayham had dated for a while and remained good friends. On this trip, they restarted their relationship. When Lindsay became tipsy and started flirting with a local, Grayham got annoyed and left for the hostel.

Jock became engrossed in conversation with a man who introduced himself as Tony. He had shoulder-length hair and a Union Jack stitched onto his jacket. His real name, which Jock would not learn until much later, was Anton Doychev. Tony was eighteen and still at school, but struck Jock as streetwise. Together they discussed the problems that the young Bulgarian had experienced just 'looking different'. Groups of youths would attack him for no reason. The conversation moved on to what it was like to live and work in Bulgaria, and then they discussed music. Although Tony's English was excellent, Jock tried to speak in Bulgarian for practice.

Just after 1 a.m. Jock and Lindsay left the Rock Bar with Tony and some of his local mates. Grayham had headed off a while before. They wanted to call him and ask if he would join them at another bar, but Tony's mobile phone was out of credit and Lindsay's had a flat battery. Not far from the Rock Bar was a little kiosk selling cigarettes, alcohol and mobile-phone credit. It was at the south-west corner of St Nedelya Square.

Fifteen or twenty young men came out of a metro underpass diagonally opposite, at the north-east corner of the square. They were shouting and throwing their fists in the air. As Tony was buying the credit, one of his friends ran by and warned them that the group of loud youths who were heading their way might be football hooligans. Jock knew he and Tony and Lindsay would stand out, as they were speaking English and had odd haircuts. Not wanting trouble, he immediately ran across the road to get away from the square, and the other two followed. The trio still hoped to meet up with Grayham, who might well be nearby, so they ducked behind a wall of pot plants outside a restaurant called the Happy Bar and Grill, which locals knew simply as Happy.

Tony had his back to the square as he battled to key the credit code into his phone. Lindsay was trying to help. Jock had crouched down but was watching the gang, the last of whose members had almost reached the kiosk opposite. Some had already crossed the road and were passing by the three friends.

Suddenly the noise changed. Now Jock could hear shouting. He stood up to see what was going on. Seconds later, he made a decision that would change his life.

. . .

28 December 2007
Sofia

As Aksenia Monova travelled to her legal practice in downtown Sofia on Friday, she worried about her twenty-year-old son, Andrei. He had not come home the night before, and his mobile phone was switched off. She tried to construct a mental map of his movements.

Aksenia lived with Andrei and her husband, Hristo Monov, in an apartment block some distance from the city centre, near the Vitosha Mountains. It was a good area but, like much of Sofia, a little shabby.

Aksenia and Hristo had met in 1976 at an entrance exam for Sofia University. They married five years later. They were both forty-nine now, and they doted on their only child.

Andrei was studying law at the private New Bulgarian University. Over Christmas, he had been enjoying a quiet break at home with his parents and some family friends.

The day before, Andrei and his father had stayed home while Aksenia went to her office. Hristo had been preparing a report on a case involving two youths who got into a fight at school. One of them had punched the other, who had died when he hit the ground. It had happened the week before in Razgrad, a city in the north-east of Bulgaria with one of the country's densest populations of ethnic Turks. Having spent 500 years under the 'Ottoman yoke', Bulgarians had little love for Turks. The dead boy was of Turkish descent. The State Agency for Child Protection had sent the trauma specialist to report on the situation. Hristo asked his son to type up the findings, and later told his wife that Andrei had seemed genuinely interested in how the parents of the dead boy coped with their loss.

Aksenia's notary practice is only a short walk from the Sofia Palace of Justice, outside which two stone lions—Bulgaria's national symbol—stand sentinel. Pigeons scattered at her approach. As Aksenia came through the heavy wooden door, her assistant could tell that she was distracted. 'Andrei came here around three yesterday, do you remember?' Aksenia asked. The assistant agreed, waiting for her to finish. But Aksenia fell silent, scouring her memory for clues. Andrei had printed out material to prepare for his upcoming law exam. Just as he was leaving, he had said he would be home late: he was going out with friends, some of them from Lozenets, the suburb where her parents lived. He had said he was not sure where they would be going.

In her mind's eye Aksenia could see her son standing next to her desk, talking animatedly. Andrei had been layered up against the cold. She stared at the empty space. 'Why is his phone switched off?' she muttered.

Aksenia had been aware that, having spent the whole Christmas period with his parents, her son was probably itching to be with his peers. When she had arrived home at 7.30 the night before, he had already gone. At the time she had not given it a second thought. She knew he was with friends, and nothing amiss had ever happened when they had all gone out in the past.

The office telephone rang. It was Aksenia's mother.

The assistant returned to her desk. This was family business, and she was feeling a little uncomfortable.

A few minutes later, Aksenia put down the phone. Now she was really worried. Her mother had heard on the news that there had been an incident in St Nedelya Square overnight, only a couple of blocks from Aksenia's office. A twenty-year-old man had died in the ambulance on the way to the run-down Pirogov Hospital. Another youth had been injured and taken to the Military Medical Academy.

She hunted for the number of Andrei's close friend, Kristian Dimov, but his mobile phone was off. Her fingers ran frantically across the keyboard to open a Bulgarian news website. Up came an article about an Australian who had been detained for questioning at Police Station No. 3.

. . .

29 December 2007

Sydney

By Saturday afternoon, Simon and Helen Palfreeman had helped their friends sail out of Pittwater, past the chain of beaches to Sydney's north, and into Sydney Harbour. They were now trying to anchor at Birkenhead, but strong winds made it difficult. Simon and Helen's friends seemed to be taking one call after another from family members, but the Palfreemans were here for some peace and quiet; their phones were turned off.

With dusk came calm, and the group was finally able to sit down for dinner in the cabin. Then there was yet another call. As the phone's owner answered it, he scrunched up his eyes. 'Simon, it's actually for you,' he said, with a baffled look.

Simon took the phone and squeezed past him to go up on deck; he was embarrassed to be holding up the start of the first course. As he passed Helen, their eyes met.

It was Simon's father, Tony. 'Jock's in trouble and Geri has been trying to track you down for the past twenty-four hours,' he thundered. 'She's sick with worry!'

Simon shook his head, exasperated. His first thought was that Jock had rushed into something impetuously, as he had been prone to do before he left Australia. Tony's voice dropped. 'There's been a stabbing incident in the Bulgarian capital, Sofia. A young man has died. We don't know much really, but I gather Jock's being held at a police station. There's no talk of any charges, though.'

'Bulgaria!' said Simon, moving further along the deck, away from the cabin. 'That can't be right. Jock's in England.'

Helen came up on deck. Her husband was now calling Jock's mother. Mary Jane told Simon she had read a wire-service story about a stabbing involving a foreigner identified as 'Joe Paul Freeman'. 'This could all be a big mistake,' he muttered in response.

The name was not Jock's, but sounded almost the same. Helen felt sick. She remembered the sporadic emails they had received the previous year. It started coming back to her . . .

He had been somewhere called Samokov.

In the Bulgarian countryside on a motorcycle.

In love with a local girl.

Simon now tried calling the Department of Foreign Affairs. It was the holiday break, so it was hard to track anyone down. When staff members did respond, they couldn't tell him anything. Since Jock was twenty-one, Simon would have to prove his son had given the department permission to divulge any details . . . if, in fact, it was Jock.

Finally, Simon came back to the cabin. He sat beside Angus and put his arm around him. 'There's nothing we can do till tomorrow.'

But underneath, his heart was racing.

Bulgaria.

Former Soviet-bloc country.

Secret police.

Poison-tipped umbrellas.

Let this be a terrible mistake.

As they sailed back up the coast to Pittwater early the next morning to get their cars, the water got rougher and rougher. No one knew what to say. One of their friends was violently seasick. Simon jumped to clean up the mess, thankful for the distraction.

'Simon,' someone scolded, 'you need to book a flight to Europe. Now.'

'I need more information,' Simon responded quietly. 'I need more information.'

A couple of hours later, Simon rang Geri in England. His sister had trained as a social worker and was used to dealing with young people in crisis, but this had hit her hard. While Australia slept, she had tried to find out more. Jock's friend Grayham had given Geri the number of the police-appointed interpreter. Geri now knew that the man in custody was indeed Jock. He had evidently gone to the assistance of some Gypsies, and somehow a young man had died from a knife wound. She had phoned the British Ministry of Defence. No one was answering.

Simon's heart raced. *Not a knife*, he thought. *Surely no one would be so stupid as to take a knife with them, much less brandish one.* But he was still not convinced it was time to act.

By midday the boat was moored back at Pittwater. As Simon adjusted the ropes, his friends insisted that he must go to Bulgaria. One even offered to organise the flight. His emotions in turmoil, Simon was not listening. He got onto the landing, then stood still, the colour draining from his face. He had no idea where to begin.

It was already too late.

CHAPTER 2

Friday, 28 December 2007
Sofia

Jock was not wearing a watch, but he guessed it was about 1.20 a.m. He was dazed, but relieved to be out of the scrum of drunken young men who seemed bent on lynching him. They had been rocking the police van and beating on its sides.

Moments before being bundled into the van, Jock had been calling out for police help. When he saw someone trying to pick up the knife, he had tried to get up off the ground, fearing one of the gang members would stab him. But this mobile cage could hardly be described as a sanctuary. The two fat policemen with him in the van were hitting him with metal truncheons, panting with the effort. When the vehicle took off he was thrown about; with his hands cuffed, he was unable to keep his balance, much less avoid the whacks to his face, chest and neck.

'What's going on?' he shouted, angry now. But neither of the cops spoke English.

As he was led into Police Station No. 3, Jock's eyes moved from one officer to another. They were staring at him. Jock pretended not to understand any Bulgarian, hoping that the cops would let slip what was going on. But when they proceeded to search him for weapons his mind froze. He stretched his arms and legs apart as they patted the length of his body. Jock wore two pairs of jeans to stave off the cold. He also wore the Army-style boots that had been his trademark as a teenager in Sydney.

When an officer removed the bootlaces and braces he was wearing over his T-shirt and under his sweater and zipped-up jacket, Jock presumed it was to prevent him from hanging himself.

The policemen handcuffed him to a stairwell railing so he could neither stand nor sit properly. They left him there for hours. This is a method of detention referred to as 'on the tram'; it was one the European Committee for the Prevention of Torture had recommended be discontinued when it started monitoring Bulgarian police practices the year after the Communist regime fell. Jock felt like an animal on display. His hands ached with the cold. He could do nothing to warm them. His body was bent and exposed, the icy air going through his jacket like razor blades.

The following dialogue is reconstructed from Jock's vivid recollection of this time.

'You are never going to see the sun again,' an officer sneered.

'You are never going to see your home again. Forget going home— home is finished,' added another in broken English.

Yet Jock had no idea how much trouble he was in. In his rush to leave Madjare, he had taken the first ID he could find, his Army card. His passport was somewhere in Grayham's house. This meant police could not confirm his nationality. Compounding their suspicions, he also had a strange haircut.

The day before Jock had flown to Bulgaria, he had met up with a fellow infantry recruit, a Fijian, in London. To celebrate being on holiday after the month of tough training they had just endured in North Yorkshire, they had taken to their No. 2 crew cuts with clippers, carving out a tiny mohawk in a style known as a trojan. The haircuts had been a bit of fun. Crew cuts happened to be fashionable in Sofia, but to the police Jock's looked odd and faintly threatening.

'You are going down for murder,' said an officer in English laced with a heavy accent. 'We're going to fuck you, dude.'

Jock said nothing.

'We're going to fuck you real good, dude.'

Jock looked up. 'I have a name. It's Mr Palfreeman. Don't call me *dude*.' He knew they were trying to get at him and he took this talk of murder as part of the general taunting. Unaware that someone had died, Jock thought he was in here because of a street fight, and that he was being set up so he would bribe the cops to let him go. When he had been travelling by train in Bulgaria the previous year, police had accused Jock and some other Australians of not having the right papers, demanding money in exchange for dropping a trumped-up charge.

'I'll call you whatever I want,' the officer continued.

'Okay, call me *dude*. I don't have a problem with that, *man*,' Jock said.

The officer's face went red. 'Don't call me *man*!'

'Well, don't call me *dude*,' Jock said, laughing. The officer lunged at him as if to throw a punch, before being restrained by several other police.

. . .

2 a.m.

At that moment, Grayham Saunders was several kilometres away in his hostel room, desperately trying to make sense of what his former girlfriend Lindsay was telling him. She was hurt and upset. It seemed that something really bad had happened to Jock.

Grayham was thirty-one, with blue eyes, a cherubic mouth and a narrow, eight-centimetre-high mohawk down the middle of his close-cropped head.

Based in Bristol and a carpenter by training, Grayham bought houses cheaply, renovated them, and resold at a profit. Two years earlier, in 2005, he had bought a dilapidated house in Madjare, a tiny village in the Rila Mountains not far from the famed ski fields of Borovets, where Bulgarian kings used to hunt. Real estate was relatively cheap in Bulgaria, and the developing market economy had made this a more attractive destination for cashed-up foreigners. There were plans for a massive expansion of Borovets, and Grayham hoped that the Madjare house would prove a nice little earner.

In May 2006, Grayham had been hanging out in the basement bar of the Art Hostel, where he always stayed in Sofia. A group of young Bulgarian hippies had come in, talking about the Rainbow Festival. Grayham struck up a conversation with an Australian who was with them. Jock had a beard and scruffy long blond hair, but Grayham had warmed to the way he had gently mocked the hippies.

Jock said he was on his way from Turkey to Bucharest, in Romania. He needed a visa to cross the border and had just discovered that the Romanian Embassy was shut. Stuck in Sofia, he had pitched a tent in a bushy section of a nearby park, camping while he waited for the embassy to reopen. Grayham was surprised to learn that Jock was only nineteen.

When Jock asked him about the house he was renovating, Grayham explained that unlike many other foreigners, who were just knocking down houses and building new ones, he believed in preserving the old buildings as part of the area's cultural heritage. This appealed to Jock. As the Australian turned to leave the bar, Grayham said he was looking for help. Jock immediately offered to give the carpenter a hand.

Still, when Jock disappeared up the stairs, Grayham thought that would be the last he would see of him. But the next morning Jock showed up at six, as Grayham had requested, and said he was ready to go to Madjare.

On the drive up into the mountains, Jock told Grayham he believed that people should work together for the good of all. He wanted to understand how Grayham reconciled his business interests with his Socialist views. He also mentioned that he wanted to join the Army. Grayham found this incongruous, given what Jock had been saying.

As they passed forests and a sparkling lake, Jock continued unpacking his thoughts on life. Grayham thought his communitarian political ideas seemed unusually sophisticated for someone his age. The Army thing was a bit strange, but Grayham gathered that it was all part of Jock's desire to do something worthwhile with his life.

The house was frozen shut, so the two men had to break in. The sight of the weird-looking foreigners must have startled the locals: many of Madjare's 300 residents were retirees. Grayham's next-door neighbour had been a police officer in the Communist era. He distrusted the pair at first, but Jock seemed to have a knack for getting on with everyone. Soon the old man was admiring their work and inviting them to ride his horse. Other neighbours dropped by with saucepans of home-cooked food. The two foreigners also made friends with some young Bulgarians in the nearby town of Samokov.

Jock refused to accept any more pay from Grayham than a local would have received. He preferred to be paid in cigarettes and keep, he said. All he wanted was a base, a purpose, and a good time in a country unlike his own. When Grayham returned to Bristol a few months later, Jock stayed to do more work on the house. Grayham had grown fond of him. When Jock finally left Bulgaria, he moved to Bristol to be near his English friend before starting Army training in mid-November 2007. Many of Grayham's friends also liked the young Australian. One of them was Lindsay Welsh.

When Grayham, Lindsay and Jock went to Madjare for Christmas 2007, it was just like old times, apart from Jock's almost clean-shaven Army crew cut. On Christmas Day, Jock's best Bulgarian mate came over from Samokov for lunch. His name was Iliyan Yordanov. They all built sleds from bits of old chairs, corrugated iron and scrap wood, and raced down the nearby hill. Grayham won.

Photographs taken that day show Jock grinning as he sits on his sled in the black jacket. His face says it all: *Life doesn't get much better than this.*

Another photograph, taken inside the house, shows Lindsay standing next to the kitchen table rolling a cigarette. Among the tools on the table is a black canvas pouch. It looks like a Leatherman multi-tool case and houses the butterfly knife that Grayham bought on the spur of the moment as he and Jock prepared for Lindsay's arrival on Christmas Eve. Grayham had wanted something more than a Swiss Army knife, something he could use to cut up vegetables. They had been in a camping and hunting shop and this one had caught his eye—it was flashy and he liked the neat way it folded up.

Such knives were illegal in England, but here you could carry any kind of knife. Grayham thought it might be useful if he had to be out at night—there were feral dogs in the area that could get nasty. It had also served its purpose in the poorly resourced kitchen.

When Lindsay returned to the hostel at around 2 a.m., she was doubled up in pain and sobbing uncontrollably. All Grayham could get out of her was that Jock was in trouble and had been taken away by the police. A gang of football fans had kicked her in the stomach when she went to help him.

. . .

A huge neon Samsung sign on the roof of the Happy restaurant cast an eerie light over the T-junction of Stamboliyski and Maria Louisa boulevards, which ran along two sides of St Nedelya Square. Crime-scene tape shimmered in the flashing light from police cars parked nearby. The area most identifiable as a square was little more than a long, irregularly shaped stretch of pavement with some chestnut trees and shrubs in planters. Pieces of broken concrete tiles from the planters, as well as broken pavers, lay scattered across the pavement. Some pieces were the size of a fist. Others were the size of three or four fists.

Experts began to collect samples of the blood that stained the area between the kiosk and the Stamboliyski kerb. In any criminal investigation, the first twenty-four hours are critical. In this case, what some police did not do in that time would become just as important as what they did.

An illuminated billboard in the middle of the square, near the Ministry of Health entrance, advertised Nescafé. 'An unexpectedly good combination,' it read. The irony was lost on the police taking down the names and contact details of witnesses. A female officer noted that at least two of the victims' friends appeared very drunk. A male officer was jotting down what some of the friends said had happened. He also spoke to the young man who said he worked in the kiosk that sold cigarettes and alcohol in the square. Near the Nescafé billboard there was a pole with a traffic camera pointing towards Stamboliyski.

Across Maria Louisa, the Sheraton security guard and car park attendants watched the frenzy of activity. But there was no such interest at the Happy restaurant on the other side of Stamboliyski. Heavily made-up waitresses in skimpy red mini-skirts were oblivious to the commotion as they cleaned tables in the American-style restaurant, where foreigners could feel at home with menus in English and football playing on huge screens. At the front of the restaurant was a courtyard known as the Happy garden, which filled with patrons in summer. It was partially walled off from the footpath and decorated with pot plants. Right now it was empty.

Following correct procedure, the male officer, who had heard the freshest accounts of what had happened, returned to his station to write up an incident report.

. . .

2.30 a.m.

Witnesses started gathering at Police Station No. 3 soon after Jock arrived. An investigator on duty prepared to interview one of the police officers who had attended the crime scene. That officer had not been the first on the scene; nor had he taken down a record of what witnesses had said. But his account gives a sense of how volatile the situation was at that time.

The statements reproduced here and elsewhere in this book are translations of the original statements made by witnesses and police. Although the statements do not include what the investigator asked, it is clear that they represent responses to specific questions. This is part of the account that forty-year-old Officer Valentin Bogdanov signed:

'On 28 December, around 1.15 . . . there was an alert about a fight with a stabbing between civilians . . . We noticed a group of ten to fifteen young people who gathered close to the main entrance of the Ministry of Health, to the left side of the entrance if you are facing it. Some of them had got hold of a civilian and they told me that he had stabbed their friend with a knife.

'On the pavement in front of the group of people I noticed a knife made of white metal and all covered in blood, and I took care that the knife was not touched or taken by anyone . . . I was concerned that someone might take the knife and stab the person whom the group was holding.'

. . .

3.30 a.m.

Galina Vodkadzhieva had received a call at 2 a.m., asking her to come to Police Station No. 3 to interpret for a foreigner. The twenty-nine-year-old had studied English at university and worked for an agency that provided police and the courts with interpreters. Police had led her to believe that the foreigner was a drug addict who, without provocation, had attacked a group of Bulgarians with a knife.

When she was introduced to the prisoner, who towered over her, he said, 'I don't know who you are. I'm not saying anything.' A man in plain clothes, who she thought was an off-duty investigator, harangued Jock, repeatedly calling him a drug addict until a uniformed cop told him to stop.

Jock clearly thought Galina was yet another police officer. She understood why. She tried to explain to him that she worked independently and was neutral. At the same time, she wondered if she had been sent to interpret for a monster. After all, someone had just been stabbed to death and someone else badly wounded.

They were led to a small room, where Galina was able to talk to Jock in private. He struck her as anything but stoned. He seemed intelligent and genuinely bewildered, and refused to talk to the investigators until he had a lawyer. He also seemed confident that the confusion would soon be sorted out and he would be on his way. It was clear Jock had no idea just how serious his situation was.

Galina went out into the corridor. From there, she could see into a room filled with young people who had been with the lad who had died earlier that morning. Some young women were crying and saying, 'How could this have happened?' No one appeared drunk or out of line. They all looked about the same age as Jock and seemed to be in shock. They were there to give statements.

It did not strike Galina until much later that these young witnesses were not prevented from discussing with each other what they had seen. Only one of them would have a blood alcohol test. There is no record of any of the youths being searched for weapons.

. . .

3.40 a.m.

One of the first to leave the waiting room and provide a sworn statement was Emil Aleksiev, a twenty-year-old finance student. He said he had been at an establishment near the Women's Market with ten to fifteen friends and acquaintances, among them Andrei Monov and Antoan Zahariev, both of whom had been taken to hospital with a knife wound.

The Women's Market is a run-down, slightly sleazy area frequented by Gypsies, beggars and groups of drunken youths. Nearby is Tolerance Square, an enclave with a large synagogue, a Catholic Church, an Orthodox Church and Banya Bashi, the only functioning mosque left in Sofia.

According to Emil, at about 1 a.m. some friends who had been with his group earlier in the evening had phoned to ask if they would join them at the nearby Solo Disco Club, at the flashier end of town. To get there, Emil's group had first gone down the steps to the Serdica metro station, which doubled as an underpass, then emerged at the north end of St Nedelya Square. To their right was the imposing limestone headquarters of Bulbank, one of Bulgaria's largest banks. It jutted out from the end of a long building that occupied most of the western side of the square and housed the Ministry of Health, a pharmacy and a kiosk. From here, it was another 250 metres or so to the Solo Disco Club, the group's destination.

As they crossed the square, the youths had broken up into smaller groups, walking at varying speeds. Emil said he was one of the slower ones. He was about ten metres from the pedestrian lights near the intersection of Maria Louisa and Stamboliyski boulevards when he became aware that something was happening behind him, at the northern end of the square.

Emil told the investigator that there was some kind of altercation in front of Bulbank but that he could not follow between whom it was taking place. He continued: 'At precisely that moment a man of around 25 years, who was about 180 centimetres tall with closely cropped hair on the side and more hair on top of the head, he crossed Stamboliyski running towards us.'

Emil did not explain how he was at the southern end of the square one minute and at the northern end the next. He went on: 'He started shouting in broken but understandable Bulgarian, with an English accent, *Ne ataka! Mahai se!*' [Don't attack! Go away!] and stuff like that. It wasn't clear exactly to whom he was shouting.

'Immediately after that he turned around, took out a knife—the blade was about the size of my palm. It was a butterfly type. He started shouting in English "Fuck fascism!" and something else I don't remember and he was heading towards us with his arm outstretched as if to stab. He didn't manage to stab anyone and we moved to cross Stamboliyski Boulevard, looking at him and trying to protect ourselves. Then I turned around and saw that Andrei, who a second ago had been next to me, had fallen on the road and his chest was all covered in blood. There was also a lot of blood flowing onto the asphalt. I realised that the man with the knife had stabbed my friend.

'At this point two bodyguards, or at least they looked like that, came from I don't know where . . . One of them took out a foldaway truncheon and opened it, saying to the guy with the knife, "On your knees, on the ground." He understood them perfectly and said "*Dobre, dobre*" [OK, OK], dropped the knife and lay down.'

Emil said they had then seen the flashing lights of police cars approaching. As police got closer, the man with the knife tried 'to run away'. Emil helped two police officers and the guards detain the man. He also called for an ambulance, which took ten to fifteen minutes to arrive—a long time. 'In the meantime our friend Kristian Dimov was trying to close Andrei's wound,' Emil added. 'He was holding his head. Andrei was not responding.'

It appears the investigator then asked him about the detainee. 'I would like to clarify that the man with the knife who stabbed Andrei was not adequate,' Emil responded, employing a word Bulgarians use to describe behaviour that can be anything from inappropriate for the time and place to alcohol- or drug-affected. 'According to me, he wasn't drunk but he was high,' Emil continued. 'He had used some kind of drug, because his behaviour was beyond logic. A blonde girl with short hair . . . tried to help the man with the knife run away while we were holding him with the police officers.' Presumably this girl was Lindsay Welsh.

What witnesses like Emil reported depended on factors such as where they stood, what caught their eye and how much alcohol they had drunk. Their accounts varied in the details, yet each reads like a complete recollection. As the folder marked *Case Number 3117/07* swelled with one witness statement after another, it must have seemed to the investigators that many quite different dramas had taken place during those five minutes in St Nedelya Square.

. . .

4.15 a.m.

Alexander Donev heard his name and went into Investigating Officer Zlatina Butchkova's office. The twenty-year-old was home on holiday from university in Germany, where he was studying information technology. In the statement he signed at 4.45 a.m., he said there had been an 'altercation between Andrei and some Gypsies' at Bulbank. 'I don't know the reason for that, but I heard that they had said, "Death to Bulgarians". The Gypsies left without anything more serious happening than an exchange of words, and so we went on.'

Like Emil, Alexander said a man had come at the group, but he did not specify from which direction. He said the man was shouting something indecipherable and waving a knife with a blade more than twenty centimetres long at 'everyone'. He also said he saw Jock stab Antoan side-on in the stomach just as Antoan was trying to stop the attack.

'The man with the knife then headed towards me, as if he was going to stab me in the chest. I kicked the hand holding the knife and someone else also managed to avoid his attack, and together we managed to retreat towards Stamboliyski. At this moment, two men came who got the man with the knife to the ground but I didn't see exactly how because I was already further on. At this moment someone shouted that Andrei had been stabbed and I saw Andrei lying on the road. There was a huge puddle of blood around him and Andrei wasn't moving.'

Then it was Kristian Dimov's turn. The Forestry University student was the friend whom Andrei's mother would try to reach later that day. Like Andrei, he was twenty years old. Kristian said he had already crossed Stamboliyski Boulevard, on the southern edge of the square, when Andrei Monov and two or three other stragglers got to the kiosk near the traffic lights. At that moment he and others 'heard something going on'. When they turned around they saw 'two other boys' and some stragglers from their group 'pushing each other'. (Like most of the witnesses, he uses the term boys rather than youths or young men.)

Kristian and others crossed back over Stamboliyski to see what was happening near Maria Louisa Boulevard, which runs along the square's eastern edge in front of the Sheraton car park. According to Kristian, one of the 'two other boys' crossed the tram tracks on Maria Louisa and ran towards the Sheraton. The other one 'who had had an altercation with the group ran away towards the metro', and Kristian and his friends continued on their way to the disco.

Kristian said he first saw Jock near the kiosk and 'in front of some kind of ministry building'. This was at the other end of the square from where Emil remembered seeing Jock. Because 'everything happened very fast', all Kristian could remember of the boy was that he was 'lean and tall, with a light complexion and light short hair' and that he would recognise him if he saw him again. He also remembered there was a blonde woman with the man.

Kristian's account of what happened next is important because it suggests that Jock was unarmed when he first appeared: '[Jock] was shouting something and took out a knife—a big one but I can't say exactly what kind of knife. He started waving it and pointing it at us as if he wanted to stab us. He wasn't aiming at a particular person from our group. But he was chasing us with the knife. So there was a huge melee. I heard a scream from our group and somebody, I don't know who exactly, told me Andrei was lying on the street.

'I went to Andrei, who was lying on his back covered in blood, and I couldn't see where the blood was coming from. There was a huge puddle of blood. I was holding his head with my left arm and I didn't know where the blood was coming from. I unbuttoned his sweat shirt, pulled up his T-shirt and someone told me that the wound was on the back, so I turned him a bit and I saw the wound on the upper left of his back ... Andrei was already dying in my hands.'

Investigating Officer Butchkova's ears must have pricked up when this young man said the victim was stabbed in the back. Accurate or not, it was a description that would stick.

. . .

6 a.m.

Maria Grozeva woke to the sound of the telephone. An investigator wanted her to come to the station. The sixty-one-year-old forensic doctor was an associate professor at the university hospital and was often called upon to give expert evidence in murder cases. She was told only that there had been an incident in which a young man had died and another was wounded with a knife. A youth was in custody. She headed straight for Police Station No. 3, where she met the suspect. He needed to be taken to the cream-brick Queen Yoana Hospital, she said, where she could examine him professionally. Two police officers drove Jock and Galina to the hospital in a police car. Grozeva drove alone. The cobbled streets were quiet. The sun was just coming up and newspaper vendors were lifting the shutters on their kiosks.

At the hospital, Grozeva took the suspect into an examining room along with a hospital staff member. In heavily accented English she explained to Jock that she needed to test his blood and urine for alcohol and opiates. She also said she would have to take a DNA sample. Jock signed a release form enabling her to do so. He was dirty and clearly exhausted.

Galina and the officers watched as Grozeva checked for blood under Jock's fingernails, between his fingers, and over his hands. She placed whatever she discovered on a white sheet of paper which she packaged up and gave to Investigating Officer Nikola Kostov. Grozeva then asked the suspect to undress so she could check him for injuries. With the investigator waiting outside the consulting room, Jock told the doctor that he had gone to stop a fight between Bulgarian youths and two Gypsies. She remembers him saying that he called out to the youths, 'Stop this fascism! Stop this fascism!' and later pulled out a knife from his pocket. But Jock said no more to her about what had happened.

Although she made no reference to it in her report, Grozeva recalls checking the suspect's head. She was not surprised by the absence of fresh wounds on his scalp. The head does not bruise as readily as, say, the face. Bruising could have appeared later. Jock might also have been hit in the head and not bruised at all.

Grozeva found three sets of abrasions near Jock's left elbow. A line of dried blood ran halfway down the back of his left forearm and another ran almost to his armpit. These came from the abrasions. She photographed Jock with his left arm and its injury facing the camera. A second photograph showed a close-up of his armpit area. He told her he could not remember being injured, but he did remember falling on the ground. He said he had a strange sensation in two fingers. She thought this suggested nerve damage, possibly from the injury to his arm.

By now Grozeva knew that Jock was suspected of having murdered Andrei Monov with a knife. She determined that he was right-handed and that he must have held the knife in his right hand. Grozeva had worked on many cases involving knife wounds, and in her experience these often produced a lot of blood. If she could find traces of the deceased's blood under the foreigner's fingernails, on his hands, or in the fibres of his sleeves, police would have a key piece of evidence that the young man had been, at the very least, in close proximity to Andrei Monov when he was fatally stabbed.

She took swabs from Jock's left armpit and his hands, and gave these to the officer. Just as methodically, she examined Jock's clothing under a magnifying glass, paying particular attention to his jacket sleeves, then packaged up his jacket and the black jeans he had been wearing outside his blue ones, and gave these to the officer as well. Try as she might, Grozeva could find no sign of blood on Jock's cuffs or person. This puzzled her, as she knew the Australian had had no chance to wash.

After examining Jock, Grozeva told him to put his remaining clothes back on. He re-dressed in his blue jeans, singlet, T-shirt and sweater.

The no-nonsense doctor was struck by the Australian's sunny disposition despite the combination of sleep deprivation and hunger that he must have been experiencing. She was taken aback as he discussed what had brought him to her country and how much he loved Bulgaria. Grozeva asked if he was concerned about being incarcerated. 'No, I have done nothing wrong,' he said. It was clear to her that Jock was not aware someone had been killed.

Jock warmed to the forensic doctor. He found her professional manner reassuring. It was the first time since his arrest that he had felt a proper process was being followed. It was also a relief not to have to wait for Galina to translate what Grozeva said. Unlike the officers at the station, the doctor treated him as a civilised human being. On his T-shirt was a picture of the first man in space, Soviet cosmonaut Yuri Gagarin. This prompted a conversation between Jock and the doctor about the changes that capitalism had brought Bulgaria. They agreed that not all of those changes were good.

However, Jock's calm evaporated when he and Galina returned to the station and police shoved him into a holding cell with four other prisoners. It was one metre square and had no lavatory. There was one wooden bench, but it was covered in faeces. There was nowhere to sit and nowhere to lie down. The floor was drenched in urine. The cell was dark, and the stench was overpowering.

In her initial report, Grozeva was able to cover only specific areas. She said that the subject was aware of what was going on around him and complained of pins and needles in the fourth and fifth fingers of his left hand. Then she described his physical wounds, details that would become critical in years to come. 'On the surface of the back of his left elbow were found 3 superficial slit-like lacerations on the skin, each one 4 or 5 mm in length with slightly bruised edges and a depth of about 1 or 2 mm,' she wrote. 'The skin around these wounds is slightly red and covered with crusted blood.' She also noted that the identified wounds in the area of the left elbow resulted from 'the action of a solid blunt object and could have been received from a fall to the ground or from a hit from a solid blunt object'.

That afternoon Grozeva mulled over the case. The fact that there was no spattered blood on the foreigner bothered her. But it was not until she received a copy of the autopsy report that she became really concerned.

. . .

8 a.m.

Viktor Georgiev finished his shift at the Sheraton. It had been a long night. It had also been a very disturbing night. It was not the sight of a knife that had upset him. Carrying a knife was not illegal in Bulgaria, and butterfly knives were readily available. Even souvenir shops sold them. Admittedly, this one had struck him as large. But what concerned Viktor most was the violence of the youths as they surrounded the foreigner, who had no option but to react like a trapped animal.

Viktor was the same age as Andrei Monov and his friends, but he knew nothing about them except that they looked like drunken football fans. Although everything had happened so fast, each moment flashed like a freeze frame in his mind as he replayed the sequence of events. When he had first noticed the group of young men and women, they had been loud but jovial. Suddenly they'd chased the foreigner across the square, circled him, pushed him to the ground and started attacking him. That was when the foreigner had pulled out a knife.

Viktor had learnt a lot about self-defence while working for the security firm. This guy had not looked like he knew how to hold a knife. Viktor had assumed he was just trying to scare off the young Bulgarians.

When Viktor and car park attendant Lyubomir Tomov heard the man calling out in English, they had left the cabin to get a better look at what was going on. After all, the man might have been a guest at the Sheraton, in which case they would have been obliged to help him. If he was not a guest, they were not supposed to leave the car park or get involved. As the violence escalated, they were in a terrible bind.

Viktor recalled how the football fans had kept attacking the foreigner, even though he had this knife. On at least three occasions, he thought, they could have run away and let the man be. But they did not. The foreigner's moves became chaotic, as happens when someone is desperately defending himself. Then the fans threw something that hit the foreigner in the head. *Bang!*—down he went. Then he got up. He called for help; he tried to get away from them.

At that point, Viktor and some colleagues ran from the car park across Maria Louisa Boulevard. As he reached the square Viktor noticed someone lying on Stamboliyski. He had been unable to see that far from the cabin, so did not know what had happened to that person. Rather than going to find out, Viktor went straight to Jock, who by then was on the ground near the Ministry of Health, protected from the youths who were still haranguing him by guards of some sort. Police turned up shortly afterwards.

Viktor and his colleagues returned to the car park, from where they watched what happened next. For the next few hours St Nedelya Square was lit up like a movie set, with sirens flashing, huge portable lights going up and people everywhere. No one approached any of them for details of what they had seen, even though they had been stationed right in front of the crime scene. At the time Viktor had hoped that he and his colleagues would not have to write up an incident report for their boss to explain why they had left their posts. He was not the kind to go reporting an incident if he didn't have to, as it involved far too much paperwork.

This had looked like just another drunken bashing, albeit a brutal one. Viktor had no idea someone had died.

CHAPTER 3

Friday, 28 December 2007
Police Station No. 3, Sofia

Chief Investigating Officer Tanya Alakusheva was in charge of the St Nedelya case. The thirty-two-year-old detective had started at Police Station No. 3 only the year before, and it was her first posting. She was thin, with dark blonde hair and green eyes. Like the other investigating officers, she had a law degree, but hers was from Sofia University, rather than the police academy.

Alakusheva had assisted on murders before, but this was by far the most newsworthy of her career. A murder in downtown Sofia involving a knife and a foreigner—it was bound to be a high-profile case. She was rostered on for twenty-four hours but would be in the station for a lot longer than that. Investigators kept a pillow and blanket on top of their battered filing cabinets for use during the downtime customary on the long shifts, but Alakusheva would have no time to rest over the coming days. She chain-smoked and stayed awake with coffee and Coca-Cola.

This was the Christmas break, and Alakusheva knew she would end up doing the lion's share of the interviews, as there were not enough people on duty. She was annoyed about shortages in other areas, too. On a case like this, she would end up using her own mobile phone, computer paper and toner. If she needed to use a car and if there was one available, she would often have to pay for the fuel.

Alakusheva would need to be in touch with the duty prosecutor all day. In Bulgaria the prosecutor oversees a criminal investigation from the start. This is different from places like the United Kingdom and Australia, where police undertake an investigation and, if they reach the conclusion that there is a case to answer, they go to the Office of Public Prosecution and try to persuade it to bring the matter to trial.

At 9.45 a.m. a knock at the door indicated it was time for Alakusheva to take down a statement from a witness. Kaloyan Karlov was a twenty-two-year-old student at the Medical University who had been out with Andrei and his friends. Kaloyan told the investigator that he had been drinking a bit, but not to the point of feeling drunk. He remembered being distracted by a scantily dressed blonde woman as he crossed Stamboliyski Boulevard. This would be the only such description of Lindsay, but its salacious nature may have contributed to later speculation about Jock. Like all his friends interviewed so far, Kaloyan had seen some kind of 'commotion' involving members of the group before the attacker appeared. He had run back to the kiosk area to see what was happening. Like Emil Aleksiev and Alexander Donev, he noted that this altercation had been with 'Roma', adding: 'I can't say which of my friends was arguing with them or why, but they were insulting each other . . . I didn't see any exchange of blows. When I came closer the argument was just finishing.'

Kaloyan said that when the argument ended, the Roma headed back towards the subway entrance from which his group had come. 'At this point I heard one or two of my group shouting, "He's got a knife, he's got a knife." I turned to the left and saw a boy with short blond hair five or six metres away, brandishing a knife and saying something in a foreign accent—"No fascism"—which he repeated two or three times.'

Kaloyan did not see who stabbed Andrei or Antoan. At 10.30 a.m. he signed his statement and left the investigator's office. Tanya Alakusheva then interviewed Vasil Velevski. He added little to what Kaloyan had said—indeed, his statement included phrases copied word for word from Kaloyan's. He reported an argument between his friends and some Gypsies, and then a man with a knife. Vasil had already told a police officer at the scene what had happened. Now he left out key details from his statement; details that might explain what motivated Jock to approach the group.

Flipping through the white folder of *Case Number 3117/07*, Alakusheva must have seen the incident report by the police officer who had attended the crime scene and recorded firsthand accounts of what had happened. But that officer was not asked to give a statement. Instead his report was either forgotten or ignored.

Meanwhile, police were talking to the media. According to the news site dnes.dir.bg/news, they had the killer. He was Joe Paul Freeman, aged twenty-one. The site quoted Investigating Officer Butchkova as saying: 'Initially, he absolutely didn't even want to communicate with the interpreter. Subsequently, he started to communicate with the interpreter; but what he says doesn't make a lot of sense, whether it's because he is under the influence or there's another reason.'

. . .

Sofia Airport
11 a.m.
Grayham drove a distraught Lindsay to the airport to catch her 12.30 p.m. flight home to England. Neither of them had any idea of how serious the fracas had been. Grayham assumed that by now his Australian friend was out of the police station and on his way back to Madjare. He expected to see Jock at the house that evening, cold and hungry but with a story to tell.

. . .

1.30 p.m.
Nineteen-year-old Antoan Zahariev sat in the waiting room at Police Station No. 3. A few hours ago, he had been released from the Medical Military Academy Hospital after doctors put two stitches in the flesh wound between the tenth and eleventh ribs on his right side. When Associate Professor Maria Grozeva examined him more than a week later, he had a scar about twenty-five millimetres long and from two to three millimetres wide. He was in good health.

Antoan was in his first year at Sofia University, studying statistical science. He had the closely cropped haircut popular among his peers and a meekness about his demeanour. His mother worked for the Blood Donation Centre and his father worked for a company that installed windows and doors. But there is no indication that either parent was with Antoan at the police station.

An officer gestured to the young man that it was his turn to give a statement and led him into the office of Investigating Officer Nikola Kostov. Antoan's interview lasted from 1.40 to 3 p.m. He said he had been partying with Andrei Monov and Kristian Dimov, among others—there were about twenty-five of them. He estimated he must have drunk 300 grams of vodka, the equivalent of six shots—'grams' is the local expression for millilitres. He said they had left for another bar at around 1 a.m. He had been halfway across Stamboliyski Boulevard when he heard some kind of 'commotion' and 'uproar' in the square behind him and turned to see what was going on.

'There was already a fight between my friends and some other people who I didn't know and had never seen before. Some of these strangers were Gypsies, I think, but I am not sure. I don't know who had started the dispute. At some point, when I went back to see what was going on, a man appeared who was around twenty-five to twenty-six years of age—at least that's how he looked to me.'

Antoan said the man had 'short hair' and was shouting loudly, swearing at them in English: 'All I could understand was that he was shouting "Fuck you." He started waving a knife around; I saw the knife had a blade that was about fifteen to twenty centimetres long . . . At first I was facing him and I got a good look at him. I think I could recognise him if I saw him.'

Antoan said none of his friends had a knife. As he and Alexander Donev tried to withdraw, Antoan remembered tripping over, his back to the attacker who was chasing them: 'After I fell forward on my hands, I heard the attacker shouting behind me. Then I stood up and, along with the other boys, started shouting at the attacker, "What's with these knives?" Then I turned slowly and he kept on shouting. I made a few slow steps to walk away from the attacker, my back to him. I then turned and saw that Andrei had fallen on Stamboliyski Boulevard, and I went to [him]. He was lying on his stomach and we turned him onto his back. I can't say who among my friends was next to Andrei there because there was such a commotion. Andrei was just trying to say something, but I couldn't understand what he was trying to say.'

At the time, Antoan was not aware that he had been stabbed. He certainly did not know who had stabbed him, but he did think Gypsies might have been involved at some point before the stabbing.

. . .

Athens, Greece
2 p.m.

David Chaplin was in his office at the Australian Embassy in Athens when he took a call from the British Embassy in Sofia. Bulgarian police had notified Chaplin's British counterpart that a British soldier in custody might be an Australian national and had said the man's name was 'Joe Freeman'. Australia has only an honorary consul in Sofia, but on 28 December 2007 she was away on Christmas holidays. The closest Australian Embassy to Bulgaria is in Greece.

Chaplin was experienced in helping Australians in trouble overseas. He had been appointed a Member of the Order of Australia for his work with victims of the 2002 terrorist bombings in Bali, where he was then Vice Consul. He had been at the hospital as the victims were brought in, and he had fought for them to be identified and given proper care. Later, he had struggled to inform and help their families.

Nothing came up when Chaplin searched the government databases for details of 'Joe Freeman'. Perhaps the young man was not an Australian national after all. Chaplin would spend the rest of the day fielding calls from Australian reporters while trying to establish the facts on this mysterious incarceration.

. . .

Sofia
2 p.m.

Aksenia Monova was still searching for news of her son, Andrei. She dialled Kristian Dimov's number again. This time he answered. Trying to sound calm, she asked the young man if he knew where Andrei was, if he had been out with him last night. Kristian's voice was barely audible.

'Could I call you back in ten minutes,' he stammered.

Aksenia's anxiety rose. Andrei's friends had always been polite and helpful when she had phoned looking for him. She tried calling Kristian again, but he did not answer.

She found the number for Police Station No. 3 and dialled it. No one answered. She then called a colleague whose husband had worked as a police investigator to see if he could help her get some information from the station. He was busy. Impatient, she phoned Police Station No. 3 once more. This time a man answered.

'Could you tell me anything about the incident in the city involving a twenty-year-old boy? My son hasn't returned home and I'm worried about him.'

The officer sounded guarded. 'What is your son's name?'

'Andrei Hristov Monov,' she replied carefully.

Still the officer said nothing about the case. Instead he asked where she was calling from. Aksenia gave him her office address and phone number. Her assistant was about to leave for the day. The rest of the staff had already gone, but Aksenia was so upset that the assistant decided to stay.

'Hang up now and call back in ten minutes,' the officer said.

Aksenia fidgeted with papers on her desk, counting every second as she waited for ten minutes to pass. She tried reaching someone at Pirogov Hospital. She tried Kristian's number again. Then the doorbell rang. Her assistant went to tell whoever it was that they were closed. The minutes dragged by. Her assistant was still at the front door.

As Aksenia checked the time yet again, her office door opened. There stood a large man with a pronounced five o'clock shadow. 'It's better that I tell you than you hear it from the others,' he said gently.

Before she could register who he was, seven or eight young men came in. One of them was Kristian Dimov. Their faces told her all she needed to know. In that moment of silence she remembered that this large man was a lawyer, the father of one of her son's friends. His wife was a public notary like Aksenia.

'Kristian! Why didn't you say anything to me?' Aksenia tried to sound composed.

'I just couldn't!' Kristian blurted out. He burst into tears.

The loud trill of the telephone on her desk broke through the moment and let him turn away. Aksenia took the call.

It was her husband, Hristo. 'Have you heard anything?' he asked, his voice cracking.

Aksenia did not dare tell him. She just said he was not to worry and that she would be home soon.

Aksenia looked up blankly. Her life was over, she thought. Then she remembered her husband. She asked three of the young men, including Kristian, to come home with her to tell Hristo. They agreed and followed her out the front door.

. . .

Police Station No. 3
2.15 p.m.
The corridor filled with police officers in a state of panic. Galina, the interpreter, struggled to follow what was going on. It seemed that no one had told Andrei Monov's parents he was dead. She watched as the drama unfolded.

Chief Investigating Officer Tanya Alakusheva was furious. It was clear to Galina that Alakusheva had left the job of calling the Monovs to a junior officer. Blame was being shunted from one officer to another. Galina gathered from the chatter that the Monovs were a well-respected family. The father of the dead boy worked for the government; he even did interviews on TV.

An officer broke the news to Alakusheva that Mrs Monova had learnt the ghastly truth by herself. It was too late. Nothing could be done.

. . .

When Aksenia Monova got home she found her husband with a neighbour. He was pacing the apartment, lost in thought.

The last conversation Hristo had had with his son was just before 2 p.m. on the previous day, when Andrei said he was going to see his mother at work. He had been running late, so Hristo had ironed a shirt for him. Andrei's 'Bye, Dad' had merged with the slam of the door.

Hristo had intended to file his report about the Razgrad death today, but while he was watching TV on his computer, a news crawl across the bottom of the screen announced that an Australian had murdered a twenty-year-old male and injured a nineteen-year old in the centre of Sofia. He had repeatedly tried calling Andrei, to no avail. He tried calling his wife. Worried, he stayed glued to the computer, and continued trying to get through to Aksenia.

Hristo's team of psychologists was often called out to tragedies like this. He knew he could use his position as an expert to get information, but he did not have the strength to try. He kept telling himself that the dead youth simply could not be his son. Then Aksenia phoned to ask if he was alone and to tell him to wait at home for her.

The sight of his wife's face as she came in confirmed his worst fears.

Although Hristo had heard Kristian's name mentioned before, this was the first time the psychologist had met the three young men who arrived with his wife. As his son's friends related the chaotic story, Hristo looked into the distance, enraged that police had not told them. It seemed that a youth had suddenly appeared, brandishing a big knife. The young men assured Aksenia that they had done nothing to provoke him and had no idea who he was. Their account got a bit jumbled and the Monovs must at times have found it difficult to follow. Indeed, Aksenia could not fully accept that her son was dead until she later went to identify his body at the morgue.

In her statement to the police investigator the next day, Aksenia said the boys told her that Andrei was stabbed twice, in the heart and the neck. She added that she had also found out he was stabbed in the back. She stressed that as far as she knew, Andrei and his friends had been trying to get away.

Whatever the young men had spluttered out to the Monovs that day, Aksenia's overriding impression was that her son had done no wrong. He was a victim of a random and vicious attack. For her, his friends' account became the truth about what happened that night.

. . .

Police Station No. 3

4 p.m.

Fourteen hours had passed, and neither Galina nor Jock had had anything to eat or drink. Jock hoped the delay had at least allowed Lindsay to make it onto her flight home to London. He did not want her embroiled in all this. She was already upset enough by the violent turn last night had taken.

As Jock sat in the holding cell, Stoiko Barborski got a call from Tanya Alakusheva, who asked the lawyer if he would represent a murder suspect, an Australian serving in the British military and on holiday in Bulgaria. A short, gaunt man with an ashen face, Barborski went to the police station and waited for Jock's formal interrogation to commence. In his canvas document bag he had a battered copy of the Bulgarian Penal Code. Its brown-paper cover was filled with his handwritten notes and doodles.

Barborski spoke no English and, according to Galina, he did not hold a private discussion with his new client. Indeed, he seemed to have written Jock off, referring to him as a murderer as he talked to Galina and the police officers. Galina started to worry. She was increasingly of the view that this young man was not being treated justly.

In an interview for this book Barborski said proper procedure was followed. Jock struck the lawyer as a tall, strong, proud young man. *His legs are huge; his hands twice the size of mine*, he thought. *Why would he have felt the need for a knife?*

A policeman nodded to Barborski, who led Jock and Galina into the small office that Chief Investigating Officer Alakusheva shared with another detective. It was 4.30 p.m. The office was piled high with files. The policeman brought in some rickety metal chairs with wooden seats. Barborski sat next to Alakusheva, opposite his client and the interpreter. What follows is Jock's and Galina's identical recollections of the exchange.

'Are you on drugs?' Alakusheva snapped. She seemed to have it in for Jock.

'No, no! I went to help a Roma who was being attacked and then the attack turned on me,' he said.

Jock felt Alakusheva was not listening to what he said about the Gypsy and the fight. Instead, she wanted to find out more about him.

'Why did you come to Bulgaria?' the investigator persisted.

'I came as a tourist on holidays from the British Army. I came to see friends.'

'No, you came here for cheap prostitutes, didn't you?'

Jock was shocked and furious. When he said nothing, Alakusheva looked at Barborski, who repeated the question. Jock recalls both the investigator and the lawyer then asked him which terrorist organisation he belonged to.

This time Jock laughed. 'The biggest one in the world—the British military,' he said. This interrogation seemed to be straight out of a KGB handbook.

'What drugs are you on?' asked Barborski, hunched over the desk, his worn-out suit hanging loosely across his narrow shoulders.

Jock turned to Galina. 'Is he supposed to be *my* lawyer?' he asked.

Tanya Alakusheva told Jock he was being charged with murder, to which he responded that he was not guilty. She then asked him to tell her what had happened.

Jock was wary. The young Bulgarian he had met at the Rock Bar, whom he knew as Tony, was already anxious about his personal security, so Jock did not want to identify him. He did not want to name the hostel or the bar they had frequented, as he liked the people who ran them. When asked where he was staying, he said Borisova Garden Park, the big park near Sofia University.

Jock knew that friends in Samokov could vouch for his character, but did not want them subjected to interrogation by police from Sofia, who, he believed, treated rural folk with contempt. Jock was close to the parents and grandparents of his friends and shuddered to think of them being subjected to the indignity of a witch hunt. They were honest, decent people who had taken him in as one of their own.

Jock's naïve determination to shield others only worsened his situation, but he did not grasp that yet. He was still convinced that the matter would soon be resolved and that the police focus would turn from him to the youths who had attacked him. He even hoped that he would not have to worry his family by contacting them until he was released and back in Madjare.

The police statement that resulted from his interrogation was thin on detail. At times it reads jerkily, because Jock is responding to questions that have not been recorded. Jock's answers have also been translated from English into Bulgarian and back again.

'On 27 December the three of us—Lindsay, Grayham and me—we came to Sofia for a night. We went to a rock bar in the centre. We stayed there for a few hours. I know neither the name of the bar, nor exactly where it is because I don't know the city. I had about three to four beers. After that Grayham suddenly disappeared. We waited for him a bit and then we left. Lindsay, a Bulgarian guy called Ivan and another Bulgarian whose name I don't know, but I remember he was wearing a leather jacket with the Union Jack on the back, we went to some place in the centre of the city, but it was closed.

'At some point we saw a group of about ten boys and a moment later we saw some other boys running away from this group of boys. Then we also ran away to the garden of the same place that was closed. No one was chasing us. The group of boys were talking about something in loud voices. During the whole time, they were across the road. At some point I saw that these boys were beating a man who I think was a Gypsy. I think this man was alone. He'd fallen on the ground and they were kicking him. I don't want to give a testimony about what happened after that.

'Grayham looks like a punk—he has that kind of haircut. He has blond hair. I guess he went back to Madjare. I don't know Grayham's surname or that of Lindsay. I think she entered the country through Sofia airport on 24 December. I think she has already left for England because she had some work to do and she'd booked a ticket for 28 December. I know that she lives in Bristol, England. I don't Ivan's know surname or where he lives. I only know that he's from Sofia. I don't know the name of the boy with the leather jacket with the Union Jack.

'I want to add that what happened was not planned. I didn't expect this to happen. I didn't resist the police officers.'

During the coming week, Alakusheva would interview a steady stream of witnesses, each with a different version of what had happened. Although she was familiar with the layout of St Nedelya Square, she must have struggled to piece together who was where, and when. Nevertheless, her job was to test these accounts against what the suspect had said, keeping in mind that he might not have been the perpetrator after all.

· . ·

The Rila Mountains
4.30 p.m.

As Grayham Saunders drove back to the village from the airport, he got a text message from Iliyan, the first Bulgarian friend Jock had made in the area: 'Where's Jock? What has happened to Jock?'

This must be serious, Grayham thought. Knowing his guest had been arrested but little more, Grayham texted back: 'Why, what's up?' Iliyan responded immediately, asking him to come to his house in Samokov.

Early that morning, Iliyan had been at work in a factory that made paper napkins when his mother phoned to say his aunt in Germany had read a report online about an Australian with a name that resembled Jock's. They were worried and wanted him to check it. His aunt emailed Iliyan the link and he printed out the story. Iliyan still has the crumpled page, a dnes.dir. bg/news article headlined 'Australian Fatally Stabbed a Youth in Sofia'. The lanky twenty-two-year-old told his mother this could not be Jock; the guy who had lived with him for three months could not have stabbed anyone.

In 2005 Jock and Grayham had been at a table near Iliyan in his favourite coffee shop, speaking English and laughing. Jock looked like a vagrant, hair everywhere; Grayham wore a mohawk. Iliyan's mates thought they looked weird and wanted nothing to do with them. But foreigners were rare in Samokov and Iliyan thought these ones looked like fun. He took the risk and introduced himself.

Iliyan's English was rough and Jock's Bulgarian rougher still, but they managed to communicate with a combination of animated gestures and a blend of Bulgarian, English and German. They shared a love of Yamaha motorbikes, music and girls. Iliyan, who was a Jack of all trades, went to Madjare whenever he could during his lunch breaks to help the foreigners work on Grayham's house. After Grayham left, Jock had briefly lived with Iliyan before moving in with a Bulgarian family.

During the harvest Jock had worked in the potato fields alongside Iliyan from sunrise to sunset for 20 *leva* (about A\$16) a day. He knew the Bulgarian words for three different kinds of potato before he could say 'How are you?' They loaded and then drove a UAZ truck with a clutch that rushed on ignition and an old Soviet engine that always rumbled comfortingly. Many times they had cried laughing as they tried to avoid ending up in the river by trying to do a sudden U-turn without driving into the row of potato plants that ran alongside it.

By then Iliyan's friends had well and truly got over their initial reservations about the Australian. Iliyan's family regarded him as one of them. Jock gave Iliyan's grandmother all the money he earned for her to look after so he would not waste it. He called her *Baba Kasa*, Granny Bank, because she kept his cash for him in a tin. Whenever he walked past her house with his little dog Walkabout, she gave him apples from her tree. After work he would chop her firewood.

Iliyan's only concern about the young man was his propensity to intervene when he saw someone in trouble. Many times he had told Jock to mind his own business or he would end up getting them both in hot water. The only thing they ever argued about was Gypsies: Iliyan thought they were human filth, while Jock insisted they were the same as everyone else and that the government was to blame for their impoverishment.

Samokov had not been the same since the crazy Australian left.

Right now, Iliyan could not concentrate, but he could not leave work because he relied on a fellow factory worker for a lift home. One friend or family member after another phoned to ask if he knew anything. All he knew was that two days earlier Jock had gone to a ski resort with Grayham and Lindsay, intending to stay the night with him afterwards in Samokov. Somehow, Jock had not been able to find Iliyan that night, so he had walked all the way back to Madjare. The next day Jock had told

Iliyan he was going to Sofia with his British friends and promised to call him when he returned.

Iliyan thought it most unlikely that Jock would have been carrying a knife. He had never seen him take one on a night out, even though his friend had seen enough violence to make carrying a weapon seem a sensible precaution.

By the time Grayham was sitting in Iliyan's small bedroom, it was getting dark. They looked out at the wall dividing the Roma quarter of Samokov from the rest of the city and searched online for more details. Iliyan said a local policeman he knew had rung him in search of Jock's passport. Samokov was a small place. Everyone knew Jock and Iliyan had been friends.

The two men drove to Madjare to get the passport and then to the policeman's house in Samokov, because the station had shut for the day. When Grayham finally got home that night, he remembered that Jock had once borrowed his mobile phone to call his relatives in Bath. Locating the number, he sent them a text message.

· · ·

Bath, England

Geri Palfreeman and her partner, Paul Henaghan, were cooking dinner for friends in their three-storey house in the postcard-pretty English city of Bath. A blanket of freshly fallen snow twinkled in the moonlight as she drew the curtains to let the Aga stove warm up the kitchen.

Her father, Tony, a political scientist, had been fascinated by the Soviet Union and on sabbatical leave had toured much of Eastern Europe by car. Tony's sense of adventure had been contagious. When Simon finished school, he had worked as a stable hand outside Geneva and on an oil rig in the North Sea, unlikely gap year jobs for someone so bookish.

Sixteen years earlier Geri had come to England in search of adventure. She had loved the country and quickly found work as a social worker. Six years later, she met Paul.

The couple did not have children, but they were close to their nieces and nephews, many of whom had stayed with them over the years. Geri looked across at the uneven row of pencil marks on one of the kitchen's walls, where each child had marked his or her height. Near the top was Jock's mark.

She was sad that her eldest nephew had suddenly changed his mind about spending Christmas with them. Jock had originally thought he would stay in his barracks for Christmas, but his Army superiors advised him against that: next year, he could be in Afghanistan. Jock thought about returning to Australia but decided there was not enough time. The Army paid for his train ticket to Bath.

When Grayham Saunders called, Jock changed his mind and swapped the ticket for one to London, from where he would fly to Sofia. Jock knew he would have to pay a fine when he got to Bulgaria for overstaying on his last trip. Then his passport went missing under paperwork at the barracks and there was a scramble to find it. Everything seemed to conspire against his getting back to the Rila Mountains.

In London, Jock went out with a Fijian recruit. To catch his early-morning flight, he would have to get the last train to the airport that night. But the two young men met up with some gorgeous girls. Jock was tempted to forgo the trip and stay in London. As one of the girls pleaded with him to keep drinking with them, Jock weighed the decision in his mind. Bulgaria won. He just made the last train and boarded the easyJet flight to Sofia on 22 December 2007.

By 9.30 p.m. on the 28th, Geri and Paul and their visitors were well into dinner when Paul noticed he had a text message. He has kept it to this day. It read: 'hi is that jock's uncle? If it is it's his friend grayham here. He's in big trouble, please call me.' Dessert was abandoned.

. . .

Australian Embassy, Athens
6 p.m.

It was not until early that Friday evening that David Chaplin finally managed to confirm that the trainee soldier in custody in Sofia was an Australian citizen. The Foreign Affairs department in Canberra could not inform Jock Palfreeman's family of his incarceration until they had permission to do so from the young man himself. Chaplin needed to get that permission from Jock as well as checking on his welfare. He decided he would go to the airport the next day and buy a ticket to Sofia for Monday morning. Since he would not have time to obtain the Bulgarian visa necessary for him to travel on his red diplomatic passport, Chaplin would have to get his office to issue him with an emergency blue one, which would let him enter the country without a visa. It was going to be a frantic thirty-six hours.

. . .

Jock's friends in Samokov had no idea anything was wrong until they saw a bTV News story about an Australian who had stabbed someone several times. Interviewed on camera, Kristian Dimov said the attacker had seemed 'high' rather than drunk. Kristian spoke in a monotone, not once looking at the reporter. His only show of expression was a slightly raised eyebrow. For most of the forty-second-long exchange, his eyes were focused on the ground.

Kristian said he had taken a taxi to see Andrei in hospital and then gone to the police station. 'They were supposed to tell his parents,' he added in reference to police. 'And in the morning when I saw the other friends, Andrei's mother called me and asked "Is Andrei with you; where is he?", and I hung up.' Kristian's voice trembled. 'What should I have told her?'

The news report also included an interview with Sonja Momchilova, described as a Monov family friend and a former spokesperson for the Interior Ministry. 'Thanks to telephone numbers that I have and the contacts that I still have, more than twelve hours after the incident, I managed to find out who the victim was, and to tell the parents,' she explained. Teary-eyed and clearly frustrated, the middle-aged woman said she then phoned someone of importance to seek an explanation, but did not get one.

Iliyan's grandmother did not trust police or the justice system. She worried what would happen to Jock now. She started keeping a scrapbook of newspaper clippings about his case and resolved not to touch the last pile of wood he had stacked until he returned.

. . .

St Nedelya Square, Sofia

As Nikolai Kotev made his way to work at the Sheraton hotel, where he was an overnight car park attendant, he saw a broken window in the building that housed the Ministry of Health. Last night someone was throwing either rocks or loose concrete pavers, so it might have been broken then. Unlike Viktor Georgiev, who had been elsewhere in the car park at the same time, Nikolai had not paid much attention to what happened before the rocks were thrown.

Taxi drivers from the Stamboliyski Boulevard rank, which was located alongside the blood-stained footpath, were standing around smoking with staff from the Happy restaurant and drivers from the Sheraton taxi rank. They talked about the fight and about the dead boy. Rumour had it that his father was an important person with connections to the police, but Nikolai had not heard of Hristo Monov.

Some said a Gypsy prostitute who had been working around the church knew what had happened. This did not surprise Nikolai. There were always Gypsies loitering in the shadows there—pickpockets, most of them, waiting for people to come out of coffee shops and bars. Gypsies also hung around the metro entrance at all hours, seeking shelter. Nikolai assumed police would already have spoken to the prostitute and to the many taxi drivers who had been in the area at that time. He also assumed they would very soon contact all the staff who had been on duty in the Sheraton car park.

With so many CCTV cameras in St Nedelya Square, he thought, it would be easy for police to work out exactly what had happened. In fact, all they would need to do would be to look through the footage taken outside the Ministry of Health building, where the arrest had taken place. But no one was asking for his opinion.

. . .

The icy streets of Sofia glittered with headlights. A police van took Jock to the Remand Centre adjoining the notoriously run-down and overcrowded Sofia Central Prison. He had not been able to contact Australian diplomatic staff, the British Army, or his family. He had no idea that his friends in Bulgaria were trying to find him. One prison gate after another slammed shut behind him. Jock was in too much shock to feel anything but numb. He later recognised this as an instinctive defence mechanism. He would need it to get through worse events to come.

Jock was strip-searched and pushed into a claustrophobically small cell with two Turkish prisoners. The cell was about two metres by four metres and had two sets of iron-framed bunk beds that were welded to the ground. Like the prison, the Remand Centre did not provide a uniform. On the bunk was a threadbare square blanket that went from Jock's neck to his knees, and that was it. There was no heating and the damp cold crept through his clothes. The night suddenly seemed impenetrably cold and dark.

All Jock wanted to do was sleep. Forever. But he knew he needed to be on guard. Jock fully expected guards to burst in and beat him, as the police had done at the station. He could hear cops laying into prisoners in other cells. Outside, the hounds of Sofia maintained their watch, marking out territory with barking that cracked like a whip and echoed down the streets and alleys, one dog after another, long into the night.

Newspapers were finalising their reports on the tragedy for the next morning's editions. The headline in the tabloid *Standard* was 'Drunken Australian Defending his Girlfriend'. The story claimed that the Australian had stabbed the two Bulgarians after they made lewd comments and gestured at his girlfriend in the metro. The popular *24 Hours* ran with the headline: 'An Australian Slaughtered Young Man near Sheraton'. The article read in part: 'The butchering happened around 1 a.m. . . . During the interrogation at Police Station No. 3 the Australian behaved inappropriately and was amused by the questions asked by the investigators. He explained that he had arrived in Bulgaria on 22 December and he stayed in Borisova Garden Park where he slept in a sack.'

The online news site dnes.dir.bg was running with 'Andrei Monov Murdered by the Hit of a Professional'. Citing bTV sources, it said: 'According to the prosecution this completely rejects the theory that the group of youths among which was Andrei Monov, son of the famous psychologist Hristo Monov, attacked the Australian John Paul Freeman. Such a hit could not have been inflicted if the Australian was acting in self-defence.'

According to the current Deputy Chief Prosecutor of Sofia, Bozhidar Dzhambazov, the prosecution is in charge of deciding what information about a case can be released to the media. Dzhambazov says that under Communism, talk of crime was banned, so since the transition to capitalism the Bulgarian public has been hungry for information. Dzhambazov adds that in their quest to satisfy that desire, prosecutors have yet to find the right balance between public expectation and the suspect's right to be deemed innocent until proven guilty.

The prosecutor in charge of Jock's case was Parvoleta Nikova. In her thirties, she had risen quickly from investigating officer in the southern port city of Burgas, a haven for smugglers, to a prosecutor in a nearby town and now to the prestigious post of prosecutor bringing cases before the Sofia City Court. This case would help make her career. It would be years before the lid was lifted on the double life Nikova was leading in Burgas when she was not required in the capital.

PART II
THE INVESTIGATION

CHAPTER 4

Saturday, 29 December 2007
Police Station No. 3
10 a.m.

Tanya Alakusheva was in her office, trying to clear enough space on her desk to set down her notepad. She had sixty days to complete her investigation and submit her report to the prosecutor. Brushing away the cigarette ash strewn across some of the files, she looked up at the calendar on the wall. Day Two, and she already felt as if she had been in this room for years.

More of the people who had been out with Andrei Monov turned up at the station to give statements.

Eighteen-year-old high school student Nikolai Rabadzhiev was not actually one of Andrei's friends; like a few others that night, he was a friend of a friend. The teenager told Alakusheva that he had not been drinking that night. Crossing St Nedelya Square, Nikolai was further ahead of Andrei and the stragglers, and he saw only brief snatches of the incident when he turned his head to see what was going on behind him.

'As we went by the Ministry of Health we passed two boys of Roma origin. I didn't pay any attention to them. Then we crossed Stamboliyski Boulevard, walking slowly. I turned around to see if the others were coming and then I saw that some of the people who were with us were walking . . . with their heads turned back to see these two Roma. I didn't hear an exchange of words because they were a long way off. I did not see conflict between them or an exchange of blows. I didn't even see them stopping alongside each other. Then we moved on.'

Nikolai told the investigator that he had noticed three people in the garden area of the Happy restaurant who he thought looked like 'skinheads or punks'. As he passed them, Nikolai had seen Jock taking off towards the square. He made no mention of a knife. Possibly because Nikolai was focused on the Happy garden, he does not appear to have seen the altercation with the Roma or the rush of youths towards the metro that other group members had described.

The next thing Nikolai saw was significant, as it painted a very different picture of what had happened between Jock and the youths: 'I turned back to see where he was going and then I saw that he had crossed the boulevard and was getting closer to the people in our group who had lagged behind. At that moment they were near the cigarette kiosk. I kept on going for a few seconds and then I heard shouts behind me. I turned around and saw that the boy had started running to the subway with people running after him. There was a commotion.'

Nikolai did not give any detail about the fracas that ensued, but his chronology of events, however fractured, is important. According to him, Jock had tried to run away before the final showdown.

. . .

Samokov, Bulgaria

Iliyan Yordanov rang Grayham and told him that, according to a story on the radio, police were still looking for a blonde American lesbian. The two men agreed that this must be Lindsay and arranged to meet at the Samokov police station.

Grayham felt he was in a Keystone Cops movie as he tried to give the officer on the front desk Tony's name and mobile number, as well as Lindsay's full name and mobile number. No one would take down the details. Through the white noise of a language he did not understand and the confusion of Iliyan's rough attempts to translate, Grayham gathered the officers just wanted him to wait to be contacted and not to leave Bulgaria.

By now both Iliyan and he were extremely concerned: Iliyan for Jock, and Grayham increasingly for himself as well.

For the rest of the day Iliyan tried unsuccessfully to find out more from the Samokov police. But downtown Sofia was well out of their patch. It seemed that one arm of the police had trouble talking to the other.

. . .

Police Station No. 3

Just before midday, Blagovest Trifonov arrived at the police station to see Tanya Alakusheva. The twenty-one-year-old was one of three young men who claimed to have seen Jock in the act of stabbing. The investigator would find his statement particularly helpful.

As the group crossed the square after leaving the metro, Blagovest said, he was at the kiosk; behind him were Andrei, Antoan, Tony, Kristian, Alexander and Emil, among others. Unlike some of the witnesses who had given statements earlier, Blagovest said nothing about seeing an altercation of any kind near the subway. He said the first sign of conflict appeared five metres from the kiosk in the direction of the metro.

Blagovest said he heard 'shouts in English', that he did not understand, coming from a 'boy' he did not know who was with a 'girl with short blonde hair'. The noise prompted Blagovest to turn around. 'The next moment the boy took out a big knife. Then he swung the knife once at Tony,' said Blagovest, referring to his friend Tony Yordanov. 'Tony managed to step back. The next moment the boy swung very hard from down to up and thrust the knife into Andrei's ribs from the left. Then he pulled the knife out [of Andrei's body] and continued brandishing it at the others. After that I was only looking at Andrei. I saw that he went pale; he clutched his wound and moved towards the intersection. I asked him if he was okay, but he didn't answer. I went after him. When he reached the road, he fell down. A pool of blood immediately formed around him.'

Blagovest said he and two others pleaded with Andrei, begging him not to leave them. Then Antoan came up to them, clutching his right side and moaning. When Blagovest lifted Antoan's clothing, he saw blood.

Like Kristian Dimov and Nikolai Rabadzhiev, Blagovest first saw Jock near the kiosk and the Ministry of Health. He recalled seeing the attacker take out a knife. This again suggested that Jock had not run into the group brandishing a weapon. Emil Aleksiev had also said the attacker drew a knife after approaching the group, but he had said that happened north-east of the Ministry of Health. There were gaps in the accounts, and it was the investigator's job to fill them in.

If Blagovest's recollection of events was accurate, the blonde woman standing next to the man with the knife might have witnessed the stabbing. Finding Jock's companion should have been paramount. Yet the chief investigating officer does not seem to have been focusing on discrepancies, gaps or missing eyewitnesses.

Tanya Alakusheva was struck by Blagovest's description of 'Tony' and his near escape from death. She assumed he was referring to Tony Yordanov, one of Andrei Monov's friends, who was still to be interviewed.

As Alakusheva opened a new pack of cigarettes, she thought about the knife used that night. It was a silver-coloured butterfly knife, one of the biggest she had come across. According to an undated report written by the Director of the Forensic Medicine and Deontology Centre at Alexandrovska Hospital, Associate Professor Stanislav Hristov, the blade was 12.3 centimetres long, and the handle unfolded to 28.5 centimetres. While the blade was sharp on only one side, it had a sharp tip. At its widest, the blade was three centimetres. There was a hilt at the top of the blade and a handle, or 'box', through which the bearer could put his fingers to steady his grip. There were speckles and sprays of blood along the sharp edge and near the hilt, as well as a small amount of blood at the tip. By the time police sent the knife away to check for blood, hair and skin, it had been folded shut.

· · ·

Alexandrovska Hospital, Sofia
11 a.m.
By now Andrei Monov's corpse had been transported to Alexandrovska Hospital and marked *Body No. 1166/07*. Three forensic doctors would

perform the autopsy. Among them was the author of the knife report, Stanislav Hristov.

In Bulgaria, forensic doctors did the job of many experts. Sometimes the investigator oversaw the autopsy, directing a police criminologist when to photograph the procedure. At other times the job was left to the forensic doctors and a hospital photographer. It is not clear how things were organised in this case, but very few photographs were taken. It is also not clear why the autopsy was not done on the night of the incident or even the following day.

In their preliminary report, the doctors gave Andrei Monov's age incorrectly as twenty-two and got his identity number wrong. They noted that Pirogov Hospital had informed them that the young man was dead by the time the ambulance reached St Nedelya Square. Describing the deceased male as 189 centimetres tall with a normal body mass, the doctors noted a cut wound in the left half of the chest on the back armpit line—in other words, below the armpit. The wound on the skin was three centimetres long and the wound canal passed into the seventh intercostal space (between the seventh and eighth ribs), touching the bottom part of the left lung and the left of the pericardium, and cutting the left heart chamber and septum. The wound canal was twelve to thirteen centimetres long. It ran from left to right, slightly back to forward and almost horizontal. There were two cuts on the victim's face and bruising on his knees.

The doctors concluded that the injury to the chest, cutting through the lung and heart, caused the death, leading as it did to severe blood loss and haemopneumothorax (air and blood in the chest cavity). The bruises and wounds on the face, and the bruises on the knees, were caused by a solid, blunt object and could have been incurred when the victim fell to the ground. They played no role in the death.

The three doctors signed the report. Within three months, however, it would be the last thing on their minds. By then, forensic medicine in Bulgaria would itself be under investigation.

. . .

Police Station No. 3

5.10 p.m.

Chief Investigating Officer Alakusheva opened the door to a dark-haired woman dressed in black. It cannot have been easy to listen to Anton Monov's grieving mother, who proceeded to recount her experiences that day. Aksenia signed her statement on the line beside the word 'Witness' and again beside 'Victim'. She looked up, her large eyes glistening. But Aksenia did not cry. She told Alakusheva how she had learned of her son's death and related Andrei's friends' claim that her son had been repeatedly stabbed, including in the neck.

The investigator thanked Aksenia for coming and shut the door after the middle-aged woman left. Although tired, she then filed the statement along with all the others and checked the experts' reports.

Andrei Monov, Antoan Zahariev and Jock Palfreeman were the only people whose blood had been taken for testing. The results for Jock and Antoan were in. There was no sign that either of the young men had taken drugs, but both had been drinking. Jock was found to have a blood alcohol concentration of 0.015 per cent and a urine alcohol concentration of 0.026 per cent. Associate Professor Maria Grozeva estimated that Jock's blood alcohol concentration at the time of the incident would have been 1 per cent promille, or 'per thousand'. This translates to 0.1 grams per 100 millilitres of blood, double the legal driving limit in Australia. Antoan's blood alcohol level at the time he was tested was equivalent to 0.18 grams per 100 millilitres. At almost four times the legal driving limit, Andrei's friend was very drunk.

. . .

6.40 p.m.

Mladen Nikolov had been bullied as a child and robbed several times as an adult, so mindless violence really angered him. He had not learnt that someone had died until he returned to his job at the kiosk in St Nedelya Square on the Friday evening after the incident. He was surprised and upset to hear that what he'd seen had gone beyond a drunken brawl.

Early the next day a female investigator called and asked him to give a statement. After two overnight shifts from 7.30 p.m. to 7.30 a.m., he was tired, but he turned up at Police Station No. 3 on Saturday evening as requested.

Mladen was a bright twenty-five-year-old marketing student who worked a few nights a week to make ends meet. As he waited to see the chief investigator, Mladen made a mental list of what he had seen and heard. He recalled that the square had been pretty busy on the night in question. He assumed that one of the many CCTV cameras in the area would have recorded the incident. Since he had been sitting in the kiosk with his back to the Ministry of Health, where much of the commotion had taken place, he wasn't sure what use his testimony would be. During the brawl he had heard a lot of rocks being thrown behind him; he had been scared that one of them would smash the kiosk window. He had turned around to see what was going on, but the little window was mostly blocked off by bottles and it had been hard to see through it. Nevertheless, he had gathered that two groups of youths were in a fight.

Mladen told Tanya Alakusheva that a man and a woman had bought cigarettes from him. Then, about five or ten minutes later, a group of about twenty young men ran past his kiosk. They were shouting 'Hey *mango!*' (an offensive term for Gypsy). 'In less than a minute this same group returned, but they were not running anymore, they were walking in a relaxed way, they were joking. I thought they were drunk, at least some of them were. There were two who almost bumped into my kiosk because they were staggering.'

Mladen said the group was heading towards the T-junction. Before the youths crossed Stamboliyski he saw them turn around, as if looking at someone. 'They started to shout and scream, I don't remember exactly what, but it was something threatening. At this point I saw two or three people—I think there were only boys, I'm not too sure—who were two or three metres away from them. Of these newly arrived boys there was one boy who was very aggressive and was spitting at the bigger group. And I was thinking—why is this one going against so many people? The people who were with that boy tried to calm him down and pulled him aside.

'The boys from the big group were also shouting something at him. Just then I saw some of the boys from the big group throwing stones at the aggressive boy. One of them bent over and took a whole tile from the pavement and threw it at him. I didn't see them hit anyone from the small group [members of which] took the stones that had fallen near them and started throwing them back at the big group. The aggressive boy and his friends started moving back towards the Ministry of Health building, so I couldn't see what was going on, but I could clearly hear that stones were thrown around.

'Then I heard clearly "Put the knife down." Literally the next moment I heard shouts of "Call an ambulance."'

Mladen was convinced that the aggressive member of the smaller group must have been the perpetrator. What he did not know was that there had been only one group and an individual—that is, Andrei's cohort and Jock. According to later witnesses, including Jock himself, Jock had been surrounded. The 'second group' Mladen identified might well have been Jock with members of Andrei's crowd behind and to the side of him, throwing things and spitting at him in a way that Mladen mistakenly thought was directed at the bigger group.

Mladen had heard far more than he had seen that night. 'I did not see a man with a knife,' he said. 'I didn't see a stabbing. I did not see anyone lying on Stamboliyski.' All he was certain of was that there was a lot of violence before someone called out for an ambulance.

. . .

8.00 p.m.

Tony Yordanov was unemployed and, at twenty-three, older than most of the other members of Andrei's group. He was referred to by other witnesses as Tony the Tall, and he would play a significant role in the court proceedings. His account placed him with Andrei, Kristian Dimov and Alexander Donev, those who had lagged behind as the group crossed the square, and who reached the traffic lights last. This is part of the statement Tony signed:

'Part of our group had already crossed Stamboliyski Boulevard when we passed by a man. I think he was a Roma but I'm not sure. He was going towards the metro. The man was saying something. I didn't understand what exactly he was saying or to whom he was speaking, so I turned back to him and asked him what he wanted. He didn't say anything specific; he kept on saying something while looking at us. I can't say whether the man was talking to me . . .

'Then some people from our group—I can't remember exactly who—ran towards that man. They stopped halfway between the subway and Stamboliyski Boulevard. There was some kind of commotion, you could hear shouting. I also went there to see what was going on. I saw no one hitting anyone. There was only an exchange of words. My memories from then are confused. I know that the Roma person left. The next thing I remember is a man with a knife in his hand next to me. He was shouting something in English and at the same time, brandishing the knife at us.'

Tony said Antoan and Andrei were on his left. The attacker was saying something about some fascists; he was aggressively brandishing the knife at everyone. 'In the next moment the boy turned to me and swung the knife from the left to the right two or three times towards my stomach. I instinctively pulled back, twisting my body . . . The knife passed very close to my body and had I not pulled away he would have hit me. Then the boy started to brandish it at my friends standing near me. I can't say who was next to me at that moment because I was just looking at the knife. I didn't notice blood on it, but I'm not sure because at that moment I was stressing out.

'. . . I tripped for a moment on one of the concrete flower pots in the square and fell on the ground and the boy came at me. I curled in a defensive position on the ground as I was trying to protect my body with my hands. At this moment someone on my right pushed the boy with the knife and got him away from me. Later I found out that this was Kristian. The boy withdrew from us and again headed after the rest. I stood up. On the ground I saw a piece of a tile. I took it and threw it at the attacker to make him drop the knife. I wasn't aiming at his head; I was trying to hit his body, but failed. Once again I tried to hit him with another piece, once again I failed.'

Tony then described how two people he thought were plain-clothes police officers got the attacker onto the ground next to the Ministry of Health and kept them all away from him.

Tanya Alakusheva added Tony's statement to her folder. He had had a lucky escape and might have become a third victim, she thought. *Small wonder that he tried to retaliate after such an attack.*

She decided that there was enough evidence for the prosecutor to finalise the charges against the Australian.

CHAPTER 5

30 December 2007
Sofia, Bulgaria

On Sunday morning the sun streamed through the Monovs' sitting-room window, snowflakes dancing for a moment on the ledge before turning to slush. Aksenia and Hristo sat together, trying to find the right words for the *necrolog*, a sheet of paper detailing the death of a loved one.

Aksenia had been inconsolable as she looked for the perfect photograph of her baby. The familiar smell of Andrei still hung in his bedroom; it was as if he had just swept through it on his way out somewhere. She had sat for a moment on his bed. The emptiness of the room overwhelmed her.

Aksenia had always dreaded the day when she would have to farewell her dear father, who was getting on in years. But Andrei had not even celebrated his twenty-first birthday. It seemed unthinkable to be taking part in this ritual of death for her son.

In Bulgaria, *necrologs* are a traditional way of transmitting news of a death. They are plastered on bus stops and on electricity poles, walls and trees, in places that the loved one used to frequent. They include a photograph of the person who has died. The eyes of the dead follow the living as the *necrologs* flutter at passersby before growing tattered.

The Monovs kept it simple. A photograph of Andrei in his suit. A cross. His name and the fact that he had died.

They posted a copy of the *necrolog* on their front door. It was the Bulgarian way of telling the world: this is a household in mourning.

That day's edition of the *Telegraph* quoted Hristo as saying, 'My son has never hit or attacked anybody. He was an extremely good child. Although I don't want to create a fanfare about [what happened to] my son until the funeral is over, the case should not be forgotten.'

Hristo Monov's wish would be granted.

. . .

Remand Centre

A guard barked at Jock that he was to get up. Two police officers yanked his arms behind him and applied handcuffs before bundling the confused Australian into the back of an unmarked car. For the first time since the attack, Jock was scared stiff. These people could make him disappear, he thought; they could kill him.

Jock sat wedged between the officers as the prison gates opened and they took off through Sofia. He could feel the officers breathing. Dread inched its way through every flinching muscle in his body. No one spoke. He had no idea where they were going.

They passed graffiti-covered buildings, some bearing the word *Ataka*, the name of the far-right nationalist party. There were also many swastikas and Celtic crosses, a symbol appropriated by neo-Nazi groups in many parts of Europe and locally by some members of the Levski Ultras, a section of a football club that had a reputation for violence.

It was only when Police Station No. 3 came into view that Jock fully exhaled. The officers removed his handcuffs, pushed him into the holding cell and locked the gate. The smell made him reel. One detainee was still there from two days before. 'What are you still doing here?' Jock asked in his bad Bulgarian. The prisoner said he still did not know why he was being held. Jock tried to explain that police had no right to hold him for longer than twenty-four hours without charging him.

An hour later, he was taken to Tanya Alakusheva's office. His lawyer was there, along with Galina. The investigator said the Prosecutor's Office would charge Jock with the premeditated murder of Andrei Monov and the attempted murder of Antoan Zahariev. She added that the charge included the attempted murder of more than one person with 'hooligan intent'. In the Bulgarian legal code, 'hooliganism' has a specific meaning that dates back to the Soviet era and refers to reckless antisocial behaviour.

All Jock took in was the word *murder*. Once again he said he wasn't guilty. The rest of the charge made little sense to him. In his mind, hooliganism referred to the behaviour of loutish football fans.

The investigator wanted to know more about what had happened that night, but Jock was reluctant to say anything. At 4 p.m. he signed a statement confirming his previous statement. The only points he added were that he had acted in self-defence and to defend the Gypsy. He said that he understood the charges.

An officer returned him to the holding cell, where Jock wrongly assumed his lawyer would see him. There was no indication that any of the hooligans had been charged, and this was starting to both worry and anger him.

. . .

That afternoon Grayham drove to Sofia, searching blindly for a police station where he could find out what had happened to Jock and report what he knew about the incident. He was on his own and spoke very little Bulgarian. Eventually he walked the streets near the large police station not far from St Nedelya Square. Eventually he asked a passing policeman where he could give information about the man whom the media called 'the Australian stabber'. He was met with a blank look. Finally, another officer pointed him in the direction of a run-down station further away, Police Station No. 3. There he warily handed over his passport at the front desk.

Waiting in the reception area for the investigator, Grayham stared at the stairwell. Handcuffed to its railing was the Bulgarian man who he had thought was flirting with Lindsay at the Rock Bar. The sight alarmed him. If the cops got the idea that he was associated with this guy, they might treat him the same way. Grayham averted his gaze and said nothing. Soon police took the fellow away to an interview room. To this day Grayham has no idea whether the man was connected to the trouble Jock was in or whether he was picked up for some unrelated reason.

Shouting and banging cut through Grayham's uncertainty. He strained to see what was going on in the cells at the bottom of the stairwell. An officer laughed and told him it was just a Gypsy. Grayham could see another kicking at the cell's bars and heard screams. At one point he saw the young Roma who seemed to be at the centre of the uproar, and who looked like a small homeless kid, in pretty bad shape.

Grayham was terrified. This was exactly what he had feared a Bulgarian police station would be like. When Bulgaria was being considered for membership in the European Union, concerns had been aired about its police and legal system. Grayham recalled seeing headlines back in 2005 about an eighteen-year-old Liverpool football fan called Michael Shields, who had been convicted of attempted murder after a brawl in Bulgaria and sentenced to fifteen years in prison. Grayham had followed the case because it began just as he was sorting out his investment in Madjare.

Shields had been holidaying with other Liverpool fans in Golden Sands, on the Black Sea, after watching their team win the Champions League in Turkey. A fight had broken out, and a barman was attacked and hit on the head with a concrete paver; his skull was broken and he was lucky to survive the attack. Shields claimed to have been in bed when the incident took place. Another British fan confessed to the crime once he was safely back in England. The British media took up Shields's case, arguing that the Bulgarian police had framed him.

In April 2006 Bulgaria's highest appellate court, the Supreme Court of Cassation, reduced Shields's sentence to ten years. The British government then successfully applied to have Shields extradited, and at the end of 2006 he began serving the rest of his sentence in a British prison not far from his parents in Liverpool. In May 2007, the European Court of Human Rights rejected an appeal by Shields. However, his local Member of Parliament, Fair Trials International (an organisation that monitors such cases around the world) and the Liverpool Football Club continued to argue that his conviction should be quashed. In the eyes of many British citizens, Bulgaria still ran the kind of show trials that had been infamous during the worst excesses of the Soviet Union.

As a prospective EU member, Bulgaria had been given hundreds of millions of euros to help it get its house in order. But as January 2007 approached, the EU had expressed concerns that the Balkan country was still not ready for accession. It had cited ongoing corruption, organised crime, and flaws in the judicial system. Bulgaria was then admitted only on the condition that Brussels monitor a program of reforms. Some Bulgarians resented this and found the outside interference humiliating. They asked what gave foreigners the right to question the Bulgarian justice system.

Given the animosity, now did not feel like a good time to be British. Grayham was slightly relieved when a young woman introduced herself as Galina and said she would be his interpreter. When they were finally called into Tanya Alakusheva's office, the investigator wanted to know why Lindsay had left Bulgaria so quickly and why Grayham had driven straight back to Madjare after dropping her at the airport. Grayham tried to explain that Lindsay had a longstanding booking on the flight to London and that they had not known someone had died.

Grayham thought Alakusheva was trying to establish whether his Australian friend was part of an organised gang of anti-fascist punks, the kind who got into fights with skinheads in Eastern Europe, particularly at football matches, and justified violence by saying they were opposing racism. He was a punk, but not that kind of punk. He recollects Alakusheva asking him, 'Was this the first time you had been to the Rock Bar?'; 'Had you met the Bulgarians there before?'; 'What's the difference between a rocker and a punk?'; 'Why do punks not like fascists?' These seemed like odd questions in a murder investigation. Grayham could see that things were even worse for Jock than he had thought. He grew wary of being drawn into the sinister scenario the investigator seemed to be constructing.

In his statement, Grayham related how he met Jock, how he came to be at the Rock Bar that night, and how he found out that something bad had happened after he left Jock and Lindsay:

'At some point Lindsay came in the room. She was very upset. She said that [she] had left the bar together with Jock and Tony [Anton Doychev], and as they were walking along the street, they saw a group of seven to ten boys. I don't know exactly what happened. But for some reason Tony told them that these are football hooligans. Lindsay said then there was a fight between these boys and Jock. She told me she saw Jock on his knees and the group of boys was hitting him. When she tried to help him, someone kicked her at the stomach and then at the back—I got the impression that Tony wasn't involved in the fight . . . Lindsay was crying and was very upset. She didn't say anything about Jock stabbing anyone or that he had pulled out a knife. She did not mention a knife.'

Grayham explained that he had not gone to police in search of Jock 'because things didn't seem so serious' from what Lindsay had told him. He added that he was also short of time: 'I'm here to work on my house, after all.' Grayham described meeting up with Iliyan in Samokov, where he discovered that Jock had been arrested and might have stabbed someone. 'I sent a message to Lindsay's mobile phone telling her to go to the local police to report the case. I also sent a message to Tony asking if all this stuff about the stabbing was true, but he did not respond. Then I decided to make a statement about the case and came of my own free will to be questioned. Last night I called Tony to ask him whether he knew that someone had been killed and whether he was going to talk to the police to explain what had happened. He didn't say anything and I haven't contacted him since. I think he is scared.'

Grayham gave Alakusheva contact details for Lindsay and Tony.

The investigator brought the statement to an end with a question about Jock's character. 'As far as I know Jock, he is not volatile,' replied Grayham. 'For the time that I have known him, he has never been in trouble.'

As Grayham waited to collect his passport, Galina muttered disdainfully: 'This is why I wanted to leave Bulgaria for good.' Grayham looked at her, astonished. She was clearly well educated and smart, but police and the prosecution were paying for her services, not Jock, and she had played a straight bat for the past two hours. 'They don't know what they're doing and they stitch people up. Your friend is in a lot of trouble and they have got it in for him,' she added.

As they left the station, Galina gave him her mobile phone number to pass on to Jock's family. They should find a new lawyer, she said.

. . .

Anton Doychev, the eighteen-year-old who preferred to be called Tony, was a student in a downtown high school and had seen a lot of violence in Sofia. But someone dying—that was different.

He could not believe what he was reading in the papers. He was sure Jock hadn't gone out to slaughter students at the traffic lights. But he didn't really know what had happened. He only knew from news reports that someone had died. He certainly didn't want to get caught up with police and the media. They scared him.

. . .

That night bTV News ran video of a vigil for Andrei Monov at the place where he died. The report described the mourners silently holding candles as they stood on the still-blood-stained pavement. It painted yet another disturbing picture of Jock, one that suggested he had been waiting across the road for a suitable group of people to attack: 'It is recorded in the case files that Freeman rounded on the young people, approaching them from St Nedelya Church and attacking them from behind. The prosecution added that the cameras at the crossing had been seized and the sequence of Freeman's actions would best be seen on them.'

Elsewhere in Sofia, the Prosecutor's Office briefed a reporter from the newspaper *24 Hours*, which published the following account the next day: 'The Australian Jock Palfreeman has stabbed Andrei Monov once in the heart with a butterfly knife. The city prosecutor on duty, Ivan Avramov, said [that] based on the results from the autopsy, the stroke was made in the back, a bit to the side. The twenty-year-old man had no chance of survival. He died ten minutes after the stabbing. Palfreeman acted in cold blood; the stroke was professional.'

If Avramov was correctly reported, the prosecutor was very wrong; the preliminary autopsy report did not say Andrei was stabbed in the back. Fact or fiction, the remark helped colour public opinion about Jock and the incident. The newspaper's account added sleaze to the mix: 'On Friday Palfreeman was bar hopping in Sofia, but he was more interested in the

shows they offered . . . He was accompanied by a blonde lady who he claimed
was British. The police are searching for her in order to question her.'

By now the image of the Australian in the public mind was that of a
homeless, drugged-up, foreign commando who went out with strippers and
had slaughtered a student in a calculated attack. There was worse to come.

CHAPTER 6

Monday, 31 December 2007
Sydney

Accompanied by Helen and Angus, Simon called by his mother's house in Sydney on his way home from the abruptly terminated boat trip. He knew Barbara would have heard about Jock by now and he wanted to reassure her that things would be all right.

Barbara Palfreeman was in tears. This was like a death in the family. She pleaded with Simon to let his former brother-in-law, a lawyer, try to sort out the legal issues. But Simon said he could not be an idle spectator; he wanted to see this through to the end. He would do whatever it took.

When they finally got home to Newcastle, Helen listened to the messages on their answering machine. Friends had booked Simon a one-way ticket to London for 2 January, the first flight available. Simon would stay with his sister before catching another flight to Sofia. Helen would stay home to coordinate things in Australia. She could see that Simon felt a bit more relaxed now there was a plan. He started pulling out all his thick jumpers and bushwalking gear. He would have to buy a coat. Daytime temperatures in Sofia averaged –4°C.

. . .

That afternoon Louis Simpson phoned Karl Ferguson. He had heard a rumour that their best mate had been arrested in Bulgaria. 'What on earth has Jock been up to now!' Karl exclaimed, half-laughing as he pictured his friend rushing headlong into some kind of mayhem. Karl, Louis and Jock had all been together at St Ignatius' College, Riverview, a Catholic boys high school on Sydney's well-off North Shore. They were part of a group who called themselves 'the Larrikins'. They spent a lot of time discussing alcohol, sex and music, though Jock did try now and then to steer the conversation to other topics.

Riverview students were encouraged to 'Dare to do your utmost,' as the school motto went, and to help the less fortunate. According to his friends, Jock's left-leaning views were out of kilter with those of many of his classmates' families, but his enthusiasm and his crash-through-or-crash approach to life drew others to his side.

Louis's older brother, Hugh, was an officer in the Australian Navy and loved his job. He had told Jock about the peacekeeping work the Australian Defence Force was doing in places like the Solomon Islands. In 2005, after Jock finished high school, he applied to join the Navy. He had grown up sailing on Sydney Harbour and wasn't afraid of hard physical work. Hugh gave him a character reference, though he was not sure how Jock would cope with the discipline. A series of mishaps stymied the application, and before Jock had the chance to try again, he decided to head overseas.

Once in Europe Jock had met up with some Greek anarchists whose work on community building projects he had found inspiring. The political talk was far more stimulating than anything he had been around in Australia.

For a while Jock worked in Bristol at the Essential Trading Cooperative that sold organic food and fair-trade household products. He lived rough in a squat house frequented by drug dealers, whom he made regular attempts to ban. He helped out at a charity that repaired bicycles for people who could not afford a car. He also volunteered at a local emergency housing organisation, and often brought homeless people back to the squat. When he applied to join the Army, which actively recruits young people from Commonwealth countries, Jock's Bristol friends chastised him for even considering military service. But some of them had also thought him mad for joining the Bristol Rowing Club. Jock was impossible to pigeonhole. He wasn't a greenie, a hippie, a punk, a Trotskyite, an anarchist or a conservative, though he had friends who happily wore one or other of those labels.

Jock had a vast general knowledge and enjoyed teasing out ideas. He explored all sides of politics and had friends of all political stripes. Indeed, he had first met Hugh at a Liberal Party function when he was flirting with signing up as a way of spending more time with some mates who were members, while also getting a better understanding of how the organisation operated.

. . .

Louis, anxious now, called his brother for advice. Hugh had a good understanding of foreign affairs. 'He's fucked,' was his response. Not knowing that the Department of Foreign Affairs had advised Simon against making any public comment, Hugh decided that if there was no better news soon, he would contact the media. *No legal system is impervious to influence*, he thought. *It's important that the court's first impression of Jock is the right one.*

. . .

Sofia

At midday the Bulgarian online news agency Focus published an interview with Hristo Monov. The grieving father framed his private tragedy as something more insidious. 'The children of Bulgaria are showing us, the adults, that we have not done enough to protect them if they can be killed in the centre of Sofia. They are children with modern thinking—Europeans. You saw them [at the vigil], they are normal children. They are all studying in elite high schools and universities.' In the coming years Hristo would again use the term 'elite' to describe to his son and his friends. During Bulgaria's Communist period, 'elite' referred to people with connections—the political insiders, the wheelers and dealers.

For Hristo, it was impossible that his son's group could be responsible for what had happened: 'Some versions [of events] are coming out that they, so to speak, attacked the Australian . . . that's terrible!' he said. 'To me [Jock] is a maniacal murderer, a man who is neither on drugs nor drunk—to kill in the back with one stroke. If you have seen my son he is a "two-metre boy" [very tall]. He was killed with one stroke; this is a professional murderer . . . This man arrived in Bulgaria with the sole purpose of killing . . . Don't forget there's psycho doping [brainwashing—presumably he meant in the Army]. The attitude of a person can be programmed and in a certain situation he can't restrain himself . . . I doubt that in Bulgaria, in the centre of Sofia someone would attack you, so why would you carry a weapon? It's scary . . . The next thing you know, someone can come into our country carrying a bomb instead of a knife and just throw it into a disco.'

According to Hristo, Bulgarian youths were not the only victims: 'What happened is an attack on the authority of the government. This can't keep happening. As a nation we must have some kind of self-defence, some kind of immunity against this scum. He can't just turn up here because there is cheap drink, cheap prostitutes and cheap drugs. If we go on like this, the best will either be murdered or leave the country. We have to stand against that . . . Today is the bail hearing for that monster. I believe Bulgarian justice will really show that our country protects its authority from violation.'

. . .

Sofia Palace of Justice
1.40 p.m.

A phalanx of guards led Jock Palfreeman out of a holding cell in the courthouse and up an ornate staircase to the bail hearing. His hands and legs shackled, the exhausted young man kept biting his bottom lip. He was still wearing his blue jeans, black hoodie and boots.

One of the many television news cameramen at court that day captured two very different images of Jock. As the accused came towards him, he filmed a boyishly good-looking young man. But as Jock moved past him and into the crush of photographers jostling for a better position, the picture showed the back of his head, with its central line of slightly longer hair.

A reporter called out in English, 'Why did you kill the Bulgarian?' Jock stared ahead and said nothing. The cameraman zoomed in on his eyes. The haircut, the silence, the fixed gaze: consciously or not, the news coverage was generating a distinctly unlikeable image of the suspect.

Stoiko Barborski was there to represent Jock. Galina was in jeans, having been called in at the last moment. She was self-conscious about her casual dress and found the media crush unnerving. One reporter wanted her to translate a question to Jock. She ignored him: her job was to translate for Jock and the court. The judge entered the courtroom and the cameras left.

In twenty-eight years as a judge, Mimi Petrova had sat on many murder cases, too many to remember. But she would not forget the details of today's hearing. The transcript of this hearing, made by an official stenographer who sat off to one side, does not include Petrova's questions or any remarks from participants other than Jock. Like the records of many subsequent hearings in the case, it is often incomplete and at times incomprehensible.

In his account of what had happened, Jock tried to head off any sugges- tion that he had been out to make a political point: 'Tony said they were bullies. He didn't say they were football hooligans. We were hiding. I saw everyone shouting and then a man fell to the ground and they started beating him. I wasn't looking for problems and trouble. I was hiding to avoid any trouble.'

Galina struggled to translate what Jock had said. The judge barked at her to speak up.

Presumably in answer to further questions, Jock added: 'I don't know what happened to this person who had fallen on the ground and was being beaten.'

The judge asked why he had crossed the road if it had all seemed so frightening. 'As a Good Samaritan I rushed to help him,' replied Jock.

Petrova pointed out that the Good Samaritan didn't kill anyone. Her voice was high-pitched, its tone shrill. Jock paused for a moment and then said: 'I intervene because I care about people. I have been attacked five or six times and always with knives. That's why I was carrying a knife. It's not that I always carry a knife.'

Resuming his account, Jock said, 'I turned around and I tried to distance myself. They started picking up rocks and I started to defend myself. The attack with the rocks was before the stabbing. I did not expect and I did not want this to happen. What do they expect if they walk together as a pack of dogs and attack people?'

Jock asked to see the CCTV camera recordings, certain that they would confirm his recollections, but there was no response to his request. He said he liked his job and could not abscond, as no one ran away from the British Army. (Privately, Jock assumed that because he had signed over three years of his life to the British Army, the Army would look after him. In this he was sadly mistaken.)

Jock told the judge about his friends in Samokov and their families, and said most of the police there knew him because he rode a motorbike. He added that he was in love with a Bulgarian girl and wanted to see her. The young man then scanned the courtroom, half-expecting to see Grayham, but his mate was not there.

Acoustics in the small courtroom were poor. The constant murmuring from the audience and the clatter of the stenographer's keyboard made it hard to hear. Galina battled to keep up a simultaneous translation. Her words disappeared into the mélange of sound. When the duty prosecutor asked that bail be denied, Jock lowered his head, trying to catch what Galina was saying.

Stoiko Barborski asked the judge to take into account Jock's clean record, stressing that his client had not yet been found guilty. While Bulgaria's legal system differs in many ways from Australia's, it does share with it the principle that defendants are considered innocent until proven guilty. Barborski pressed the judge to release his client on bail so that he could better arrange his defence.

Jock piped up: 'The police haven't interrogated anyone other than those who were involved in the incident. There are no independent witnesses. Technically Grayham and Lindsay are, but they didn't see what happened. Naturally the boys say they didn't attack the Gypsy because without this person on the ground I look like a psychopath.' Although Jock could not have seen the media coverage of his case, he had hit the nail on the head.

Jock asked to have his hair cut and be given a suit. Years later, Hristo Monov would cite this request as proof of the defendant's inability to understand the seriousness of his crime and lack of regret for what he had done. Other than his school uniform, Jock had never owned a suit, but he had grown up believing that a suit was essential attire for weddings, funerals and court appearances. He had worn one to Simon and Helen's wedding; he wanted one now. Not to wear a suit in court would be disrespectful. For all the topsy-turvy life he had lived since leaving Australia, Jock had a deeply conservative streak; he believed in doing things the right way so everyone knew where they stood. 'I would stay in Samokov with my head down,' Jock continued. 'And I would appear in court wearing normal clothes and a normal haircut . . . I am a man of honour with beliefs, and that's actually what got me into this situation . . .'

Jock felt totally alone. He was cut off from family and friends. He had no consular assistance. He did not know that Grayham was outside, circling the enormous Sofia Palace of Justice, searching for someone who would let him in, frustrated and freezing, because it had now started to snow. The iron gates at the front of the building were padlocked shut for the holidays.

The judge had made up her mind. Jock had run towards Andrei Monov and his friends to stop them making such a lot of noise, she said. As he did so, Jock had brandished a knife that he 'specially carried on him'. Petrova believed the evidence against the defendant was overwhelming; even Jock's friends had supported the unanimous account of fourteen witnesses so far. The judge said the group had done nothing to provoke Jock; 'No one needed his interference.' In her view, Jock's claim that he had wanted 'to protect an unidentified person' originated in misinterpreted initial information from a police incident report, in which an officer described a witness account of 'an altercation between two groups, the defendant going to help the smaller group from the bigger one'. Petrova claimed that Jock had then developed an alternative version, 'involving some Gypsy'. Her conclusion was striking: 'There is no evidence that this Gypsy existed. If the person was as "badly beaten" as the defendant Palfreeman claims, he could scarcely have run away so quickly.'

Yet Petrova had drawn on only part of the incident report. She did not refer to the officer's account of what Andrei's friends had told him. With the investigation barely begun and despite evidence to the contrary, the court had rejected Jock's claim that there had been an attack on a Gypsy. Jock had no defence.

Had Grayham been in the courtroom, he might have been surprised by the judge's finishing touch: 'Even Grayham says that "As far as I know Jock, he is not volatile," that is, his statement says that he doesn't know Jock well. He claims he has visited him twice and helped him with the repair work on the house he bought.' Rather than take from this statement that Jock was not an aggressive person, Petrova concluded that Grayham and Jock scarcely knew each other. It was a harbinger of the misinterpretations of witness statements that would be a hallmark of this case.

According to Jock's recollection, Petrova was crying as she refused bail. Galina recalls how theatrical the judge was. Stoiko Barborski thought nothing of it: in his experience, Judge Petrova was always emotional. Before Galina had a chance to translate Petrova's concluding remarks, the guards cuffed Jock and dragged him to the door. Twisting his head back in an effort to see Galina, he called out to her: 'What did the judge say? What is going on? I don't understand.'

With the wooden courtroom door in front of him now, Jock shouted in confused desperation: 'Wait a minute!' If Galina responded, her words were lost in the rapid clicking of shutters as photographers took shots of the guards yanking Jock into the huge hallway outside the courtroom.

Petrova remembers mulling over the case afterwards. 'He didn't say I did it,' she would later say in an interview for this book. 'But he didn't deny he made the hit, either.' Petrova was not responsible for determining Jock's guilt or innocence, but she said, 'I was just astonished to see that such a young person was full of hatred.' As well as hating Bulgarians, she decided, this Australian was 'racist' and 'led by this feeling of superiority'. Someone so arrogant and dangerous was capable of anything.

CHAPTER 7

Monday, 31 December 2007
Sofia

David Chaplin spent the morning at the British Embassy in Sofia, where he was briefed on the few known facts about the Palfreeman case. He was not aware that Jock had already fronted a judge. That afternoon his British counterpart arranged for Chaplin to visit the prison with an interpreter. After an hour waiting outside for papers to be processed, he was taken by a prison guard to a small interview room. A glass panel separated him from Jock; they had to use a telephone to talk. To protect himself against the cold, Jock had the hood of his sweater over his head. Chaplin thought this made him look intimidating. Guards waited outside the room as the young man told him what had happened. Gradually Chaplin warmed to him. When Jock paused for breath, Chaplin explained that there was an Australian government representative based in Sofia who would check up on him while he was in prison and attend court hearings.

As a guard led him into the corridor, Chaplin ran into Jock, who was being escorted back to his cell. Chaplin took advantage of the unexpected encounter to give Jock a golf magazine he had brought with him and ask him if he had spoken to his family.

Jock said he could not make any calls without a phone card for a fixed line and the prison did not sell credit. Shaking his head in dismay, Chaplin dialled Simon's number on his mobile and handed Jock the phone. At this, two guards lunged at Jock, but the diplomat stepped between them and demanded that they get their supervisor. Jock was impressed by Chaplin's gutsy impulse to intervene. He could not imagine his father acting so quickly. Not that Simon was a wimp; he had just always seemed cautious, almost to a fault.

. . .

Newcastle, Australia

Exhausted, Simon and Helen had gone to bed early, even though it was New Year's Eve. The phone on Helen's side of the bed rang at about 2 a.m. She scrabbled about in the dark, trying to locate the receiver.

'Helen, it's Jock.' His voice was faint. He paused and then rushed on. 'I'm so sorry, so sorry. I didn't want to have to involve you and Dad.'

Helen passed the phone to Simon, who rubbed his eyes and tried unsuccessfully to calm his son. 'It's all right, Jock . . . We love you . . . Are you OK?'

Jock was not making much sense.

'I will be there as soon as I can,' said Simon, trying to sound more confident than he felt, his hands shaking. 'Hang in there.'

Jock burst into tears. His father's willingness to drop everything tore down the protective wall Jock had built around himself. The phone cut out.

. . .

Simon had met Jock's mother, Mary Jane, when he started university. She was studying dentistry; he was studying medicine. She encouraged him to go on adventures like rafting down Tasmania's wild Franklin River. Theirs was an attraction of opposites—she was a vibrant character with very definite views, he was quiet and scholarly.

Simon had grown up with his six siblings on an orchard at Wilberforce, on the bank of the Hawkesbury River. Like latter-day Huckleberry Finns, he and his younger brother would disappear for hours, making rafts and floating them on the dam. Later, at Riverview, Simon discovered a more bookish side, and became a first-class student of Latin and Greek.

Simon had graduated and was specialising in pathology when his first son was born. Even as a baby, Jock stood out. He had an enormous smile that was shaped like a watermelon and he was always active. Simon had loved taking him in a backpack on day-long bushwalks. Bobbing along, Jock would listen with his father to the calls of birds, which Simon tried to identify. Jock can still mimic with uncanny accuracy the cries of a white cockatoo, a magpie, a hawk, a currawong and a whip bird.

When Jock started to walk, Mary Jane and Simon tried putting him in a playpen with four sides but no bottom to keep him in one spot while they attended to domestic chores. Within minutes they would turn to find the little boy pushing the pen to wherever he wanted to be.

Spencer was born a year and a half later. When the boys started school, Mary Jane grew more interested in politics; she was later elected to Mosman Council as an alderman. Her mother had been one of the first women admitted to the New South Wales Bar, and Mary Jane had grown up with a strong sense of justice. A feisty advocate of residents' rights, she was often at odds with the mayor and fellow council members.

Angus was born when Jock was seven. By the time Angus was a toddler, Simon's relationship with Mary Jane had become strained. When Jock was in his last year of primary school, the marriage broke down. Simon's ultimate decision to leave the family home was all the harder to make because his own parents had divorced: his father had left Barbara with seven children, three of them still young, when Simon was at university.

After a year at the local high school, Jock switched to Simon's alma mater, Riverview. The teenager had very firm views about fairness. If he saw other children being bullied by teachers or fellow students he intervened, even when he scarcely knew the victim. Occasionally his conviction and impulsivity led to schoolyard scuffles.

Jock's aunt Geri wonders whether he was bullied at some stage and whether that experience informed his compulsion to help the underdog. Jock's Riverview friend Karl Ferguson remembers that when Jock started there, he was teased every so often about the blue-tinted glasses he wore to help correct what appeared to be dyslexia. Another Riverview friend, Marty Silk, remembers Jock making it clear to would-be bullies that he was not a walkover. Marty thought Jock must have had a hard time at his previous school and had resolved never to stand by and watch others, particularly younger ones, go through the same thing. Jock was protective of his younger brothers; it made sense he would stick up for other kids their age.

Every year the Palfreeman cousins would go away with their parents and their grandmother, Barbara, to a house on the New South Wales coast. Jock was fearless and a bundle of energy. Without warning, he would disappear for hours and then return with stories about the group of kids he had just met on the beach and the amazing things they had done together.

From a young age Jock had strong opinions on every subject under the sun. He challenged teachers on issues as diverse as the existence of God and the ethics of capital punishment.

When Jock was in Year 9, Helen and Simon married, and he moved in with them: he resented his mother's acrimony about the divorce. Unsettled, Jock wanted to try another school. With the promise that he could return later if he chose, Jock left Riverview and spent Year 10 as a boarder at the expensive Anglican King's School, Parramatta, going home to his father and Helen on weekends.

Now fifteen, Jock joined the West Parramatta branch of Resistance, a Socialist youth organisation. Some former volunteers there remember seeing him after school, in the King's distinctive grey blazer with its red-bordered sleeves and being struck by the disjunction between the privilege his uniform suggested and the beliefs Jock espoused.

In July that year, Jock participated in several student rallies protesting against the then government's policy of holding asylum seekers in detention. He asked permission from the school to attend, and it was granted. But when the local *Parramatta Advertiser* photographed Jock in his uniform behind the school gates, things took a different turn. According to the accompanying article, Jock was encouraging others to join him in protest. Simon was called to the school to explain his son's behaviour.

After a year, Jock returned to Riverview. There he helped form the Riverview Student Peace and Unity Congress, and later joined students from across the state in protests against the war in Iraq.

Jock's friends remember him as the one who stayed sober to help others get home, the one they could always count on when someone got into trouble. A strong character, Jock tended to be loved or loathed by his fellow students. Even so, these were happy years for him. He had wonderful mates, and he threw himself into team sport, particularly rowing.

Loud and messy, Jock was no angel at home. His father battled to convince him to stay at school and complete his Higher School Certificate. Jock was bright. He liked military history and was fascinated by human conflict. Yet his hyperactive nature made sitting still in class difficult. Sitting for exams was close to impossible. He wanted to be out working with his hands. In the end, however, Simon won, and Jock finished his final year of school, the highlight of which was rowing in the First Four.

On hearing of his arrest, Jock's former house master and rowing coach, James Busteed, wrote him a glowing character reference that ended: 'My lasting memories of Jock during his time at the College is of a young man with a friendly, open personality and a positive outlook on life that made him popular with his peers and also the staff with whom he came in contact. He was passionate about his interests, socially aware and prepared to speak out for what he felt was right. He willingly and unselfishly would go out of his way to help others and to involve and include those who may feel isolated or marginalised.'

. . .

Remand Centre, Sofia

Jock was thankful to have the company of his two Turkish cellmates. In a combination of French and Turkish, they kept reassuring him things would work out. While he did not believe them, he was grateful for their concern. One was in for attempted murder after stabbing another Turk; the other had been found at a border checkpoint carrying a pistol as he travelled from France to Turkey on a bus. Their stories about life outside prison gave the Australian some reprieve from his anxiety.

With no radio or telephone, Jock had no idea of what was going on in the world. None of them had a watch, so he lost all sense of time. When he heard fireworks going off outside, Jock assumed it was New Year's Eve. He banged on the cell door to ask the guard for the date, but no one came.

Unable to sleep, he turned to the magazine the Australian consular official had given him: *Golfing Australia*. But by now Jock had read it so often he knew every word.

The fireworks went off again the next night. And the night after that. Each time, Jock thought it must be New Year's Eve. He felt trapped in a twilight zone.

Again and again, Jock tried to retrace the sequence of events of that fateful night, but the harder he tried, the more confusing it all became: a blurry swirl of faces and gestures and shouts.

. . .

Wednesday, 2 January 2008
Police Station No. 3

Five days had passed. According to the court file, it was only now that Tanya Alakusheva wrote to the Ministry of Health requesting CCTV recordings from outside its building in St Nedelya Square. Jock had asked in court to see the videos, and much of the testimony gathered so far suggested that at least part of the melee had taken place at that location.

Friday, 28 December, had been a working day, and personnel at the ministry would have been on duty. Even if the investigator had not made an immediate request for the recordings themselves, she could have asked for them to be retained. In an interview for this book, Alakusheva said she had been too busy to write the request until that Wednesday. In any event, she added, police officers were responsible for gathering all the evidence at the crime scene and providing it to her; it had been their job to tell her about the recordings.

. . .

Newcastle, Australia

Jock's story was all over the front page of the *Sydney Morning Herald*. The report included comments from Jock's brother Spencer and old friends like Hugh, Louis and Karl. But it also claimed that Jock had confessed his guilt to Sofia police. As Simon Palfreeman finished packing his suitcase, he tried not to look at the newspaper rolled up on the bedside table. Right now he seriously doubted that he was up to the job of helping his son. Unlike Jock, he was not an intrepid traveller. Nor was he assertive by nature. If conflicts or danger arose, he preferred to avoid them.

Helen and Angus went with him to Sydney airport. It was a sombre send-off—very different from the one Jock had received on New Year's Day two years earlier.

Once on the Qantas flight, Simon took out the *Lonely Planet Guide to Bulgaria* that he had found in a bookshop. Inside was the letter Angus had given him to pass on to Jock. He hesitated, then opened it.

Dear Jock,

I really miss you. Every time the back door opens I keep feeling, I keep thinking I'm going to hear your big voice calling out how is everybody, where is everybody and I really miss that. Come home.

Angus

Tears rolled down Simon's face. It was the first and only time he cried for Jock.

Driving back to Newcastle, Helen looked across at Angus. He was a quiet young man, and it was hard to tell how this crisis was affecting him. Helen's thoughts turned to Simon. She knew he was in agony, worried for Jock, utterly unable to believe he could have committed murder. She also knew he hated feeling so uncertain about what was the best course of action. He was methodical by nature and craved order.

Simon headed a section of a large pathology practice, where he oversaw the operational standards of several regional offices as well as taking blood and tissue samples and studying them under the microscope. For him pathology was like detective work. He loved the challenge of figuring out just what was abnormal in the cells he was staring at. He often worked alone, reviewing slides and dictating reports. Now and then he would look up and see the photograph on his desk of the three boys and Helen on Simon and Helen's wedding day.

Simon was a stickler for rules and believed in following them to the letter. He had been inside a police station only twice before: once about a parking ticket; once when his two older sons had attended a teenage party in Chatswood on Sydney's North Shore that had turned nasty. But Helen knew her husband would do whatever he could to help his children. It was one of the things she loved about him. Neither she nor Simon had the faintest inkling that Jock's plight would dominate their lives for years to come.

. . .

Sydney

Gemma Jones is a reporter for the *Daily Telegraph*, a popular Sydney tabloid. She remembers the morning of 2 January as a frantically busy one. Among other jobs, she had to confirm the name of the young Australian arrested in Bulgaria. Even that was proving difficult. Then a young man rang who claimed to have information about the detainee. She arranged to meet him in Martin Place that afternoon.

James Atack came with his friend Matt, who did not want Jones to publish his surname. They told Jones they had been stabbed at a teenage party in Chatswood on 30 December 2004 and blamed Jock Palfreeman for what had happened. Matt showed the newspaper's photographer a scar on his torso that he said was the result of a knife wound.

Jones recalls that the young men described a chaotic situation in which no one saw the weapon that caused the injuries. She checked with police, who confirmed that there had been a fight involving knife wounds on the night in question. It struck Jones as odd that a former Riverview student who was not known to police would have been involved in such a fracas, but with her deadline fast approaching, she started to write.

That night the *Daily Telegraph* website bore the bold headline 'Bulgarian Stabber Accused Before'. The article read in part: 'James Atack and his friend Matt, both 20, revealed yesterday they told police that 21-year-old Jock Palfreeman was behind an attack in 2004 which nearly killed them.

'Both men were knifed three times in the vicious assault—with the wounds missing vital organs by millimetres. "It just hurts to know he has done it to someone else, I was a millimetre away from dying," Matt, who was too afraid to have his last name published, said yesterday.'

The story was picked up around the world, including, of course, in Bulgaria. It would play a key role in shaping public opinion about the Palfreeman case.

CHAPTER 8

Thursday, 3 January 2008
Sofia

It was the day of Andrei Monov's funeral.

Zlatin Tepsiev looked out his window and took a long drag on his cigarette. More snow had fallen overnight, and Sofia was ankle deep in it. A few days before, Andrei's father had phoned to ask if Tepsiev could help with arrangements for the funeral. He had felt honoured that the Monovs had come to him.

Tepsiev had been head of the Levski supporters' club for about nine years. Levski is one of Sofia's leading soccer clubs. It is named after Vasil Levski, Bulgaria's national hero, who was executed for organising a revolt against Ottoman rule in the nineteenth century.

Andrei had been a keen Levski fan and had gone to almost every match. In Sofia, football is very popular and very tribal. Each club has multiple fan clubs, each with a particular identity. Andrei belonged to Levski's South Division, with which the Levski Ultras are also aligned. The Ultras are a fan club notorious for loud chanting, flares and smoke bombs in the stands, mayhem and thuggery.

Tepsiev thought most criticism of the Ultras was unwarranted—as he saw it, fights between fans of rival teams were normal and natural. Levski's traditional 'enemy' team was CSKA. Levski had originally been the police team, while CSKA stood for Central Sporting Club of the Army.

Levski's team colour was blue; CSKA's was red, and its symbol was the red five-pointed star of the Communist Party. For Tepsiev, Levski embodied the spirit of resistance against the Soviet domination of Bulgaria during the Communist era, when the sporting arena was the only outlet for defiance. To be a Levski supporter was also to be a true patriot.

The Levski Football Club had issued a formal statement supporting the family of its fallen fan. To honour the young man, Tepsiev had arranged for supporters to carry wreaths featuring blue flowers.

Tepsiev had a son Andrei's age. As he stubbed out his cigarette, Tepsiev's thoughts turned to Hristo and Aksenia Monov. *To bury your child must be every parent's nightmare.*

. . .

London

By the time Simon's flight touched down at Heathrow Airport, he had been travelling for close to thirty hours. He fired up his laptop to email Helen that he had arrived safely. Up came the *Daily Telegraph* article. Reading it, he was stunned. At the time, he had been upset that Jock and Spencer were caught in a fight involving knives. He had taken Jock to a police station to give a statement but had no reason to believe that either son was a perpetrator.

As Simon understood it, ten to fifteen youths had gate-crashed a party at the home of one of Spencer's friends. One of the youths had been out to get Spencer because he thought the seventeen year old had been seeing his girlfriend. When Spencer got wind that this fellow was on his way, he had phoned Jock, who was at a friend's house nearby, and asked for help. Jock went to protect him. As the gate-crashers jumped a fence to get in, a fight broke out. Jock, who had just turned eighteen, gave a statement to the police.

Of course you never know what really happens in something like that, Simon thought. *And you can't just assume your children are lily white.* But as far as he was concerned, that had been the end of it. The police never called back. He could not understand why the two young men would make such an allegation after all these years, and at a time like this.

Whatever the truth, some key facts were missing from the newspaper story. First, three men had been taken to hospital with knife wounds, including Spencer's friend Andrew Mair, who had not seen Jock anywhere in the fight. As Andrew lay on the ground groaning, Jock had appeared out of nowhere, taken him to a bathroom and called an ambulance. Second, after investigating the incident, the police had not charged anyone.

Dazed and tired, Simon boarded the bus for the two-hour ride to Bath, where Geri was waiting for him. Simon had always been the perfect big brother. As children, Geri and her siblings would get up in the morning and find him calmly cutting seven sets of sandwiches for the school lunches. They all still teased him about the time his primary school class voted him most likely to be Pope because he had earned so many good behaviour points.

When Geri had finally got through to the right section of the Army, it took a while for office staff to find any details about Rifleman Jock Palfreeman, 30038840. Journalists had encountered the same problem, and some interpreted this as a sign that the Army was washing its hands of him. Once it was established that the recruit had been on holidays when the incident happened, the answer was a pretty blunt 'Can't help.'

Like the rest of the family, Geri had been puzzled by Jock's determination to join the Rifles, an infantry regiment whose 6th Battalion had a detachment in Bristol, where he was living. He had gone through six months of filling in forms and undergoing interviews, as well as extensive personality and fitness testing, before being accepted. He had rated well on the general aptitude test and could have gone into any career in the Army, including one in the Medical Services. According to Jock, he chose the infantry because he wanted to be with the regular soldiers. He was proud and excited to have made it.

In his first four to five weeks of training, the closest Jock got to a weapon was a lesson or two on rifle cleaning. According to the Army, knives are prohibited in the barracks, and Jock and his fellow recruits had been a long way off learning how to use them.

In letters to Geri, Jock was full of enthusiasm for his new job. He sent a photo of himself in uniform in the snow, holding a sign that read 'Yipes'.

Geri imagined him laughing as he mimicked the cartoon character Road Runner, who uses the sign to mock Wile E. Coyote's misfortune. The routine of Army life seemed to suit him, and she wondered if in fact her nephew had craved order ever since his parents had divorced.

As the bus got closer to Bath, Simon focused on his tiny spiral-bound notepad. Simon is a compulsive list writer, and he uses the notepad to keep track of what he needs to do. The more anxious he becomes, the more he studies it. Right now the pad was full of questions.

. . .

Remand Centre, Sofia

Grayham Saunders was finally admitted to visit Jock, who was overjoyed to see him. When Jock told him he had pocketed Grayham's knife as they had left for Sofia, Grayham went pale. Jock laughed. 'It's me who should be scared,' he said, trying to lessen his friend's distress.

As Grayham left for the airport, the newspaper headlines shouted from the kiosks, all trying to outdo each other with new insights into the murder. The local *Telegraph* ran with an embellished version of the news from Australia: 'Twenty-one-year-old Australian Jo Paul Freeman, who has been arrested in Bulgaria, has been accused of another stabbing in his home country,' its story began. It claimed the Sydney youths had both been 'stabbed three times, as the knife went through millimeters away from vital organs'. Included in this newspaper's coverage was an interview with an anonymous friend of Andrei's who claimed to have witnessed the attack in St Nedelya Square. He declared that Jock stabbed Andrei 'in the back', once 'in the left auricle of the heart', and once 'very close to his spinal cord'—none of which claims matched the preliminary autopsy report. Denying that he and his friends had provoked Jock, the youth said they had only thrown a rock at him after the stabbing. When asked why, the youth was reported as saying: 'Because we were afraid to approach him, as he could stab us, too. We found a rock and threw it at him to calm him down.'

The newspaper *24 Hours* took the scandal further with an article headed 'The Australian Who Stabbed Two Trained as a Butcher'. Among his many part-time jobs in Sydney, which included child care and construction, Jock had worked at a butcher's shop. His role was to barbecue and serve sample sausages outside the shop on a Saturday morning in a bid to draw customers inside. When he got older, Jock advanced to making the sausages and serving customers. He was not trained in butchering meat and was not allowed to use knives except to cut sausage links. When Jock told his boss about the stabbings at the party in Chatswood, the older man had warned him that anyone working in a butcher's shop should steer well clear of knives outside work, because if anyone near them was cut, it would immediately be assumed that they were guilty. Indeed, for Bulgarian readers, the news out of Australia merely confirmed that the suspect was not only a vicious killer but a practised butcher with a history of knifing people.

The double-page spread in *24 Hours* included interviews with a group of Andrei Monov's friends, some of whom had known him for much of his life. 'There would not have been a single parent who would deny that he looked the best in his suit, he was very handsome,' Gabriela Videnova was quoted as saying. She had been a classmate of Andrei's at the prestigious First English High School and would be a regular attendee at the ensuing trial. '[Andrei] was very serious and at the same time very light-hearted, he had a big soul. He acted as if he was absent-minded. He was always joking, as if he never had a pen or a notebook, but for the exam on constitutional law he came all dressed up . . . and he sat down and wrote and wrote . . . Of course, he got an A. He had unique charm—tall, slender with a great body and smile. He was always very attentive to girls. No negative side, none.'

Among the friends quoted were two who had been with Andrei the night he died. 'He was very keen on justice. Always!' said Kristian Dimov. 'That's why he studied law. It was as if there was something knight-like about him.' Emil Aleksiev elaborated: 'In November there were clashes between [football] fans and one man was killed,' he said. 'He demanded justice. We said to him that the man is dead, he's gone. But he insisted that, despite that, there should be justice and there should be retribution.'

Apparently Andrei believed in an eye for an eye.

. . .

10.30 a.m.

As Andrei's parents prepared to leave for the cemetery, the investigation into their son's death continued. Two plain-clothes police officers arrived at the Sheraton to escort Viktor Georgiev and his colleague to Police Station No. 3. With no access to a police car, all four of them took public transport.

The only reason Viktor and his colleague had filled in an incident report was because they assumed police would want to interview them in the days after the incident, and didn't want to be caught out not having explained why they had momentarily left their posts that night. Viktor's supervisor had phoned a few days after the incident to say his employees might have been witnesses. Viktor was annoyed. He would have preferred to avoid all this. Nevertheless, he calmly took Tanya Alakusheva through what he had seen that night. His version of events was to prove inconvenient for some.

According to Viktor's police statement, he and Lyubomir Tomov had been in one of the two parking-lot cabins in front of the hotel. At approximately 1.30 a.m., they saw a group of about fifteen to twenty loud young people come out of the metro exit across the road to their right, chanting 'Levski' and singing as they moved towards Stamboliyski Boulevard.

Although both of the Sheraton workers could see this clearly, they did not pay much attention to the youths until they noticed them chasing a young man who was running from Stamboliyski Boulevard towards the metro. Viktor said the group caught up with the 'boy' near the metro entrance, pushed him to the ground and started attacking him. Viktor's statement continues:

'They were kicking him for about 30–40 seconds. It was chaotic and indiscriminate and, as far as I could see, their hits were not very strong. At that moment my colleague and I got out of the cabin and stood next to it. Then one of the boys from the group started to pull his friends away from the man on the ground, trying to stop the fight.

'At that moment the boy on the ground stood up and I could clearly see him holding a knife in his hand. I did not see when he took out the knife or from where, just that at this moment he was holding a knife with a big blade, probably a long one, about palm-sized. The knife was silvery. The boy waved the knife about two or three times from left to right towards the group of boys around him. The group started to step backwards. At the same time the boy started to advance towards them. He continued to hold the knife, pointing towards the group of boys, but he was not brandishing it any more.'

Viktor said he and his colleague had been opposite the action and only twenty metres away when he saw the whole group, including the boy, reach the entrance of the Ministry of Health. At that time the boy was holding the knife but still not brandishing it. While Viktor went inside the cabin to alert others, he kept watching the unfolding events through a window.

'. . . I saw one of the boys from the group go behind the boy with the knife and throw some kind of object at him, which, as far as I could see, hit him on the head. I don't know what exactly hit him. I can't describe the boy who hit him. Then the boy with the knife fell to the ground for a moment. He propped himself on one arm, though I don't know exactly which, and then he stood up again. Then some of the boys in the group started throwing rocks at him.'

Viktor said this prompted him to seek out his colleague from the hotel entrance and that in doing so he had missed a few moments of the fight. After that he and two others had crossed Maria Louisa Boulevard.

'Just in front of the Ministry of Health there was a man with a strong build, who was short with short dark hair, wearing camouflage trousers and a light-coloured jacket. This man was pinning the boy with the knife to the ground. The boy had squatted. I also saw that the knife was on the ground about three to four metres away from them, in front of the kiosk.

'The boys from the group were around. The boy who was on the ground was shouting in English "Police!" and close to him there was a girl who was dressed in a white jacket. She was shouting something in a foreign language, I couldn't discern in what language exactly. She was obviously very upset. Almost immediately a police van turned up . . . When the police came, the boy tried to run away; I don't know why. Then the well-built man with the camouflage trousers stopped him.' Viktor finished by saying that this had been the moment when he and his colleagues had returned to the car park, concerned about leaving their posts unguarded.

As he left the police station, Viktor felt confident he had told the female investigator the truth as he knew it. A fortnight later, he resigned from the security job at the Sheraton, feeling it was time to move on.

. . .

Police Station No. 3
12.45 p.m.
Just as Andrei's funeral was getting under way, Viktor's fellow car park attendant, Lyubomir Tomov, entered the chief investigator's office to give his statement. He was an economics student and, unlike Viktor, worked not for a security firm but for the Sheraton itself. Lyubomir told Alakusheva that he and Viktor had seen a group of fifteen young men and women come out of the metro chanting 'Levski' and singing a club song loudly as they walked across the square. At some point the noise had stopped abruptly. His statement continues:

'About five minutes later I saw a few of the boys chasing a boy in the direction of the metro. I couldn't say at this point whether the boys were from the group that passed earlier. Ten metres before the entrance to the metro they caught up with him, pushed him to the ground and started kicking him. I can't give a description of the boy who was running or of those who were chasing him. First three or four boys kicked him, and some others ran and took over from them and also started kicking him. There was no coordination in their actions . . . Whoever wanted to, just went in and kicked him. All this time the boy was on the ground.'

Lyubomir and Viktor painted a similar picture of a group of football fans chasing the young man across the square to the metro entrance and then attacking him. But they differed on when the 'boy' produced a knife. Viktor says it was while they were beating him. Lyubomir says that at some point the youths left the boy on the ground and headed for Stamboliyski. At this point he got up, brought out a knife from a pocket in his jacket and started walking towards the group. Lyubomir says a girl next to Jock shouted something in English, which prompted the group of youths in front of him to turn around. He adds: 'When they saw the knife in his hands, most of them ran away; but one or two of them tried to kick it out of his hand. They failed to do so.'

Like Viktor, Lyubomir says Jock then followed the group as they continued to move away from the metro towards the intersection of Stamboliyski and Maria Louisa boulevards. Lyubomir says Jock was swearing in English but not pointing the knife at anyone in particular.

'They kept on like this until they were at the telephone booths at the corner of Stamboliyski Boulevard. I didn't see the boy brandishing the knife at anyone in particular. Then my colleague and I went into the cabin to call the security guards. From there I saw that, near the 24-hours kiosk, the boys from the group were throwing pavers at the boy with the knife. He was trying to protect himself from the rocks. At this point he had his back turned towards us.'

Lyubomir adds that a Sheraton porter called Kris was the first to go to the scene. Lyubomir was three or four steps behind Viktor as they ran across Maria Louisa Boulevard. Andrei Monov might well have been stabbed then and, if so, they missed it. The porter was never interviewed, but he may have been there in time to see what happened.

Lyubomir says that when he reached the square he saw a 'well-built' man holding the boy to the ground, one of the two men variously described by witnesses as bodyguards and off-duty police officers. Lyubomir does not mention whether he saw the knife, but does recall one of the group members was shouting at the boy: 'This one has to die.'

. . .

Boyana Cemetery, Sofia

Boyana is a suburb full of winding roads in the foothills of the Vitosha Mountains. It used to be a favourite retreat for Communist leaders and apparatchiks; now it is home to the very wealthy. The Monovs live close to it.

The Boyana cemetery sits on a hill near the bottom of which is a small Bulgarian Orthodox church lined with mediaeval icons. Sofia has a chronic shortage of burial grounds, so procuring a grave site here would not have been easy.

According to media reports, between 200 and 300 people attended Andrei's funeral. On this freezing day, young faces were contorted with grief and the cold. Older heads were bowed. The mourners carried chrysanthemums and roses, carefully counted to ensure there was an even number. In Bulgarian tradition, the only time one gives an even number of flowers is when someone dies. A group of Levski fan club members stood together and sang the Bulgarian national anthem. Andrei's Levski sweater and scarf lay on the coffin as seven of his friends carried it down the church steps and up the hill to his grave site. The snow was almost knee-high on either side of the cleared path. The church bell tolled.

It was not just the patriotic gestures that marked the funeral as unusual. The line of mourners walking through the deep snow included Mihail Mikov, a lawyer turned Member of Parliament who knew Hristo and Aksenia from university. Within four months he would be the Interior Minister, in charge of the Bulgarian Police. Also present were the deputy Environment Minister and former legal adviser to the President, Chavdar Georgiev, and the recently appointed head of Bulgaria's highest court, Professor Lazar Gruev, a close friend of the Monovs. No one at the cemetery that day could have been in any doubt that this was a well-connected family.

The church bell continued to toll as the mourners watched the coffin being lowered into the grave. Hristo Monov was the first to step up and throw dirt onto the coffin. He stumbled as he backed away, and a friend caught his arm to steady him. Aksenia Monov then moved forward, bent to see her son's coffin for the last time and, supported by a friend, also threw down a handful of dirt. Having navigated the ice and that final farewell with a hesitant dignity, she turned away from the grave.

· · ·

Alexandrovska Hospital, Sofia

At some point that same day, the chemist at Alexandrovska Hospital filed her report on the alcohol content of Andrei Monov's blood. She had received a sample from the doctors who performed the autopsy. The reading was 2.9 promille: 2.9 milligrams per litre, or 0.29 per cent, an extraordinarily high concentration and almost six times the legal driving limit in Bulgaria and Australia. This suggested Andrei had been what would generally be regarded as staggeringly drunk and might well have found it difficult to stay upright.

. . .

Police Station No. 3
4.10 p.m.
Late on the afternoon of the funeral, twenty-two-year-old Martin Stoilov walked into Tanya Alakusheva's office to give a witness statement. The fourth-year student at the Forestry University was another friend of Andrei and would be the most coherent witness to claim he saw Jock Palfreeman in the act of stabbing. His account painted a different picture of the melee from that provided earlier in the day by the Sheraton workers.

Martin said that night he and Andrei had been out with Levski fans. He recalled that as they entered the subway three or four of them sang 'Shumi Maritsa', an old national anthem that was banned under Communism. It is a battle song that describes a blood-stained river and the brave Bulgarian warriors who are prepared to die for their country.

Martin said the group emerged from the metro in dribs and drabs. He was about fifty metres ahead of the stragglers, among whom were Andrei, Antoan and Tony. As Martin crossed Stamboliyski, someone alerted him to something going on involving the stragglers: 'I turned around and saw Tony and a stranger gesturing and talking in loud voices, but I didn't hear exactly what they were saying. I could clearly see that the two were standing about three metres from one another.' Unlike some of his friends, Martin did not describe the stranger as a Roma.

'I didn't see them exchange blows,' he continued. 'I just heard them exchange words in a loud voice. With that I ran to them to see what was going on, because the other man didn't want to leave and I thought he was looking for trouble. I saw that a man stood at the tram tracks opposite them, gesturing to the stranger, as though urging him to leave.'

Martin said the men took off after seeing him and others approach. A few of his friends 'shouted something' at the strangers and he told them 'just to forget about them and move on'. After taking a few steps back towards Stamboliyski, Martin heard someone call out, 'This one's got a knife.' Thinking the two strangers must have returned, he turned around and saw someone waving around a knife from left to right.

The next section of Martin's statement makes chilling reading: 'We started to pull back and the man kept on brandishing the knife and saying something to us, and I heard him say "Get back" a few times in Bulgarian. Then he started shouting something about anti-fascism. Some of my friends told the boy to drop the knife as they were retreating, but he kept on coming at us. We were walking backwards. I didn't dare to turn my back on him because I thought, if I start running, he will throw the knife at me. We were almost at Stamboliyski Boulevard; we had nowhere else to go. Then the boy came very close to us; he kept on brandishing the knife at everyone, whoever happened to be closest to him. When that person stopped, the man went towards whoever hadn't pulled back yet.'

Martin's next words would became a critical part of the case against Jock: 'Then I saw how the man stabbed Andrei and Antoan . . . one after another. I can't remember which one he stabbed first, because for me this was a big shock and I am confused about the order of these two blows. However I clearly saw how at some point the man came very close to Tony "the Tall" and tried to hit him with the knife. Tony managed to pull back and the knife passed very close to his chest. Andrei was next to Tony and was watching what the man with the knife was doing. When he failed to hit Tony, the man swung his knife at Andrei, who didn't manage to react and I saw how he stabbed him on the side with the knife, with the blade facing inside, on the left in the chest.

'Andrei immediately grabbed the area [where he had been injured] with both hands. At the moment when the man hit Andrei, he was opposite him.' When Andrei moved away, Martin lost sight of him: 'At first I thought Andrei had been only scratched, as the blow was fleeting and I didn't think it had caused a serious injury.'

Reflecting on how Jock went about the attack, Martin said: 'I want to add that the whole time he was delivering the hits with the knife, the man acted very cold-bloodedly, as if he had done that before. When he tried to hit someone with the knife, he would hit them from the side with the blade pointing inside. His actions were quick and rehearsed. He wouldn't let anyone get past him.'

Martin then said two men with guns arrived at the Ministry of Health entrance, and told Jock to drop the knife. 'When [Jock] saw them, he stopped for ten seconds, then bent over and very carefully put the knife on the ground. Then he himself fell to his knees and put his hands on his neck. It was just like in the movies. The man showed no fear or anxiety, neither at this moment nor after that, nor earlier when he hit Andrei and Antoan.' Once police had the man in a police van, Martin could hear punches being thrown and saw the van rocking.

Martin's observation that the hits happened one after the other suggests the attack on Antoan took place at the same location as the one on Andrei, a detail that would prove important to determining the degree to which Jock had been provoked. This account puts the lie to suggestions that Jock stabbed Andrei in the back but supports the claim that Tony 'the Tall' Yordanov had a lucky escape. It also suggests that Jock managed to trap the group of football fans singlehanded, even though they were in a large open space flanked by two major roads on which, at 1 a.m., there would have been little traffic.

. . .

Bath

By late in the afternoon of Andrei's funeral, Simon was at his sister's house, huddled around her Aga trying to catch up on what she knew of Jock's movements until now. That night Grayham Saunders and Lindsay Welsh drove to Bath from Bristol for dinner with Simon, Geri and her partner. Simon was relieved to meet his son's friends and hoped they could shed light on what had happened. With their weird haircuts and multiple facial piercings, the new arrivals certainly looked different from Jock's Sydney friends. But as they ate salmon and a pomegranate salad, Simon started to see why Jock was so fond of them.

Grayham talked at a million miles an hour. Lindsay was less confident; she was clearly still traumatised and found it hard to organise her recollections. She said Jock had been in good spirits at the Rock Bar—drinking, but not too much. Later, she, Tony and Jock had hidden from some drunken football hooligans. At one point Jock had got up to see what was going on, then suddenly run off. She had called out, 'Come back! Come back!' But he was gone. Tony had still been tapping numbers into his mobile phone, trying to key in his credit code, and had his back turned to the hooligans.

Lindsay explained that she hadn't been able to see what attracted Jock's attention because she was crouching and a wall of plants blocked her view. Not knowing where she was, she had been scared that Jock would disappear into the night. She had gestured for Tony to come with her, but he seemed even more nervous than she was, so she took off across the road on her own and found Jock on the ground moaning.

She had screamed, 'Jock! Jock!' Some of the youths around him pushed her over and kicked her hard in the stomach. They looked as if they were about to kick her in the head, but at that moment Tony appeared and led her away.

Three days after she got back to Bristol, Lindsay had gone to see a doctor. According to his notes, Lindsay said she had been assaulted and now felt dizzy. She had a bruised right buttock and right temple. Her abdomen looked and felt normal. Lindsay had notified the Bulgarian Embassy and local police but no one had contacted her for details. Members of Andrei's group would later deny that any of them assaulted her.

Grayham said he had heard the gang was out to get Jock and anyone connected with him. He had also heard that the boy who died came from a family with clout. Rumours were swirling in Sofia, he said. By the end of dinner, Geri was alarmed—not just for Jock, but also for her brother's safety.

Simon looked calm enough but his legs felt like jelly. He knew no one in Bulgaria and was now even more uncertain whom he could trust to look out for his son.

. . .

That evening Simon's father took a solar-powered lamp to the cliff top on his farm at Wollombi, New South Wales, about one and a half hours' drive inland from Newcastle. A flick of the switch, and it lit up the drought-stricken land.

Tony Palfreeman was seventy-six and had lost an arm to skin cancer years before, but he had the constitution of an ox and still gave the occasional politics lecture at Macquarie University, in Sydney. He paused to catch his breath, then said defiantly, 'Comrade Jock, this light will stay on until you return.'

. . .

As the Monovs read the allegation that Jock had been involved in a knife attack before, their rage intensified. *If only the Australian authorities had done their job properly, Andrei would still be alive! Who were the attacker's family and what had they done to see him walk free from that earlier incident?* The News Limited article became a touchstone for Andrei's parents. The killer had been gearing up for this killing spree. He had invaded their country and their lives.

A website was set up in memory of Andrei. It gave him the status of a national martyr, likening the blood-soaked roadside where he had been killed to Christ's cross on Golgotha and the gallows on which the national hero Vasil Levski had died.

CHAPTER 9

Friday, 4 January 2008
Bath

Simon Palfreeman had no time for jet lag as Geri and Paul helped him turn the second floor of their house into a control room. Paul brought up on his computer Google Earth aerial views of Sofia Central Prison to give them a sense of where Jock was being held. All Simon wanted to do was get him out of there.

The first step was finding a suitable lawyer for Jock. Simon had little idea of how the Bulgarian legal system worked, let alone who was best for the job. The Department of Foreign Affairs in Canberra had given him a list of criminal lawyers in Sofia, but it was not permitted to recommend one.

Friends had given him the names of one lawyer in London and two in Sofia. Simon phoned the British lawyer, who strongly advised that he use a Bulgarian one. Simon then tried calling the local lawyers, but one was away on holidays and the other did not want to take on the case because he knew Andrei's family. Simon was running out of options.

Someone suggested that he contact the London-based non-profit organisation Fair Trials International. Someone there suggested he call a lawyer whom the group often used to monitor cases in Bulgaria and who spoke English. His name was Dinko Kanchev, but Fair Trials did not have his mobile or office number. All it had was a number for the Bulgarian group Lawyers for Human Rights, of which Dinko had once been president.

Simon started dialling. If this number did not answer, he did not know what he would do. A man answered; it was Dinko. By chance, he had just dropped by the Lawyers for Human Rights office. He agreed to take the case provided certain stipulations were met, the most important of which was that everything be done strictly by the book.

Simon was relieved. He had heard that buying your way out of trouble was commonplace in countries like Bulgaria and worried that someone might try to pressure him into paying a bribe. He hated the very idea of corruption.

Now, he thought, the Bulgarian lawyer would assemble a team that could include Australian or British advisers. That team would see Jock through, leaving Simon to worry only about his son's psychological well-being. At worst, he guessed, it might take six months and a couple of trips to Sofia to sort this all out. Delighted to have finally found a lawyer for his son, Simon readily agreed to Geri's request that he stand against the kitchen wall so she could put a pencil mark there to show his height. It was almost level with Jock's.

. . .

Remand Centre, Sofia

Jock sat on his bed, shivering. He had called his mother, using the phone card the Australian consul had given him. She talked so much he shouted at her to be quiet and listen, worried he would run out of credit and be left alone once more. By now Jock realised he was in serious trouble. Grayham had given him an idea of how the incident was being reported. Other detainees had told him they had heard he was the only person who had been arrested.

Over and over, memories of that night flashed through Jock's mind. He found it hard enough to hold onto his recollections, much less make sense of them. He wondered if he was going insane as voices in his head clamoured, *Is the judge right? Was I imagining the attack on the Gypsy? Did I kill someone? Did I do it in cold blood?* There was so much he could not remember.

. . .

News stands in Sofia were doing a brisk trade that morning with newspapers full of stories about the funeral. They mixed emotional tributes by grieving friends, graphic firsthand accounts of the events surrounding Andrei Monov's death, and rumours that were reported as facts.

The newspaper *Labour* quoted anonymous friends of the dead man who depicted Jock as the kind of dissolute foreigner many believed came to Bulgaria to have a good time on the cheap, with no regard for the country or its people. Claiming he had been drinking at the Happy restaurant, the article said, 'The Australian was drunk after 5–6 beers and a shot of tequila and he shouted at people walking between the tables, he stood against them as though inviting them to fight. When police asked the staff there why they didn't do anything to bring the customer into line, some said: "We thought that he's just another drunk British guy."'

Despite the lack of supporting evidence, the prosecution would later attempt to table this article in court.

. . .

6 January 2008
Sofia
Simon gazed out of the aeroplane window at a stunning range of snow-covered mountains. On descent into Sofia he could see white fields dotted with abandoned factories. Sofia's airport is named Vrajdebna, which means 'hostile'. The cold went straight through Simon as he left the terminal; he drew his coat tighter and got into a taxi.

On the way to his hotel, Simon passed decrepit blocks of apartments with peeling paint and electrical wiring gaping from walls where the plaster had fallen away. Washing hung out to freeze on rusted balconies, and graffiti was everywhere. The Cyrillic lettering of the street signs only increased the strangeness of the city.

On the road, the latest Mercedes and Porsches sped past horse-drawn carts hauling anything from plastic piping to old tyres, and the cheaply made cars that were once prized possessions for Soviet–bloc families—Ladas, Moskviches and Trabants. Lines of people waited for buses on cracked pavements strewn with litter, their sombre faces swathed in coat hoods, hats and scarves; cigarettes drooped from their lips as though to warm them.

The traffic grew denser as the taxi turned into the historic downtown of Sofia, going clatter, bump, clatter, bump over the potholes. The driver could not park outside the Radisson Hotel, as the road in and away from it was snowed in. That did not stop him from charging Simon four times what the ride should have cost. Simon protested, but he still ended up paying double the usual rate. He then dragged his suitcase fifty metres to the entrance through snow thirty centimetres deep. The Radisson would be comfortable, but Simon could afford to stay there for only a few nights.

He had just got settled in his room when the telephone began to ring. It was News Limited's London-based European Bureau Chief, Charles Miranda. Simon politely told him he had nothing to say and hung up. He rang David Chaplin, the consular official, and they agreed that since the prison did not allow visitors on weekends, they would meet in the morning. He rang Dinko Kanchev, who said he had postponed his holiday so as to meet Simon and Jock.

Simon ventured outside. He wanted to get his bearings before he saw Jock, but, increasingly paranoid, he was wary of going to the scene where it had all happened. He did not want to upset Andrei Monov's family; he also feared young men seeking revenge on random foreigners. As he neared St Nedelya Square, Simon paused for a moment, then quickly turned away. He did not see the makeshift shrine about a metre from where Andrei had collapsed. It was at the base of a billboard bearing a Sisley fashion advertisement with a back-lit photograph of a young couple embracing. A candle was burning on the pavement and the remnants of many others were scattered around it. Leaning against one of the billboard's supports was a framed photograph of Andrei with his arms outstretched, holding a Bulgarian flag: smiling, confident, tall and good-looking. Friends, football supporters and strangers touched by the tragedy had left bunches of flowers nearby, but their petals had frozen and the colour from their wrapping paper was leaching into the snow.

. . .

7 January 2008
Sofia
8.30 a.m.

David Chaplin met Simon in the Radisson lobby. With him was Australia's honorary consul in Sofia, Indiana Trifonova. A Bulgarian national who had studied in Australia, Trifonova was bilingual. In the taxi to Sofia Central Prison, she provided a brief summary of local media coverage of the tragedy. Simon was appalled.

Three days before, the Bulgarian *Telegraph* had published a story under the headline, 'Australian is Also Killing Snowmen'. It referred to a YouTube video Jock had made of some friends of his beating up a snowman in the winter resort area of Perisher Valley, New South Wales. The young man in the video was not Jock but a dark-haired school friend. He was with two girls, one of whom, Ash Hart, Simon would later come to know well.

As their taxi approached the dark stone wall of the prison, the Australians fell silent. The entry to the Remand Centre was at the side. Trifonova did all the talking and filled in the paperwork. After an hour of waiting in the snow, they passed through a primitive metal detector and were patted down. Then a guard led them up a stairwell. Simon looked down the long, empty corridor, not knowing for a moment what to do.

When the consular staff and Simon were led into a small room, Jock was already there with a guard. He was behind a glass barrier and he seemed to be making an effort to look upbeat. The last time Simon had seen him, Jock was tanned and fit, with wild curly blond hair. Now he had a crew cut. He was dirty, unshaven and shaking from the cold.

Just seeing Jock alive gave Simon a rush of relief. But he was anxious, too. At any moment the guards could tell him to leave. Simon picked up the phone on his side of the glass. Jock spoke quickly and spiritedly. As had often been the case in Australia, Simon was finding it hard to make sense of what his son was telling him. The pressure was excruciating. Simon knew that if he could not understand Jock, no one else would. His son seemed to be jumping from one topic to another and genuinely bewildered by the fact that he was the only one who had been arrested.

One of the guards suddenly gestured that their time was up. Jock tried to look calm, even though his teeth were chattering. Simon watched as the guard led his son out of the room and then got up to leave. Jock was in the corridor. For a moment Simon lost his reserve and gestured to the guard, who did not react. Interpreting that as a yes, he took off his new coat and passed it to Jock. He wanted desperately to hug his son, but the guard's stolid expression made him hesitate, and his courage dissolved. It would be some time before Simon would feel strong enough to try again. In the meantime, Jock's fellow detainees would often ask if he would swap Simon's coat for something they had that he coveted, like cigarettes. He always refused, and the coat remains one of his most precious possessions.

Back in his hotel room, Simon wrestled with Jock's account of the fatal night. His son had always been prone to hyperbole, but he had seldom actually lied. Jock seemed to find it hard to accept that someone had died. Simon felt that his son's distress about this was genuine. *Jock's heart would have been in the right place, if not his head*, he thought. At the same time, he wondered how much of what Jock thought was happening had actually taken place. Had he been well intentioned but mistaken? The group of young men might well have been doing nothing wrong.

Over the coming days father and son would return many times to Jock's recollections of what happened as Simon struggled to piece together a chronology of events. He could not understand why Jock had taken a knife out with him that night. When Jock had described the knife, Simon had become even more concerned. He had grown up on a farm and was accustomed to using pocket knives in the bush. Simon had not seen a butterfly knife, but he gathered it was a lot bigger than a foldaway red Swiss Army knife.

What he could not grasp at all was Jock's claim to have no memory of the moments when Andrei Monov and Antoan Zahariev must have been stabbed. He had kept at his son about that, but Jock looked blank every time Simon probed for detail.

It was not that he distrusted Jock, but Simon liked to think things through carefully and logically. The pathologist in him always wanted corroborating evidence. He wished he could read witnesses' statements and expert reports on the knife, the wounds and any blood found at the scene.

Jock had said he did not want Simon to believe him just because he was his son, but because what he said was true and what he did was right. Based on Jock's higgledy-piggledy account, Simon was finding that difficult. He did not know that Jock himself was not entirely confident of his recollections. Father and son were locked in a dance of doubt.

. . .

By now the investigation was in its eleventh day. Tanya Alakusheva had the disk of video recordings collected from CCTV cameras at the metro and the intersection of Maria Louisa and Stamboliyski boulevards. Her colleagues at Sofia Police Headquarters had sent it three days before. Presumably she had reviewed the video evidence: CCTV images, however indistinct or incomplete, might at least help sort the facts from fiction in the various witness accounts. All that was missing were the recordings from the Ministry of Health building outside which Jock had been arrested.

That afternoon, the secretary of the Ministry of Health signed off on a response to Alakusheva's request for the recordings from its building in St Nedelya Square. According to him, there were two surveillance cameras at the building. One faced the square; the other was behind the building. His letter outlined what Alakusheva should have expected to see from the footage:

'During the day the video surveillance covers the area from the entrance of the ministry to the corner of Stamboliyski and Maria Louisa Boulevard and part of the intersection between the Ministry of Health and St Nedelya Church. During the night the surveillance is limited and the only part that can be seen is the lit area in front of the ministry's entrance for a radius of around ten metres.'

But there was a problem: 'Due to an already outdated computer system, the recordings from the cameras are kept only for the last four days. As a result, the recording of the night of 28 December leading into

29 December 2007 has been already automatically deleted . . . and so cannot be given to you.'

The Ministry's confusion about which night's recordings were required was a minor point. Far more significant was that the investigator had made her formal request for the recordings just after the disk was erased.

That was not the only mistake. Seven weeks later, the secretary of the Ministry of Health would respond to a request from Prosecutor Parvoleta Nikova for the CCTV material. In this letter he would state that in fact there were two cameras outside the entrance of the Ministry of Health, the second monitoring a fifteen-metre strip along the building towards Bulbank and five metres in front of the entrance. It might have taken in the area near the metro where Jock claimed the Gypsy was beaten, particularly if that was closer to Bulbank and thus the Ministry of Health. Certainly, either or both cameras might have shown the final melee.

As if that wasn't curious enough, the ministry secretary stated in the same letter that 'Due to a failure in the electric supply on 26 January 2008, the computer hard drive has been damaged and cannot be used.'

In the coming months, the saga of the Ministry of Health's CCTV recordings would become more and more bizarre.

CHAPTER 10

8 January 2008
Remand Centre
6 a.m.

Early on Tuesday morning, guards shouted at Jock to get ready for court. Hunger gnawed at him. Breakfast here was soup made of macaroni and water, which made him gag. It was a minimal version of the traditional Bulgarian dish *macaroni na furna*, pasta doused in eggs, sugar, cheese and milk and then baked.

Simon had bought Jock some clothes, but to wash them Jock had to shower fully dressed. He was allowed only one short shower a week and he was not allowed one today. His request for a haircut continued to fall on deaf ears. Simon had not yet been able to find him a suit.

By 7 a.m. Jock was in the back of the police van and on his way through the dark streets of Sofia. The back door opened and guards led him a few paces across a laneway and into the holding cell on the ground floor of the vast Sofia Palace of Justice. There was no toilet here and the cell reeked with urine and faeces.

. . .

8 a.m.

Simon was pacing his hotel room. It was way too early to leave. The court hearings didn't start until 10.30. He felt very alone and desperately missed Helen and her calm, organised approach to problem solving.

Stoiko Barborski would be the defence lawyer at today's bail appeal hearing. Jock had complained that he still did not have copies of the witness statements he had requested, and that he'd been unable to contact either Barborski or Galina.

Simon had not met Barborski, and that worried him. The only experience he'd had with lawyers had been when he and Mary Jane had divorced. His idea of how courts worked came mostly from watching episodes of *Perry Mason* as a teenager, but he knew enough to sense that what was happening here in Sofia was not right.

By 9.30 a.m. Simon was in a suit and making his way on foot to the Palace of Justice, a stone's throw from where Andrei Monov had died. His neat backpack looked out of place as he walked up the granite steps, past the giant sculptures of lions, through security and into the vaulted hall with its thick columns and polished stone floor. Stained-glass windows filled the hall with patches of bright light. David Chaplin and Indiana Trifonova were already there. He followed them into one of the small courtrooms that flanked the hall, and they found seats at the back.

Reaching into his suit jacket for a notepad, Simon looked around. There were a lot of people here. He wondered if the parents of the dead man were among them.

Hearing a scuffle at the court door, Simon turned to see what was going on. Jock was walking down the aisle, surrounded by guards. Camera crews and photographers buzzed around them like locusts. As Jock passed his father, he nodded at him. Simon's heart missed a beat—his son's hands were clasped behind him in steel handcuffs.

At least thirty journalists pushed forward, bumping into the wooden seats in their attempt to get up the aisle. Jock was at the front of the courtroom now, but he had disappeared into the swarm. Video cameras were in his face. Simon was horrified. *Click, click, click* went the stills cameras, like guns firing. Simon jumped up. 'Stop that! Stop that now!' he called out, without thinking. Someone pulled him back, saying, 'There's nothing you can do; just calm down.' The photographers continued taking shots of Jock.

Simon could see the interpreter, Galina, and the lawyer at the front of the court. A panel of three judges entered. The cameras left. Resplendent in a floor-length crimson velvet robe, a duty prosecutor addressed the bench. The honorary counsel tried interpreting for Simon, but she found it hard to hear the proceedings.

Jock stood at the front surrounded by guards. The handcuffs were off now, but his hands were still behind him. He rubbed one wrist and then the other. Simon stared at the familiar torso, broad-shouldered and well built.

The prosecutor wanted to present new evidence. He drew the judges' attention to Martin Stoilov's police statement, pointing out that this witness had seen the moment when the accused stabbed Andrei Monov and Antoan Zahariev. He said nothing about the two other witnesses who had given evidence on the same day as Martin and who had seen most of what had happened that night—the workers at the Sheraton, Viktor Georgiev and Lyubomir Tomov.

Taking some pages from his file, the prosecutor said he now wanted to tender the *Daily Telegraph* article with the allegation about an incident in Sydney three years before, together with a translation. He also presented an article that claimed the British Ministry of Defence 'had refused to help the defendant'. He argued that the news items should be included as evidence because they shed light on the accused's character.

The prosecutor then pointed to the story in *Labour* of 4 January in which the perpetrator had been described as drinking to excess at the Happy restaurant. Jock remembers interrupting him to protest against the submission of the newspaper articles, which he said were factually incorrect. Barborski agreed, pointing out that under Bulgarian law they did not qualify as evidence. The judges accepted only the new witness statement. The newspaper articles, however, would remain in the court file.

Barborski then asked that Jock be granted bail, arguing that he was not a flight risk and could stay with Grayham. The prosecutor said Jock's action had 'rudely violated civil order' in Bulgaria and constituted an expression of 'blatant disrespect for both society and its institutions'. He pointed to the *Daily Telegraph* article once again. 'Even though he has no priors, the information about him shows he did some similar acts in the past. Even though these are only newspaper and internet articles from here and elsewhere in the world, and even though this evidence is not collected in the proper manner, they are out there in the public domain.'

Barborski said the prosecutor's argument was circumstantial rather than factual. Jock argued that the prosecution had relied on the word of friends who would have agreed to support each other's stories, despite there having been many other people in the square that night. He suggested that the witnesses had left out some of what had happened so as to leave him with no motive. But Jock did not understand that the charge of hooliganism effectively circumvented the need for motive, since it referred to a random antisocial act.

The chief judge said eleven witnesses had identified Jock as the perpetrator of both the murder and the attempted murder. The judge added that the kiosk worker's testimony was particularly significant, as he was an independent witness and the incident had taken place outside his kiosk.

The court denied Jock bail, finding that, without an acceptable address in Bulgaria, he was a flight risk. 'You're lucky we no longer have the death penalty,' Barborski said to his client. Guards snapped the handcuffs back on and led Jock through the cameras and out of the courtroom. Simon caught Jock's eye momentarily, but then his son was gone; he tried to speak to Barborski, but the language barrier made that impossible.

Both English and Bulgarian-speaking reporters approached David Chaplin outside the courtroom. Among them was a News Limited reporter, who asked if it was true that Jock was not happy with his lawyer. Chaplin said he was aware of that and was working on it. Simon steered clear of the journalists, not wanting to talk publicly. No one seemed to recognise him as the father of the accused. Unfortunately, by not refuting what was said in court, Simon missed a chance to stem the misreporting.

When Indiana Trifonova took Simon through the Bulgarian media coverage of the hearing the next day, he felt as if he was living in a different universe from that of the reporters. The Bulgarian *Telegraph* claimed he had bought a house for Jock so that his son would have a permanent address for bail purposes.

But it was News Limited's account that disturbed Simon most. Its newspapers reported that Jock's female companion, 'who is known only as Susan', had returned to Sofia and been interviewed by police, but had now fled the country. Simon gathered 'Susan' was Lindsay, who he knew had neither fled nor been contacted. As he read on, his concern about misinformation grew. 'Palfreeman's lawyer, Stoiko Barborski, said the charges could be changed as further evidence was being gathered by police. "It may now be proved he did it, but he may not have been in his right mind—unstable—at that time, and not responsible for his actions."'

Simon sat back in his chair, appalled. Barborski's comment to the reporters would only have compounded the Bulgarian media's bad impression of Jock: he was now crazy, as well as being a homeless, trained killer known to police. Could it get any worse? Simon was confident of only one thing: in this unfolding disaster, the lawyer Fair Trials International had recommended could only be an improvement.

. . .

Remand Centre, Sofia

That afternoon Simon went to the Remand Centre with Dinko Kanchev to introduce the lawyer to his son. He was anxious. He hoped the meeting would go well, that Jock would agree to brief Dinko, and that the three of them would agree on a path forward.

Dinko was in his late fifties and married to a judge in Bulgaria's highest appellate court, the Supreme Court of Cassation. With his handlebar moustache, ever-present Victory Blue cigarette, and deep, deadpan voice, Dinko looked like a KGB spy from Central Casting. He was unhappy with aspects of the legal process in post-Communist Bulgaria and glad that the government was making some reforms.

Bulgaria's legal system was still heavily influenced by Stalinist law. The push was now on to bring it into line with the shared principles of the European Union, but much of the language used in the Sofia Palace of Justice was a holdover from the Communist era. If the allegations of backroom deals were correct, corruption was also a holdover from the transition to capitalism when Bulgaria resembled the Wild West.

A new article, No. 281, had recently been added to the Bulgarian Criminal Procedures Code that was designed to prevent police from concocting false statements behind closed doors, a practice that Dinko had seen all too often as a defence lawyer. Article 281 allowed the prosecution or defence to object to the use in evidence of witness statements that had been given only to police. The intention was not to white out inconvenient evidence; it was to guard against police manufacturing evidence. But Article 281 had implications that lawmakers failed to foresee. Jock's case would expose these flaws.

As Dinko and Simon waited in the snow outside the prison, a tanned young woman approached them. Simon did not notice her at first. Pigeons hovering around him took off as her footsteps got closer. At the sound of her Australian accent, Simon looked up. It was Ash Hart, the girl in Jock's snowman video and a friend of his from Sydney.

Ash had gone to a Catholic girls school not far from Riverview, and she and Jock had been close during their senior years. She had just completed her second year of officer training in the Royal Australian Air Force and had heard about Jock's plight while on holiday in Paris. She had immediately set out for Sofia, a trip that had taken several days owing to the snowstorms in the Bulgarian capital. She had not told her parents or her commander; she didn't want to worry her family or get into trouble with the Air Force. For security reasons, the military needed to know where all its personnel were when they were abroad.

When Ash had tried to visit Jock that morning, police had been notified that a blonde English-speaking woman was at the prison and she had been taken to Police Station No. 3 for questioning. Galina had been there to translate. Convinced that Ash was Lindsay Welsh, the police investigator insisted that she make a statement about the incident in which she had been involved. Ash kept protesting that she wasn't Lindsay. But the more she shook her head in response to the barrage of questions, the more insistent the investigator became. Galina quietly explained that in Bulgaria shaking one's head means yes, while nodding means no.

Dinko and Simon took Ash with them to see Jock. He grinned when he saw her. 'I want you to meet Mr Dinko Kanchev,' said Simon, anxious that Ash's unexpected presence not eclipse the mission at hand. Dinko was still coming through the door and Jock could not see him; he certainly did not know the lawyer spoke English. 'Oh, fair Dinko!' Jock said with a laugh, then started to say something to Ash. Simon threw him a Stern Dad look and said Jock should talk with his lawyer privately first. He and Ash would wait at the door.

Jock told Dinko what he remembered about the night. Dinko's face was inscrutable, but he said the strength of public feeling about the case, fuelled by the media reports, meant they had a tough job ahead of them. Jock was under no illusions on that front. He appreciated Dinko's direct manner and was relieved the lawyer seemed honest. Jock had expected a Bulgarian lawyer to suggest they bribe the investigator, the prosecutor and court officials. By the end of the visit, he had a new lawyer.

Afterwards Ash took a taxi to the airport to catch her flight back to Canberra. Simon and Dinko went to a coffee shop near the courthouse to nut out details. The lawyer lit up one cigarette after another as he took the polite foreigner on a Cook's Tour of Bulgaria's judicial system. Simon hung on every word.

Dinko explained that Jock would be deemed innocent until proven guilty and that guilt had to be determined beyond reasonable doubt. Consequent to this, both the police investigation and prosecution were obliged to examine all sides equally. The lawyer then said that Jock could plead not guilty on the grounds of self-defence and defence of another person. According to the Bulgarian Penal Code someone who perceives a threat can harm the person he believes is attacking himself or someone else. The court would have to determine if the amount of harm he inflicted in the course of defending himself was commensurate with 'the nature and danger' of the attack. It could find him guilty of defending himself with excessive force. The court could release him without punishment if it found that Jock had exceeded the limits of 'inevitable self-defence' because he was frightened or confused, and was attacked by more than two people and at night. Simon nodded his head: similar principles applied in Australia.

As Dinko talked, Simon realised that the Bulgarian judicial system worked very differently from anything he understood. In the English

Common Law system practised in the United Kingdom, the United States and Australia, lawyers engage in argument and counter-argument in an effort to convince a jury of the validity of their cause, with the judge as adjudicator. Like France, Bulgaria used a form of the inquisitorial system. Here a trial is more of a fact-finding exercise, in which the judge tries to gather as much evidence as possible before retiring to weigh its merits and reach a decision. In the lower court, three lay people assist the judge in assessing the evidence. They come from a small pool of citizens—often, but not necessarily, with a legal background—and are variously referred to as 'lay judges', 'professional jurors' and 'court assessors'. The prosecutor and the defence team, including the defendant, can request that certain evidence be heard and can question witnesses within limited parameters. But they are not the only parties to the trial.

Dinko said that it was possible for victims of a crime to mount a claim for damages. If they did so, their case would run at the same time as the criminal trial. 'But the victims have a financial as well as emotional incentive to see a conviction recorded,' Simon said, taken aback. 'Surely this constitutes a conflict of interest!'

'That's up to the judge to control,' Dinko responded.

Simon peered through the haze of cigarette smoke, unsure what this would mean for Jock's trial. He accepted that an unfamiliar system could still function effectively. Nevertheless, this strangeness unsettled him. He jotted down notes.

Dinko then explained that most Bulgarian senior judges, prosecutors and lawyers—himself included—had been trained during the Communist era. At that time, crimes were graded by the degree to which they affronted the state, rather than individual rights. The addition of 'with hooligan intent' to his charge meant that Jock was accused as much of attacking the Bulgarian state as of attacking two young men.

Simon asked about bringing together a team, possibly including Australian or British lawyers. Dinko said he would take the case only if he had sole carriage of it. He would be solicitor, barrister and office staff. He would not work alongside lawyers from England or Australia, or Bulgaria for that matter. That was not how it was done here.

Simon frowned. This was unexpected, but he would have to accept it. 'So how can I help my son?' he asked.

Bulgarian law allowed for an immediate family member to act as part of the defence team. Dinko recommended that Simon sign on, because this would give him access to Jock in prison beyond the normal two visit days a month, and would provide him with access to the case file once the investigation was complete. Ultimately, it would also mean he could sit at the bar table alongside Jock and examine witnesses in court.

Simon was nervous. He had no legal training. He knew nothing about Bulgarian law. Another relative might be able to do the job better. On the one hand, he could see that becoming what was known as Jock's 'defender' was probably the only way he could get access to all the witness statements and expert reports and also have enough time with Jock to get to the bottom of what had happened. On the other hand, he dreaded what might be revealed in the CCTV recordings and the forensic tests. What if Jock was entirely to blame? How would he deal with that? What if he let Jock down?

Pushing his doubts aside, Simon agreed on the spot. This was his son and, come what may, he wanted to ensure that he was dealt with fairly. He did not want to be stuck at the back of a courtroom, cut off from proceedings. Taking part seemed the only way he could come close to understanding Jock's accusers. If Jock was convicted, at least Simon would know exactly what had taken place. He just hoped that by taking this step he would not do his son any harm.

. . .

Thank God Dad's here, Jock thought as he sat on his bunk. He may have sparred with his father during high school and in the year before he left Australia, but Simon had always been the person he had turned to for help and advice. Where Jock would rush into things, his father approached them methodically. Jock respected Simon's capacity for clear thinking, something he felt the lack of right now. His father was meticulous about following the rules and, as far as Jock could see, he always did the right thing.

After Jock's parents had divorced, Simon had continued taking his sons to Mass on the weekends they stayed with him. He had wanted them to grow up with the Roman Catholic faith and tradition that he and Mary Jane shared. But he no longer received Holy Communion. When Jock once asked him why, Simon explained that the Church did not accept divorce, so when he left Mary Jane he had forfeited his right to participate.

Simon's aversion to conflict could be infuriating. They had already argued over media coverage. Jock thought they should get his side of the story out, to balance what he regarded as the lies being spread.

Simon was dead against saying anything publicly. Like the Department of Foreign Affairs, Dinko had advised him to steer clear of journalists. Courting the media would be disrespectful and wrong, given this was now to be a matter before a court.

Dad has absolutely no idea about how people and systems operate here, Jock fumed. *He sees everything through rose-coloured glasses.*

CHAPTER 11

10 January 2008

Stoiko Barborski took a call from Tanya Alakusheva, who had originally given him the Palfreeman brief. She told him the Australian had a new lawyer. He wondered if other lawyers had said bad things about him to Jock's father. Ever since the first bail hearing Barborski had been approached by lawyers offering to take charge of Jock's case on a pro bono basis. The law was a dog-eat-dog world and a high-profile case was good for business.

Ego bruised and feeling abandoned, Barborski went to see Jock. He still remembers asking Jock if there was anything he needed. 'Just a Kalashnikov,' Jock said animatedly as he pretended to hold a gun. 'So I can shoot my way out of here.'

In an interview for this book, Barborski recalled he had heard from police that there was CCTV footage showing what had happened. *He stabbed our boy in the back, in the heart*, the lawyer thought as he left the Remand Centre.

. . .

A police fingerprint expert reported to Tanya Alakusheva that there were no 'dactyliscoptic traces' on the butterfly knife Jock had carried. In layman's language, that meant no fingerprints—neither Jock's nor anyone else's.

The next day the investigator requested DNA testing of the knife, Jock's clothing and the samples of blood taken from the crime scene. It would be some time before those results came through.

. . .

Aksenia Monova was even more distressed now. Since the murder, her father had stopped eating and seemed to have lost his will to live. Andrei had been his only grandchild.

When Aksenia and Hristo married at the end of 1981, they had wanted to start a family at once, but it took five years. Her pregnancy had been difficult; she spent the last seven months of it in hospital. In August 1986 there was an earthquake, and all the pregnant patients had fled the hospital. Aksenia refused to leave her bed. If she was going to have a miscarriage, she thought, it would be then. When she and her unborn child made it through unscathed, she was sure that God or Nature had given her a survivor.

Aksenia's parents helped raise Andrei. Indeed, he spent so much time at their home in Lozenets that he built up a group of friends there, with whom he played football. As Andrei grew, his grandparents took him to piano lessons and to maths and English tutors. Andrei played volleyball, and they took him to training.

Right now her mother was on the phone in tears. Aksenia hurried over to her parents' place, hoping she might be able to persuade her father to drink some soup. By now he was very unwell.

. . .

The prison provided a single serving of watery gruel for lunch and dinner. Once a week there was half a cow's liver served in one piece in warm water. There was no fresh fruit or vegetables. The meals were brought to the Remand Centre from the prison kitchen. By the time they arrived, much of their content had been stolen.

Jock was a hardy young man and used to living rough, but Simon knew that poor nutrition combined with the bitter cold would quickly render him vulnerable to disease. Now that he was Jock's defender, Simon could see his son as often as he wanted on weekdays. His attention turned to making sure Jock was properly fed.

It was difficult to establish what was allowed in and what was not. Some foods he got past the inspection desk one day were ruled unacceptable the next. Simon wanted to get things right and avoid doing anything that might give the authorities reason to hurt his son. The arbitrary application of rules he did not understand rattled him.

With a good sense of direction, Simon quickly worked out how to navigate his way around Sofia and found the Women's Market, which was near Maria Louisa Boulevard. Gypsy children chased each other around abandoned Russian cars. Scruffy, lean Roma youths sold handmade axes and brooms. Fat women with their hair held back by colourful scarves urged him to buy roasted chestnuts and cigarettes. Simon could not remember ever having seen a Gypsy in Australia.

Among the goods for sale were knives—pen knives, long knives in leather sheaths and butterfly knives, all costing between 3 and 15 *leva*, which equated to the cost of a cup of coffee and a sandwich in Sydney. Knives were certainly more commonplace here than at home, but the idea of carrying one as a form of protection remained anathema to him.

Simon could not find all Jock wanted in the market. His first request had been for a watch and a calendar. Not knowing how much time was passing played strange tricks on Jock's mind. Another day, he asked his father to bring in a chess set. It had to be a wooden one to be allowed into the prison. Finding one was tough. Simon had to search back streets for small shops with limited stock on half-empty shelves. Shopkeepers did not speak English. Their signs were in Cyrillic. When he finally found a wooden chess set on the other side of the city, Simon felt a small surge of triumph. Getting the things Jock wanted made him feel he was doing something for his son, if only making his time in prison a little more comfortable.

. . .

Remand Centre, Sofia

From Day 1 in the Remand Centre Jock had known he would have to figure out who he could trust and who he should avoid. The rough and tumble of school playgrounds and sporting fields had taught him that ignorance makes you vulnerable. Now Jock was hyper-alert, always on the lookout for signs of danger. He could tell that the guards were equally wary of him; some of the detainees kept their backs against the wall if they had to be near him. Small wonder, given what they were all hearing about him on TV and in the tabloids.

During the hour each day that the detainees spent in the generously named exercise yard, Jock got to know two young Russians. Sasha was an amiable drug addict. Vasia was a lock picker and a thief; this was the second time he had been charged, so he knew the ropes. Jock watched how he survived and copied him. For that hour outside in the snow, Jock felt he had a friend.

When a Roma detainee passed to Jock through the wire in the exercise yard a newspaper clipping about the snowman-bashing video, Vasia translated it for him, roaring with laughter. Vasia and Sasha would soon become Jock's cellmates. Sasha left for a while, but prison was to become a revolving door for him; he would be released, only to be arrested again.

. . .

Each time Simon went to see Jock, he learnt a little bit more about his adventures during his two years away from home. Simon was taken aback by how much violence his son had encountered.

One night Jock had found himself alone in an alley in the southern Bulgarian town of Pazardzhik. Out of the shadows stepped a skinhead, who lunged at him with a knife. Another time, he was camping on the Black Sea and woke to find a naked girl cowering in the corner of his tent. Eventually he established that she had been raped by someone who had her girlfriend trapped in a nearby shack. Without thinking, Jock went to help, leaving the naked girl in his tent. He laughed as he told of the happy endings to each tale. During one visit, when Jock started on yet another story, this time involving a Gypsy, his father interrupted him. 'Jock, Jock, Jock, slow down,' said Simon. 'Why on earth did you stay here so long?'

Jock stopped and stared at his father. 'Are you insane? I was meeting the most wonderful people along the way.' Jock explained that after the

Pazardzhik attack, he started to take pepper spray with him when he went out at night in a new city. On returning to Bulgaria for Christmas, he had tried to buy the spray in Samokov but the shops there were out of stock.

'But Jock, why the knife that night?' Simon asked gently.

'I don't know,' Jock said glumly. 'It was next to my ID card on the kitchen table. At the last minute I just grabbed them both when Grayham was in a rush to leave and then I didn't think any more about it.'

Simon walked back to the city centre to clear his head. Jock still sounded like the boy he had helped to raise, but Simon could see that to understand how this whole debacle had come about he needed to know more about the people Jock had met here and the experiences he had shared with them.

By now, Simon had moved into a serviced apartment. To stay in touch with Helen, he would email from an internet cafe called The Inferno, run out of a lean-to with no heating. It was so cold there that he found typing difficult, but night after night he would write to Helen about what had happened during the day, and then search the net for news and other information about Bulgaria. He became fascinated by Bulgarian history, language and contemporary politics, and began to understand what it was that had drawn his son back to this country at the other end of the world.

. . .

15 January 2008
Police Station No. 3
2.30 p.m.

Anton 'Tony' Doychev entered Tanya Alakusheva's office, where she quizzed him about his conversations with the accused.

Tony explained that he had met the Australian and his two English friends at the Rock Bar at around 9 p.m. on 27 December. He had drunk two or three beers; he thought the others had had about the same amount. He said he had not taken drugs and did not see the others taking drugs. The investigator wanted to know what the group had discussed. He said: 'Jock, Lindsay and Grayham told me that they are anti-fascists. I explained to them that in Bulgaria most political youth organisations have a far-right orientation—football hooligans and skinheads . . . Personally I don't have political beliefs. I told them about the animosity between right-wing football hooligans and the small number of left-wing organisations. I told them that there are fights here between those two groups . . . I told them that I have been attacked by football hooligans and skinheads, just because of the way I dress, and that they should be careful. We talked like that for several hours.'

Tony said the group of youths emerging from the metro were 'yelling' and 'chanting'. He had warned his companions that 'these were probably football hooligans' and they should 'get away' from them.

The trio had crouched behind the wall at the Happy restaurant. As Tony keyed the credit code into his mobile phone, Jock asked him whether the youths had just attacked someone. 'I answered that I didn't know; I didn't see. At this moment I looked across and saw a group of twenty boys standing on the other side of the road, as if they were about to cross.'

Tony said the boys had stopped yelling and chanting by then. He noticed that occasionally other passers-by seemed to be deliberately walking a bit further away from the football fans. But Tony seems not to have seen the 'altercation' with what were variously called 'Roma' or 'strangers'; nor did he see any members of the group advancing towards them.

The next thing Tony noticed was Jock running. Like Nikolai Rabadzhiev, who was near him at the time, Tony was not focused on the square. He was preoccupied with his mobile phone and he may not have seen what led to the incident, looking up only when the melee was well underway: 'They started yelling and scattered. Until then the boys were standing in two lines. After Jock went among them they spread around him in a circle. Jock was in the circle and that's why I couldn't see him well. But I saw that Jock was pushing the boys. I couldn't see exactly what he was doing because they were all moving chaotically. I think they exchanged blows, but I am not sure.'

Tony said that Lindsay rushed after Jock, calling out that he should come back. By the time Tony reached the site of the confrontation, the boys had knocked the Australian to the ground, where he lay on his stomach. Tony heard the youths calling Jock a *chorbar*, an offensive expression for a CSKA fan. He saw one of the youths kick Lindsay 'in the waist'.

At the bail hearing several days after the incident Jock had denied that Tony had described the youths coming out of the metro as 'football hooligans' and insisted Tony said they were 'bullies'. Tanya Alakusheva was interested to hear that the suspect had a political objection to football hooligans. This fitted in with the picture of the killer she could see emerging from the witness statements. In the final section of Tony's statement, one can imagine her asking the question: 'Why did the foreigner attack the boys?'

'We got on really well with him,' Tony said. 'He seemed intelligent and well balanced. I can't explain his behaviour at the square. I'm sorry for what has happened there, for the injured boys and for Jock himself. I guess Jock attacked the boys at the square because he had decided that they were far-right football hooligans, because everywhere in the world they are aggressive and get into fights. I guess Jock decided to attack them first, before they beat him to it . . . I personally didn't think that they would attack us, because we were standing to the side, and I thought that they would pass by us. However, I guess Jock thought so.'

The interview lasted almost two hours, roughly the total length of time that Tony had spent in Jock's company.

In a few days' time it would be Tony's name day. For Orthodox Christians, a name day is like a second birthday. Tony shared his name day with the injured Antoan Zahariev and with Tony 'the Tall' Yordanov. He was scarcely to know the extent to which his testimony would become entwined with those of the young men he had feared that late-December night.

. . .

18 January 2008

Jock was playing chess with one of his cellmates when guards came and took him to another part of the Remand Centre. All he knew was he was about to see some doctors, and he was glad of the distraction. Galina was there to translate.

Professor Boris Shtarbanov shook the accused's hand. A tall, thin, balding man in his early seventies, he explained that he was a forensic psychiatrist and that the police investigator had asked him and his colleagues to assess Jock's state of mind. Accompanying Shtarbanov was forensic

Dr Simon Palfreeman with Angus, Jock and Spencer in 2003. SIMON PALFREEMAN

Geri and Jock Palfreeman in Bath on Jock's first day in England at the start of his trip away from Australia, in January 2006. GERI PALFREEMAN

Jock going to work in Samokov, 2006. JOCK PALFREEMAN

Jock at the Infantry Training Centre at Catterick in Northern England. JOCK PALFREEMAN

Lindsay Welsh rolls a cigarette as Grayham Saunders fixes a window in his Madjare house. Grayham's butterfly knife is on the kitchen table near the white bowl. JOCK PALFREEMAN

Grayham Saunders and Jock Palfreeman sledding on the hill overlooking Madjare, Christmas 2007. Jock is wearing his badged jacket. JOCK PALFREEMAN

The village of Madjare, where Jock Palfreeman stayed in the house that Grayham Saunders was renovating. RON EKKEL

Iliyan outside his house, next to the Roma wall. BELINDA HAWKINS

Memorial to Andrei Monov at the base of the billboard near where he fell on Stamboliyski Boulevard. BELINDA HAWKINS

Necrologs at Andrei Monov's grave in Boyana Cemetry. BELINDA HAWKINS

Freeze frame from subway CCTV camera showing Andrei's cohort coming out of the metro. The youth with a white stripe on his jacket on the left of frame is wearing a beanie but soon removes it. BELINDA HAWKINS

Freeze frame from the traffic camera on Maria Louisa Boulevard showing Jock as he runs across St Nedelya Square. BELINDA HAWKINS

Freeze frame from the traffic camera that shows Andrei Monov's group chasing one of the two people. The 'stranger' or Gypsy is on the far right, then the youth with lots of white on his jacket, followed by the youth with a stripe across his jacket.

BELINDA HAWKINS

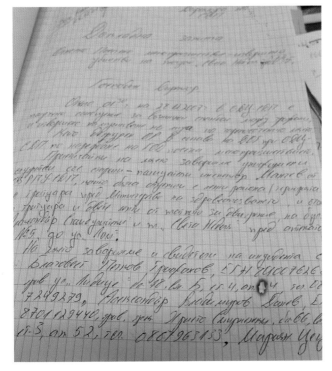

The incident report with cigarette burn and bearing Alakusheva's name.

BELINDA HAWKINS

The northern end of St Nedelya Square. The edge of the metro can be seen on the left with Maria Louisa Boulevard and the Sheraton car park to the left. The pot plants of Bulbank are to the right with the building housing the Ministry of Health. In the distance are the kiosk, Stamboliyski Boulevard and the Happy Garden. SIMON PALFREEMAN

A Roma cart near St Nedelya Square. BELINDA HAWKINS

The Ministry of Health entrance where Jock was arrested is to the right. The final melee took place between the tree in the middle of frame and the kiosk on the right of frame near the top of frame. BELINDA HAWKINS

One of the two cabins in the Sheraton car park facing Maria Louisa Boulevard and the south end of St Nedelya Boulevard. BELINDA HAWKINS

Simeon 'Simo' Panev, the Roma Jock helped at a rock concert in 2006. RON EKKEL

Jock Palfreeman with his brother Spencer on a special prison visit in 2008.
SPENCER PALFREEMAN

Sofia Central Prison. DOBRIN KASHAVELOV

Sofia Palace of Justice near St Nedelya Church. BELINDA HAWKINS

The police mug shot
from the morning
of the incident.

Приложение 1

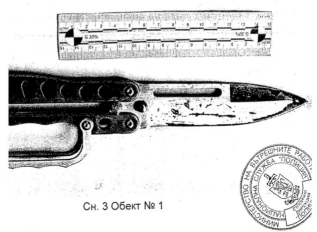

Сн. 3 Обект № 1

The butterfly knife.

Antoan Zahariev shaking hands with Aksenia Monova (sitting), and Tony Yordanov shaking hands with Hristo Monov in the Sofia Palace of Justice hall during the appeal. DOBRIN KASHAVELOV

Antoan Zahariev at court.

Prosecutor Parvoleta Nikova.

Simon Palfreeman and Dinko Kanchev at court.

Judge Georgi Kolev.

SUPREME ADMINISTRATIVE COURT

Associate Professor Maria Grozeva.

DOBRIN KASHAVELOV

Dr Krassimir Kanev. BELINDA HAWKINS

Judge Mimi Petrova. SOFIA CITY COURT

Hristo Monov and
Aksenia Monova at
court. DOBRIN KASHAVELOV

Jock in prison. DOBRIN KASHAVELOV

Dr Simon and Helen Palfreeman in Samokov. BELINDA HAWKINS

Jock in his part of Cell 17. BORYANA DZHAMBAZOVA

psychiatrist Dr Elka Stoycheva and psychologist Dr Lilyana Behar. Jock was pleased to be with new people, and the conversation flowed easily, despite the need to pause for translation.

Shtarbanov had retired in 1994, but he still gave expert advice in criminal cases. He had examined hundreds of murderers during his long career. As head of the three-member panel, he had been given a list of the charges against Jock and copies of the police witness statements, as well as the estimate of Jock's blood alcohol content at the time of the incident. In this initial interview, the panel wanted to start gathering information about Jock's background, his early childhood development and his behaviour as a teenager.

In its report, the panel included detail of when Jock smiled and laughed as he answered questions. It noted that Jock had behaved appropriately during the examination and had understood that its primary purpose was to determine whether he was sane.

Jock told Shtarbanov how he had worked his way around Europe 'in construction, in a butcher shop, in agriculture, in farming . . . in a kitchen, on a ship, in a hotel, in a kindergarten'. So far, he said, 'I have visited England, Austria, France, Greece, Turkey and Bulgaria. I became a professional soldier to get an English passport. This is the fifth time I have come to Bulgaria. I like it. I have friends here.'

Asked specific questions about his health, he said, 'I smoke a packet a day, I drink a bit. I have never had concussion.' He then laughed as he added, 'I have never been admitted to a psychiatric hospital, so far!'

Jock said, 'I'm loyal, honest, hardworking, I'm assertive, I'm usually in a good mood, I have a good sense of humour. I'm not aggressive—well, that's not an absolute given.' He told the doctors of a time in Samokov when someone had tried to steal his motorbike. He had wanted to beat the thief, he said—but not badly. Iliyan had persuaded him not to. The panel misconstrued this. Probably because of a glitch in the translation, the report says that Jock had started beating the man, but not badly.

'I do not hold grudges against people,' Jock said. 'I help the underdog. At school they told me I was the Bully of the Bullies. After [leaving] school I grew a beard and they called me Robin Hood.'

Shtarbanov had warned Jock that he should not regard the examination as a time for unconsidered confessions and should keep to what he had discussed with his lawyer. Jock understood, but he decided to tell the experts what had happened anyway. They noted what he said in their report.

Jock said the day before the incident he had gone sledding. When he came to Sofia with his friends he had about four or five beers and a shot of tequila. 'I wasn't drunk,' he explained. 'I was under the influence—yes!—but not extremely drunk. Actually, I'm not the bad kind of drunk—I'm the laughing drunk. When I drink, I'm cheerful and I love everyone!'

He recalled that in the square, 'There were people running around us and a boy who was with us said, "Let's get out of their way, these are football fans, they attack." We hid next to a pizza restaurant, in the yard, and waited for them to pass by. I looked—a few people were beating a man on the ground. I ran to there to help him and shouted "Run." They moved away. I bent over to check how the man was, then the people came towards me again. I waved the knife; they threw pavers from the pavement. Then they came closer to me, they hit me on the head. I fell, then I stood up and waved the knife to protect myself. Everything happened very quickly; I can't say if and how I wounded someone. Bodyguards came from somewhere—they kicked my knife away. They turned me on my stomach and actually they protected me from those who were throwing pavers at me. Police officers came and I was relieved, because I wanted them to take me, because I didn't know who the others were. The police officers took me away. They hit me a bit.'

Jock smiled as he recollected the fat officers puffing with the exertion. But he finished his account solemnly. 'They brought me here and that's it. Everything here is lawful.'

That month the experts would make two further trips to the prison to carry out specific psychological tests on Jock in a bid to establish if there was any sign of the aggression needed to have committed such a terrible crime. In their report the experts would describe Jock as 'sociable' and 'well meaning', with no 'psychotic tendencies'; he thought 'with a normal pace and structure, correctly and logically'; he was 'emotionally lively . . . with a sense of humour and irony'.

The experts would find that Jock was warm and spontaneous, rather than narcissistic or domineering, and that he reacted instinctively to what he perceived as unfair treatment of others. They would conclude that: 'he has lots of energy . . . he makes decisions very quickly and he puts those decisions into action immediately. That's why it is possible in some extreme situations he could react a bit aggressively instead of just assertively. This is not due to a high level of aggression in his character, but is an expression of his desire to get results right away by finding an immediate solution to the problem, which is a feature of his character.'

The panel would also interview Simon in his small apartment. It found that Simon and Jock shared a sense of decency and openness. But Simon seemed more cautious than his son. Responding to questions about Jock's character and personality, Simon said Jock was more like his mother, who was 'quite strong-willed'.

Interviewed for this book Stoycheva said the culture of carrying knives in Bulgaria concerned her but given the number of knives on the streets of Sofia, she could understand why Jock had carried one that night. What was unusual was that he ran in among a group of football fans. Everyone knew that football fans could be violent.

Stoycheva said that of all the accused murderers she had examined, Jock had seemed the least likely to have committed the crime of which he had been accused. He had been happy to talk about what had happened that night, something most defendants would not do. He had told the panel that he did not know if he had stabbed the boy. She had seen a lot of pathological liars and this young man seemed like an honest person.

Also interviewed, Shtarbanov said he thought that when Jock saw another youth being beaten, he had run into a situation whose danger he did not fully grasp. When he realised how badly outnumbered he was, the Australian may have pulled out a knife with the expectation that this would scare away the attackers. Jock's rush into harm's way might have been foolhardy, but he was far from mad.

CHAPTER 12

19 January 2008

Geri had flown to Sofia for the weekend. Simon wanted her to join him on a trip to Samokov. He was keen to meet Jock's local friends, hoping they might help him better understand what had drawn his son back to Bulgaria. But first Geri visited Jock. Because her job involved visiting young people in prison, she was less upset to see her nephew in remand than his other relatives might have been. She understood why he had rushed in to help a stranger. Jock saw things in black-or-white terms. When she was his age she had been much the same.

As the bus climbed the mountain to Samokov, Simon almost felt like a tour guide. He pointed out the roadside stalls selling potatoes, a speciality of the area. Then the ugly smoke stacks of the town came into view. This had been an iron mining centre in the Middle Ages, and for all its proximity to the snowfields of Borovets, Samokov remained an industrial hub.

As they got off the bus, Iliyan Yordanov was waiting for them, grinning from ear to ear. His family were keen to meet Jock's father and aunt. So too were his friends. They went to the bar and the coffee shop where Iliyan and Jock had spent so much time together.

Iliyan was limping. When Simon asked what had happened to his leg, he laughed. Jock had bought a Suzuki VX 800 to get around Bulgaria. When the Australian left Samokov for England after his first visit, he had entrusted it to Iliyan. One night Iliyan was riding home drunk and had a crash that left him in a coma and with a badly broken leg. The bike was fixed now, and when Iliyan had seen Jock in remand, he had suggested that he sell it to raise money for him. Jock had threatened never to speak to him again if Iliyan did that, because the bike had so many happy memories attached to it.

As they talked, more of Jock's friends turned up. Dobri Danchev, a good-looking young business student, had been charged with hooliganism when he was seventeen after he smashed up a seat at a football match in Sofia. His winter clothing concealed a gallery of tattoos: an eagle atop a swastika on his arm, *skin* on his left wrist and *head* on his right, the word *Bulgaria* across his back, a man holding the Bulgarian flag with a Celtic cross in it across his chest, a portrait of Vasil Levski on one shoulder and the words *Ultra Blue Levski* in a Celtic cross on the other.

There were two girls who spoke excellent English. One of them was Sonja Nikolova, Iliyan's cousin, whose house they visited. Sonja's mother recalled how they had tried in vain to get Jock to wash and brush his long, unruly hair. Bulgarian youths tended to have very short hair. With his fair hair, freckles and bushy beard, Jock stood out. He had made them all laugh. The friends brought out photographs of Jock, recalling for Simon and Geri the adventures he and Iliyan had shared, like riding to the Black Sea on the Suzuki wearing World War II helmets.

Jock's friends recalled the heated debates they used to have. The Australian, for example, had his own perspective on the Gypsies who lived in Samokov. He criticised his friends for dismissing all Roma as thieves; they thought he was naïve. Dobri didn't mind admitting that he and his friends beat up Gypsies. It was to try to change their behaviour, he said. For the Bulgarians it was almost a sport. Jock didn't think that was right, and spent hours arguing about it with Dobri.

After Jock left Bulgaria in early 2007, some of Dobri's skinhead mates picked a fight with a group of young Gypsies in the centre of Samokov. One Gypsy, Asparuh Asenov, was beaten to death. Dobri was not involved: he had decided against going downtown with his mates that evening.

This was the incident Hristo Monov had described in his opinion piece 'Gypsies versus Bulgarians: Two worlds on a knife edge'. In Hristo's view, this confrontation was the culmination of years of pent-up frustration among young ethnic Bulgarians: 'Our children won't tolerate [having to drive] their nice cars, which they have bought with their own money, past stinking carts on the streets of a European capital. Nor will they allow their taxes to be spent on the welfare of people who have chosen to rely on the state because it's more profitable not to work.'

Many of Jock's Samokov friends shared this view. While most of them disliked violence and thought Dobri and his skinhead mates went too far, they understood why that group hated Gypsies. What they didn't understand was why Jock did not hate them, and why he was always trying to help them.

They told Simon about a Gypsy Jock had met when they were all at a rock festival in the Rila Mountains. Simeon Panov, whose nickname was Simo, had found God early in life and moved away from the Gypsy ghetto. At the festival he had been set upon by skinheads, who called him *mango*, 'Gypsy filth', punched him in the face and stabbed him in the foot with a knife. Simo had made his escape, but when the skinheads searched him out, Jock took him under his wing. The pair had become firm friends. All Jock's Samokov friends had got to know Simo. But, they added, he was not like other Gypsies.

Geri asked about Jock's former girlfriend, whom he had once mentioned to her. 'They were not long together, but I gather she's taken this whole thing really hard,' said a young woman called Diana 'Didi' Alexandrova. 'Rightly or wrongly, she feels it's her fault that Jock returned to Bulgaria.' That would be as much as Simon and Geri would learn about the girlfriend. Jock refuses to talk about her to this day. Out of respect for the young women concerned, he says, all his romantic relationships are off limits.

Iliyan took Simon and Geri to meet Tihomir Pashev, a forty-five-year-old former military captain with whom Jock had lived in the months before he had left for England. Tihomir said he had instinctively felt Jock was trustworthy. The young man had been a friend to his older daughter and a big brother to his youngest, helping her with homework, and even going to a parent–teacher session when Tihomir could not go himself. Jock was hardly a domestic saviour—his idea of shopping for the household had been to buy Coke and biscuits—but he had helped with the chores and filled the house with joy.

Tihomir had enjoyed talking with Jock and found him to be intelligent and thoughtful, if full of contradictions. On the one hand Jock was against capitalism and war; on the other hand he wanted to join the Army. When Tihomir had asked him why he did not go to university, Jock had said one day he wanted to be a trade unionist, a leader of some sort, but he wanted to start from the bottom and work his way up. Tihomir had sensed that Jock took a scatter-gun approach to life: he wanted to do a lot of things all at once.

'You seem to know my son well,' Simon said. 'He needs some character references.' Tihomir interrupted and offered to write one.

The question that Simon and Geri kept coming back to was why Jock had been carrying Grayham's knife that night. Dobri said that carrying a knife was commonplace in these parts. He himself had stopped carrying a weapon for self-defence only after his skinhead friends' fight with the Gypsies had ended in a death. Tihomir said it was a Bulgarian custom to give young men knives. He had wanted to give Jock one. Jock had kept a pocket knife in his room but seldom carried it. Iliyan said that when he visited Jock in remand he had repeatedly asked him why he had taken a knife that time, but got no answer.

Back in Sofia that night, Simon groaned when he discovered that Sydney's *Sunday Telegraph* had posted a photo of Jock beside one of the actor Matt Damon, claiming they looked similar and saying the Australian had acquired 'star status' in internet discussion about the case. It was just more gossip. He wanted to stick to facts.

. . .

21 January 2008

Aksenia's father died. She would later tell the Sofia City Court that he had just stopped eating after Andrei was murdered. In essence, he had died of grief. Another *necrolog* went up on the Monovs' front door, and the couple prepared for their second funeral in less than a month.

CHAPTER 13

22 January 2008

As Anton 'Tony' Doychev walked up the steps of the Sofia Palace of Justice, he was nervous, unsure what was expected of him. In Bulgaria a prosecutor can require witnesses whose evidence is deemed particularly significant to testify before a judge well before a trial begins. Such statements carry far more weight than witness accounts given to a police investigating officer.

Simon walked up the same stairs. He and Jock and Dinko would all be in attendance as Tony testified. Simon felt a mixture of anticipation and dread.

As Jock was led down the aisle, he caught sight of Tony. Their eyes met. Jock nodded and started to smile, but then stopped, knowing that would be a bad look.

When Tony was called to the witness microphone, the judge, Chief Investigating Officer Alakusheva, Dinko, Simon and Jock all asked questions. But the transcript records only Tony's answers. The prosecution clearly wanted Tony to say that Jock had been fired up by the discussion about fascists in the Rock Bar and had shown signs of aggressiveness even there.

However, Tony testified that he not seen any sign of conflict at that point: 'We weren't drunk. In my opinion we were sober—we only drank beer.' He repeated the version of events he had previously provided to the investigator, adding that the youths 'chanting like a choir' were 'football hooligans'. He went on to detail what happened after Jock ran from the

Happy garden to the square: 'I saw two or three boys going towards Jock with their arms outstretched . . . Jock was moving backwards, withdrawing. Jock's hands were in the position to protect himself. Before the group started to go towards Jock, his arms and hands were in a normal position.'

Tony said that when he eventually followed Lindsay to where Jock was lying, one of the youths threatened to attack him if he went any further. 'I heard them saying that Jock was from CSKA . . . They thought he was a fan of the other football team . . . I didn't see him with weapons during any of the incident.' He said he saw the youths holding onto Jock before some 'bodyguards' intervened. Jock had been shouting out for police. It was not until police officers escorted Jock to the van that Tony saw the bloodied knife on the paving, one to one and a half metres from the kiosk and five metres from the Ministry of Health. At that moment, Lindsay ran towards the van and two of the youths attacked her: 'I can't remember whether she fell on the ground or she just propped herself on the ground. There were red spots on Lindsay's clothes—I don't know what they were . . . She asked me if Jock had stabbed someone, because obviously she was close to the body that was on the ground . . . We could not imagine that Jock would be capable of doing something like that . . . I asked her once if she had seen the stabbing and, as far as I can remember, she said no.'

Tony now added a sentence that would become important to later court deliberations about Jock's intent: 'Lindsay tried to stop the attack, and that's why she was running after Jock.' Read on its own the sentence could suggest Lindsay saw Jock attacking the group. It could also be referring to Jock under attack from the group.

Tony explained that Jock had been trying to protect them from the group. Of the threat posed by Andrei Monov and his friends, Tony said: 'Based on their shouting and chanting . . . based on the type of clothes and haircuts, I thought they were hooligans . . . The way the boys were looking at me frightened me.'

As he returned to his seat, Tony wondered how the hooligans would react if they found out what he had told the court. He asked the judge if his name and personal details could be suppressed. Both Tony and the defence were led to believe that would happen.

When Simon visited Jock in jail that afternoon, they talked about Tony's testimony. Simon was taken aback by the references to neo-Nazis and rockers. Jock thought the prosecution were bent on proving he was motivated by gang allegiance. Simon was uncertain. He knew Jock liked to stand up for the underdog. Was it possible that he had lashed out unprovoked at a group of football hooligans, just to make a political point?

Tony's statement that he did not see the attack on a Roma which Jock claimed had prompted him to run into the group of football fans, and that Lindsay 'tried to stop the attack' would acquire a significance he could never have foreseen. Without knowing it, the young Bulgarian had become a witness for the prosecution.

. . .

23 January 2008

Giving his version of events to police, the manager of the Happy restaurant said no one at the restaurant had noticed anything out of the ordinary that night, contrary to an earlier media report that Jock had been causing trouble there. He said the restaurant's security guard had been indoors the whole time and saw nothing of the melee.

. . .

28 January 2008

Halfway through the investigation, police telephoned Nikolai Kotev and told him to come by the station. On the night in question, he had been on duty in the cabin on the other side of the entry to the Sheraton car park from the cabin where Viktor Georgiev was working. Nikolai was no stranger to police procedures, having started his working life as a warden in a low-security prison during the Communist years. These days he preferred to stay as far away from police as possible.

In his statement to Alakusheva, Nikolai explained that he had been standing outside one of the car park cabins talking to a taxi driver called Emil, who drove a dark-blue or black Mercedes. Nikolai could remember most of the registration number and gave the details to the investigator. She must have been aware that in Emil she potentially had a new eyewitness.

Nikolai said that, while he was facing the Sheraton, the taxi driver was facing the square. At some point, Emil observed that there seemed to be a fight going on. Until then, Nikolai hadn't noticed anything. When he finally turned around, Nikolai saw 'a big group of boys' stretched between the Ministry of Health and Stamboliyski. They were constantly moving between the two points, clearly agitated. Some of them had surrounded a man on the ground and were trying to kick him. Three or four people had tried to stop them. Nikolai moved a bit closer and saw a young man lying on Stamboliyski. He was bleeding profusely. A youth next to him was shouting, 'Andrei, don't die.' Nikolai returned to his cabin, but Emil later told him that he thought the bleeding boy would probably die.

Emil was not the only potential witness Nikolai provided to the investigator. He also said there was a woman standing opposite the scene during the melee: 'Then a female Gypsy came to us, saying those over there got into a fight and one stabbed the boy with his knife. I don't know the name of the Gypsy. I only know that she is a prostitute and a pickpocket in the area. I haven't seen her since.' With one month left to complete her investigation and submit her report, Alakusheva now had the information needed to track down two additional independent witnesses who could test the version of events provided by both the accusers and the accused.

CHAPTER 14

4 February 2008

Hristo Monov entered the investigator's office. As a psychologist, he often met with people who had lost children. Now he was the grieving parent.

The statement he provided to Alakusheva was brief. Its tone was strangely detached, as though he was an expert providing evidence rather than a father in mourning. The investigator read back the statement so Hristo could check that it was correct. He leaned forward and signed it, then picked up his overcoat and left.

. . .

Ivan Ivanov finally submitted his findings. He was in charge of the DNA section of the Institute of Forensic Science and Criminology, which came under the jurisdiction of the Interior Ministry. This was a fairly straight-forward case: he had been told who was the perpetrator and who were the victims. Although nothing about the results really surprised him, there were some curious anomalies. Ivanov located a 'smudge' of Andrei's blood on the left sleeve of Jock's jacket. The smudge was located ten centimetres below a zipper that ran between the shoulder and the elbow. This was new information. Associate Professor Maria Grozeva, who had initially examined Jock, had been sure there was no blood on his sleeves. The investigator who had collected his clothes noted only a reddish smudge on the inside lining at the back of Jock's jacket.

Ivanov also identified two 'not big' spots of Jock's blood on his 'dirty' black jeans. They were next to each other on the front left panel immediately above the knee. Four samples of blood taken from the pavement near the Ministry of Health belonged to the deceased.

One knife had been taken from the scene—from the pavement near the Ministry of Health. Testing had already failed to locate Jock's fingerprints on it. There was blood on the knife, which Ivanov identified as that of Andrei Monov. He found no trace of Jock's DNA, not even on the hilt, which would have been in sustained contact with Jock's hand, particularly if he had used any force. There was no sign of Antoan Zahariev's blood, either on the knife or on Jock's clothing. Nothing in the DNA testing connected Jock to Antoan's stab wound.

As he read through the test results, Ivanov thought it possible that the quantity of the deceased's blood on the knife had overwhelmed any from the injured victim. It was also possible that Antoan's wound was superficial so it produced little, if any, bleeding. Certainly Ivanov had not been able to identify Antoan Zahariev's DNA in any of the blood samples taken from the pavement.

The test results did not prove that Jock had stabbed either Andrei Monov or Antoan Zahariev, nor did they rule out the possibility that he might have. Yet they did cast doubt.

. . .

Tanya Alakusheva wrote to the forensic doctors who had performed the autopsy on Andrei Monov to request more information. First, she asked, was it possible that the incision in Monov's chest had been made with the knife provided for testing? Second, what had been the force and direction of the blow that resulted in the incisions? Third, was it possible to determine the relative positions of the person delivering the blow and the victim at the time of the blow?

The experts were provided with all the witness statements and expert reports collected to date. In an undated report, the head of the forensic department, Associate Professor Stanislav Hristov, concluded that Andrei Monov had died from a single wound to the left side of his chest that had penetrated his left lung and heart. He added that death would have been 'inevitable' even if there had been 'timely, highly qualified medical help'. Death had occurred very fast as a result of the victim's severe blood loss. Hristov surmised that, given the degree of injury, Andrei would briefly have been able to make limited movements before losing consciousness and falling to the ground. The injuries to his knees and face would have occurred during that collapse.

Hristov finished his report with a line that would resonate with the prosecution and the civil claimants while raising doubts about his competence in the minds of the defence. He found that the injury was inflicted by a blow with 'considerable force'. For Alakusheva, this represented expert evidence that the accused had intended to kill.

But, away from the Palfreeman case, Hristov's professional integrity was about to take a hit.

· · ·

5 February 2008

On Tuesday afternoon four more police officers came to the chief investigator's office to give evidence.

First was forty-three-year-old Slaveiko Tsonkov. He recalled that he and his colleagues had been at the other end of Maria Louisa Boulevard when a passing taxi driver stopped and told them about a fight in St Nedelya Square. When they arrived at the scene, which was teeming with people, Tsonkov said he was briefed by unnamed officers already at the scene who told him that 'a group of about ten boys had got into an argument and then a fight with one or two Roma individuals. We did not come across Roma individuals at the scene. But we also found out that another individual, a foreigner, had attacked them with a knife to protect the Roma.'

Officer Krassimira Stoyadinova was next. She gave much the same version of events as Tsonkov. Viktor Lyubenov's and Petar Katsarov's statements include similar copy-and-paste details.

The incident report these officers had filed on the day of the tragedy had provided far more information than they gave in their statements.

The incident report described Tony 'the Tall' Yordanov and Alexander Dimov as 'behaving almost inadequately', a Bulgarian term for drunk and disorderly. Just as they did in their witness statements, the officers had said 'colleagues' told them that 'a group of around ten boys had a quarrel and a fight with one to two Roma and another boy—perhaps a foreigner—ran at them to defend the Roma'.

By now twenty-two police officers had been interviewed. Bizarrely, the officers who had been first on the scene continued to be unidentified, even though they had taken down vital first impressions from eyewitnesses. Chief Investigating Officer Alakusheva had the details of at least one officer who had spoken to Andrei's friends at the crime scene about what had happened. His incident report was signed for her on the day she took charge of the case. Alakusheva's name and the date are handwritten above the signature. Judge Mimi Petrova had either seen the report or heard about it. Presumably the prosecutor had, as well. Over the coming years, almost everyone who mattered would know about both incident reports except Jock and his father.

· · ·

Early that evening Antoan Zahariev returned to Police Station No. 3. He would later tell the court that he did so at the request of police.

After Antoan described the group coming out of the metro, his account of what happened changed slightly but significantly. Instead of 'I think there were Gypsies', now there were 'boys'. Instead of a 'fight', there was an 'argument'. It seemed that Antoan was now at pains to stress the innocence of what he and his friends had been doing.

According to his first statement, the only English he had been able to make out was 'Fuck you'. Now he recalled 'No racism, no fascism' and 'C'mon', a term he regarded as 'provocative': it was as though the attacker had been 'urging us to attack him', he said. He also recalled more details about the attacker: 'His movements were sudden, directed at whoever was in front of him. The hits were short, forceful, aiming to stab. He was holding the knife with the blade upwards.'

The passing of time might well have brought memories to the surface that had eluded Antoan on the day of the incident. It could also have provided him time to consider the implications of his first account.

. . .

6 February 2008

It was the fortieth day since Andrei Monov's death. According to tradition it takes this long for the spirit to pass on to the other world. The Monovs brought wine and food to leave at Andrei's gravesite. The spirit needs sustenance to help it on its journey.

At the Boyana Cemetery, Aksenia lit a small candle and stood quietly. She could see Andrei in her mind's eye, his arm around her, laughing. For a moment he was there with her. But as she bent over to put the candle at the head of his grave, the image dissolved. The ground was frozen and unforgiving. She had never felt so alone.

Hristo Monov rang Zlatin Tepsiev, the head of the Levski fan club. He asked if Tepsiev could get some turf from the sacred home ground of the Levski football team to grow at the foot of his son's headstone and along the length of the grave.

Tepsiev could think of no better way to remember the young man, who should have been preparing to celebrate his twenty-first birthday in a couple of weeks' time.

CHAPTER 15

12 February 2008

With the investigation now entering its final quarter, Associate Professor Maria Grozeva was about to re-examine Jock. She needed to measure his height, his arm length and the distance from his elbow to his fingertips, to ascertain where he would have stood in relation to both Andrei Monov and Antoan Zahariev.

Before heading off to Police Station No. 3, Grozeva flipped through file notes on Body No. 1166/07. She wanted to refresh her memory of the case and of the wounds inflicted on the two young Bulgarian men. She frowned as she examined the photographs of Andrei Monov's ribs. Something was not right here.

Unlike many of her contemporaries, Grozeva had decided early in her adult life to follow what she believed, rather than what she was told to believe. Her parents had been well-connected members of the Communist Party. She had gone to the school where the children of the well connected went—the school, now called the First English Language School, that Andrei Monov had attended. She had been a member of the party. The protection of her connections meant that she had been able to do what she thought was right in her career without worrying about whom she might upset.

Grozeva was concerned about the quality of forensic medicine in Bulgaria. In her view, at best it was slapdash and out of date. At worst it was criminal. She was currently heading a panel investigating the role of forensic doctors in a scandal involving the sale of body parts to an American-based company. One of the doctors they were investigating was Associate Professor Stanislav Hristov, the expert in charge of the final autopsy report on Andrei Monov as well as the report on the knife Jock had carried.

In an interview for this book, Grozeva recalled that after she examined Jock, she had turned to Tanya Alakusheva and said in Bulgarian, 'Look out. This case may not be as straightforward as you think. That knife [held as evidence] is not necessarily the knife.'

According to Grozeva, the investigator brushed her off. 'We have blood samples,' Alakusheva said.

But that did nothing to assuage Grozeva's concerns. The autopsy report and one of the accompanying photographs bothered her. The picture showed cuts in two adjacent ribs, one cut deeper than the other. This suggested a double-edged knife like a dagger. But the knife held as evidence was single-edged. To make such cuts, a single-edged knife would have had to twist as it passed between the ribs and simultaneously nick one rib with its tip. Yet the nature of the wound made this extremely unlikely. Was it possible that another knife had been involved?

Grozeva was surprised that the doctors who performed the autopsy had not excised the damaged section of the rib cage to test whether the suspect's knife could have caused the cuts. When she came to write up her second report, Grozeva checked what kind of mark the knife left in cardboard. The result only made her more worried. Perhaps the police should not be so certain they had the killer.

. . .

Dinko Kanchev played with his moustache as he waited for Tanya Alakusheva to take his client's statement. When Jock was charged he had reserved his right to explain what happened after he ran to help a Gypsy. He had wanted to speak to his father and to have his choice of lawyer with him before he did that. It is not clear why it took so long for the investigator to get Jock back to her office. The Palfreemans were relieved the day had arrived.

The room was small and the window shut against the cold. Jock, Dinko and the investigator were chain-smoking. Simon could hardly breathe. The investigator typed as Galina translated. Her colleagues walked in and out to get things.

At this point the only other witness testimony Jock knew about was that of Anton 'Tony' Doychev. Grayham had visited Jock just before he left for England, so it is likely the two had discussed the incident then, including what Lindsay had told Grayham. But, other than what he read in newspaper reports, Jock had no idea what the dead boy's friends had said to the police. He knew the kiosk worker had been interviewed, but he did not know what that witness had said, either. He still had no idea that other independent witnesses existed, among them the security guard at the Sheraton, Viktor Georgiev.

What Jock told Alakusheva would be extremely important in terms of gauging the accuracy and consistency of his recollections. Simon believed that, if surveillance cameras had recorded any of the lead-up to the incident, much less the fateful moment, a future court would be able to compare the video evidence with Jock's statement. His son's credibility was on the line.

In his most complete account of events so far, Jock began by explaining that while Tony and Lindsay had crossed Stamboliyski to buy credit for Tony's mobile, he had waited near the Happy restaurant. As always, Jock's words were immediately translated into Bulgarian for the record; what follows is a translation back from that official version.

'Then I heard noise and shouting coming from the Serdica metro station. I looked in that direction and I saw a group of many people, I can't say exactly how many. I asked Tony why people were running. Then he told me that the people who were shouting were hooligans. I am not quoting him exactly, but he said it was a big group of drunken men and it would be better for us—along with everyone else—to stay away from them. But we couldn't leave because we had to find Grayham . . .

'I can't remember who suggested it, but we decided to hide in the Happy garden. We ducked down there in the garden between two rows of low bushes or some sort of rails, I can't remember which. We wanted to hide. Tony was squatting next to me and Lindsay was next to him. At that moment the noise stopped. Tony and Lindsay were talking and trying to load the credit into Tony's phone. At some point the noise started again.

We heard shouts and screams, the tone of some of which sounded like swearing. The shouting was ferocious.

'Then I looked over the rail and I saw the group of men surrounding two other men who were lying on the ground, and they were kicking them brutally . . . I turned to Tony, who was charging his phone, and asked him if the group was attacking someone. I think that Tony said nothing, I'm not sure—he was busy with his phone. During that time Lindsay was busy worrying about Grayham and was also looking at Tony's phone.

'When I saw what was happening on the opposite side, I ran towards the group of men. I crossed Stamboliyski. Taking into account that there were a lot of men, I went around them. I didn't run directly at them. But [after] crossing Stamboliyski, I passed between the group and the cigarette kiosk. I didn't want to have a clash with this group at that moment; I didn't want to attack them. I just wanted to stop the beating of the Gypsies. I don't know why I decided that these two men on the ground were Gypsies; but, even when I was at Happy I decided that because of the [way] Bulgarian culture [works]. I also saw that their hair was black, although most people have black hair. I could see the colour of their hair as I could see very well from Happy, as far as one can see that distance.

'When I came close to the group, I saw that one of the men had squatted and was punching the man on the ground in the head. The rest of the men were standing next to him, kicking the man from time to time. This was happening around three metres from the entrance of the Ministry of Health in the direction of the Serdica metro station. I pushed aside the man who was beating the man on the ground.

'Then I knelt down to the man on the ground to check how he was. I thought that the Gypsy was unconscious. I grabbed him by the shoulder to see whether he was going to react, but there was no reaction on his part. I asked him in Bulgarian, "*Dobre li si?*" [Are you all right?]. The man was either unconscious, or was so badly beaten that he couldn't move and didn't say anything. In the meantime, some of the other men there kept on kicking him from time to time.

'I looked up to see what was going on with the other men. Half of the group was moving away towards Stamboliyski. The other half continued kicking the man on the ground. No one hit me at that moment; maybe they thought I was part of their group. I stood up and started yelling in Bulgarian to the men there, "*Nazad, nazad!*" [Get back, get back!]. Then the men around me started pulling back towards Stamboliyski for about a metre and they were still facing me. I stood up and went to stand between the man on the ground and the men. I told these men in Bulgarian, "*Nyama ataka,*" by that I meant "Don't attack him."

'At that moment the part of the group which was moving further away came back towards us. The people who were in front of me started coming at me, so I took out the knife from my upper-right-hand pocket on the outside of my trousers. I took the knife out with my right hand and opened it. Then I lifted it up to the level of my head and I repeated "*Nazad, nazad!*" in Bulgarian. I thought that, when these men saw the knife, they would go away. I just wanted them to move away from the Gypsy. He kept on lying on the ground behind my legs without moving. Then the men started to come at me, even though I was holding the knife up. They called me a "*Pederast*" [an offensive word in Bulgarian for homosexual]. Then one of the men who was diagonally on my left side at ten o'clock, and was standing on Maria Louisa Boulevard, started yelling, "No, no, come away; he has a knife," because more men from the group were coming at me at this moment. That man was taller, so he stood out from the group.

'Then the people next to me stopped, but the other group members continued to come closer towards me from the direction of Stamboliyski. Then the man who was standing on the road came back to the footpath and started pulling back those who were coming at me as he was trying to stop them getting close to me. All this time I held the knife above my head, waving it around, not to attack anyone but so that everyone could see it. With my left arm I gestured to the men in front of me to indicate that they should back off. At this stage I had not touched them.

'Then those who were close to me turned around and started to retreat towards Stamboliyski. I was following the group and kept on shouting, "Get back, get back." My goal was to make them go away, but at that moment I thought that, if I turned my back on them to help the man, they would attack me. So I was walking slower than them to put some distance between us. They were walking quickly, half running ahead of me. From time to time they were looking at me, but kept on going.

'The group was almost at the intersection when some of them crossed the Boulevard, but most of them stood spread out between the intersection and the [pharmacy and Ministry of Health] building. I was about ten metres behind them. I turned my back on them and took maybe five or ten steps. Then I turned back and, about half a metre behind me, I saw one man who had obviously been half running up behind me. When I turned around he stopped. At this moment I saw his right arm lifted to the height of his shoulder, his hand clenched in a fist and pointing forward. I didn't see him holding anything in his hand. I thought he was swinging to hit me. So I started waving the knife in front of the man, making the shape of an X. At that moment I was trying to block him and protect myself. I didn't want to hit or injure the man; I just wanted to scare him away with the knife. At this moment the man started to pull back, still facing me. I stopped waving the knife and stayed put.

'I noticed that the rest of the group was coming at me, surrounding me from the right and the left. Then they started to throw concrete pavers at me. I suppose they had got them from around the tree that was on the corner. They hit me three times on my left elbow with the pavers. The last time, I lost my balance and fell to the ground. At this time I was trying to protect myself with my left arm. I realised that, if I didn't stand up, I was lost. That's why I was quick to jump to my feet. The whole group had moved and surrounded me in a circle and gradually they were tightening the circle around me, so I started waving the knife in front of me. I didn't want to stab anyone. They threw three or four more pavers at me and then they stopped. Then they started hitting me.

'They hit me five or six times. I guess they were punching me, because I couldn't see exactly how they were hitting me. I can't say who exactly was hitting me as there were a lot of people around me and everything happened very quickly. At that moment I was just trying to keep my balance so I wouldn't fall over again. I don't remember swinging the knife at this point, because at this point they were beating me. I didn't see anything in the hands of the men who were around me, apart from the concrete pavers.

'The next thing I can remember is a man in a black fluffy jacket, who I suppose was a bodyguard. Along with this man there were two or three others. One of them was holding a black truncheon in his left hand and they stood between me and the rest and they pushed me to the wall of the Ministry. As soon as these men came, I raised the knife above my head so everybody could see it. I didn't want to hurt anyone. I knelt down and stretched my arm forward, putting it in front of me on the ground. Then I put my hands on the ground so they could see them. I said in Bulgarian "*Nyama problem*" [No problem]. I knelt right in front of the Ministry of Health, about a metre in front of its doors.

'Then the group started spitting on me and trying to attack me, but these men stood between me and them and protected me. I said in Bulgarian, "*Iskam politsai*" [I want police]. Shortly after that I looked towards Stamboliyski and I saw police. I tried to get up, but the bodyguards tried to grab me. I managed to push them aside to make way for the police. I kept saying to the bodyguards, "There's no problem. No problem. I'm not a problem." So when the police arrived, no one was holding me. I could have run away if I had wanted to, but I handed myself over voluntarily. The police came and I put both my arms out to let them handcuff me. The police officers pushed me against the entrance of the Ministry of Health. There they handcuffed me with my hands behind my back. Then they took me to the police car and drove me to Police Station No. 3.'

Jock's account was not quite the same as what he had told the investigator in the days after the incident. At first he had said the group was beating one Gypsy; now he said it was two. The investigator does not seem to have picked up on this discrepancy. In this statement Jock made only a fleeting reference to two Gypsies before his recollection focuses on 'the man on the ground'.

Jock locates the attack on the Roma only three metres from the Ministry of Health entrance where he was ultimately arrested. His lack of familiarity with St Nedelya Square and the chaos of the moment might well have hindered his capacity to judge distances. Yet Jock's estimation correlates with where two of Andrei's friends, Emil Aleksiev and Alexander Donev, told the investigator that something happened. It suggests that the bashing that the workers at the Sheraton had described was actually midway between the metro and the long building with the Ministry of Health. If that was the case, there was far more chance that one of the Ministry's cameras would have captured what had happened.

For the moment all that mattered was getting Jock's statement down on paper. Simon and Dinko were able to ask Jock questions before the document was completed to help him clarify what he had said.

'What were the issues you discussed in the Rock Bar on Lavelle Street?' asked Dinko. 'Did you discuss with Tony the attitude of certain youth groups towards the minorities?'

'We talked about life,' Jock said. 'We also discussed how in Bulgaria football hooligans are sometimes racist and they attack minorities. We were telling each other stories that we knew of. I told him how a racist from Samokov had beaten up a Gypsy with his fists. I have been attacked many times—in Pazardzhik, Samokov and Varna, and during a rock festival in the Rila Mountains. All these attacks against me were with a knife and I was always attacked from behind.'

'Was that why you had a knife on the night of 28 December 2007?'

'Absolutely!'

'Was the knife yours?' continued Dinko.

'No,' said Jock. 'Grayham bought the knife to use for cooking at Madjare. Grayham didn't know that I took the knife from there, and when he found out, he got angry with me.'

'When you saw the group of people, did someone tell you they were football hooligans?'

'Yes. I was told this by Tony and the friends, who were with him.'

'When the group initially retreated and you were going after it, what happened to the Gypsy on the ground?' Dinko said.

'He was still lying on the ground.'

'Did you see where and when the Gypsy went?'

'No.'

'What was your motive for going towards the group to begin with?'

'I wanted to stop them killing the Gypsy. I did not hear him call for help beforehand or when I went to him. There was a second Gypsy with him whom the same group was beating, but the second Gypsy got up and left at some point. I can't describe the Gypsies' faces, and if I saw them I couldn't recognise them.'

Simon then threw in a question of his own. 'When was the first time you realised that someone had been seriously injured or had died?'

'At the police station. I found out from the police officers at Police Station No. 3. I saw some blood on the knife after I placed it on the ground next to me, when the bodyguards came, but I didn't know where the blood was from. My adrenaline was high; it could have come from me. I was very worried when I saw it.'

After two hours of questioning, Tanya Alakusheva handed Jock his statement to sign. Simon then asked the investigator if he could touch his son. 'Da, da, da,' she said briskly, her eyes on the paperwork she was finalising. Simon took that as consent. He hugged Jock, whose initial stiffness softened into the loving embrace of childhood.

In the next three and a half years, they would have only one other chance to hold each other so close.

. . .

For some days now, Jock had been talking about asking Andrei Monov's parents if they could consider discussing what had happened that night. Jock knew the trial would go ahead regardless; he just wanted them to know all that he could tell them about the last five minutes of their son's life.

Simon agreed that, if the tables had been turned, he would want such a meeting. As it was, the shortage of concrete evidence was causing him much anguish: did what Jock believed had happened really happen? Surely Andrei's father too must wonder about the accounts he had read in the newspapers and heard from his son's friends. If nothing else, Simon wanted to offer some small solace. At least he still had Jock; Hristo Monov had lost his son forever. But Dinko advised against making such a request: it would not be well received, he said.

For the time being, Simon had to return to work in Australia. He had almost exhausted his holiday and compassionate leave and would have to ask for long-service leave. His boss had been sympathetic, but the pathology laboratory could not run indefinitely without a supervisor. Simon missed the routine of checking slides, and the sense that, in identifying abnormalities, he was helping to save lives. It was a very different feeling from the impotence he felt here.

. . .

Jock replayed the 28 December incident in his mind over and over again. After a while a new frame with the Roma joined the jumpy series of images in his head. His recollection was changing slightly.

After he had pushed away some of the gang members who were beating the Gypsy who was still lying on the ground, even the most persistent had pulled back. Now he thought he recalled following them for five or six metres to make sure they did not resume the attack, then returning to the man on the ground to check on him.

Suddenly he had heard footsteps. His heart was racing. He started to run. The gang was at his heels and closing on him. Some of them tackled him. All he could see were faces and fists. At that moment, he had pulled out the knife. He did it to scare the youths away. It worked. As they moved off, Jock walked behind some of them to ensure they did not double back and come up behind him.

Ultimately, Jock gave up trying to fit this new frame into the sequence. Maybe it was better to leave things as he had told police. Simon would get confused if he started changing his story. And maybe he was imagining things.

CHAPTER 16

19 February 2008

Today, a Tuesday, was a special day in Bulgaria: the anniversary of the day Vasil Levski, leader of the anti-Ottoman resistance, was hanged. But the work of the courts went on as usual. Two of the group members who had told the investigator they saw Jock in the act of stabbing testified before a duty judge. (Alexander Donev was abroad and not compelled to return.) Jock was present, along with Dinko and Galina the interpreter.

Martin Stoilov went first. Aspects of his account now changed. This time he did not mention that some of the group had been singing 'Shumi Maritsa' (the national battle song) as they came out of the metro station. Once again Martin described an encounter between some of his group and two 'strangers'. Again, he said he and his friends went after one of the men so that he would understand there were a lot of them; the man took heed, running towards the metro. But this time Martin then described a confrontation he had not mentioned to the investigator and which seemed strangely out of keeping for a group that was merely trying to scare someone away: 'When we went there, my friends started to deal with that man,' Martin said. 'They started to shout something—"Who are you?"—or something of the sort. I can't remember who the man was because I was further away. I pulled my friends away and it was over . . . At the next moment I just turned around and I thought that everything had finished when I heard someone shouting, "This one's got a knife." I turned around immediately and I saw a stranger dressed in black clothes, brandishing a knife in his right hand . . . He started to shout in bad Bulgarian, *"Nazad, nazad"* [Get back, get back] and went towards us.'

In his first account, Martin had not known who was stabbed first. Now he thought it had been Antoan. He noted that Andrei had been the only other person to see Antoan stabbed and had immediately run 'away along the road'.

'We had gathered again close to the kiosk and at some point we moved chaotically to the entrance of the ministry near a tree,' Martin continued. 'Then the stranger struck out at Tony, who was opposite him, with horizontal movements of the knife towards his chest. Tony tripped and fell, someone pulled him away, I don't know who, and I think it was Kristian. At that moment Andrei was very close to Tony and Kristian. The stranger made two or three very quick steps towards Andrei, who didn't have enough time to move from his position, and he swung out his right arm and hit him from the left on the side of the ribs.'

Martin pointed at his left armpit and the upper part of his rib cage. 'The hit was very fast and strong.' According to Martin, Andrei 'immediately grabbed this area' and ran towards Maria Louisa Boulevard limping.

Chief Investigating Officer Tanya Alakusheva took the witness back to the moment when he saw Tony 'the Tall' Yordanov with the two strangers. 'Did you see an exchange of punches during the conflict between your friend and these two people in the beginning?' she asked.

'I did not see an exchange of punches,' replied Martin. 'Everything was about an exchange of gestures and words.' But in the next breath he said that when he got to the metro, he had tried 'to calm them down'. He did not explain how a harmless exchange of words near the kiosk prompted Tony and others to run after the stranger and then to become so agitated as to require pacifying.

Alakusheva wanted to determine how the defendant had stabbed the victims. She asked Martin if the action was 'like an arc'. 'The knife was coming from below. The arm was reaching to the level of the chest and was directing it straight at the body,' he replied. 'Both the hit to Antoan and that to Andrei happened very quickly and were forceful because the body bounced away from the hit.'

Dinko Kanchev asked him to describe what the group had been doing as they came out of the metro.

'We were talking, maybe a bit loudly because we were fifteen people. Maybe we shouted something, but we were doing nothing wrong. I don't remember what we were saying or shouting.'

Dinko Kanchev asked Martin if he had ever noticed any aggressive behaviour towards the blond boy.

Martin explained that some of the group had thrown dirt—but only dirt, not pavers, and only at the accused's feet.

Jock turned to Galina. 'Did he say dirt?' he said. Galina nodded. 'Are you sure you translated that right?' Jock persisted, perplexed.

'Yes, he said dirt,' Galina replied with a hint of disbelief. At that, Jock laughed; Dinko frowned at him.

Martin now did not specify when this had happened, saying only that the group had gone on the offensive because the defendant had been 'pushing us to the street and we had nowhere to go'.

The investigator asked him if the dirt throwing had been before or after Antoan was hit.

'It was after the hit to Antoan and before the hit to Andrei,' stuttered Martin. 'I'm not quite sure, but that's what I think.'

Then it was Jock's turn to ask questions. In the court transcript, the witness and Jock sometimes refer to each other as 'you' and other times as 'the defendant' or 'the witness'. That is because in this court all parties direct their questions and answers to the judge. At times the judge may rephrase a question. Owing to the incomplete nature of the court transcripts, the questions and answers often read oddly.

Jock remembers asking the witness where Martin and his friends were in relation to him when he was allegedly attacking them. The transcript records the following response: 'They were opposite him . . . we were all facing him . . . He didn't let us get round him,' Martin then appears to have corrected himself. 'I can't say that all fifteen people were facing him, but when someone went to the side, he would go after that person immediately, so we were pulling back in groups and didn't even try to get round him.'

'Did I stop anyone from leaving?' Jock asked, through the judge.

'We were running away, but he was coming after us,' Martin replied, also through the judge.

'Did you see Andrei running towards me?' Jock continued.

'Andrei was trying to protect himself from him [Jock],' Martin said in closing. 'I didn't see him running towards the defendant.'

Blagovest Trifonov was next to enter the courtroom. He described the moment when Jock stabbed Andrei: 'After he thrust [the knife] in Andrei's ribs, he just stood like a cyborg and continued to brandish the knife towards whoever of us was closest. He wasn't stunned. There was a tree just in front of the ministry and that's where the person in question swung and, because Andrei was one or two steps away from him, with one quick, short hit he stabbed him.'

(When Jock later mulled over what Blagovest had said, he wondered if he had looked 'like a cyborg' because he was dazed. Maybe he had been knocked out briefly. If so, that might explain why he could not remember hitting anyone with the knife.)

Blagovest added that all Andrei and Tony were doing at the time was shouting at the accused to put away the knife. 'In my opinion Andrei did not provoke him at all,' he said.

Jock then began his examination: 'Did you see me stabbing Andrei in the area of the ribs, under the armpit?'

'Yes.'

'Why then wasn't his arm blocking his armpit?'

The judge objected to the question. Jock and his lawyer suspected that Andrei might have been in the act of throwing a paver at Jock and had his arm up when the knife struck as Jock waved it in an X pattern to keep the youths away from him.

Dinko rephrased the question: 'When you saw him hitting Andrei, what was the position of Andrei's left arm relative to his body?'

'He was standing with his arms stretched to the side of his body and he was explaining something to the blond man. He was saying something like "Put the knife away."'

Dinko continued: 'Could the left arm of the injured person have prevented the hit with the knife?'

'I saw how he stabbed my friend with the knife, and then I felt my life was in danger,' responded Blagovest, evading the question. 'All of our lives were in danger. We didn't carry knives.'

Jock asked, 'What was I wearing?'

'Dark-blue jeans. Some kind of black shirt. I think it had braces. I think there were braces with the trousers. He was tall. Blond. It was dark.'

'How could he see the braces?' Jock asked, through the judge.

Jock remembers this question making the witness freeze for a second. 'They were on top of the clothes,' Blagovest finally answered.

For Jock this was a critical moment. That night he had been wearing two pairs of trousers. The inside pair had been held up with a belt. The outer pair had been looser and needed braces. He wore his sweater and his zipped-up jacket over the braces. Officers at Police Station No. 3 had confiscated those braces, along with his boot laces. *For sure, this witness has been worded up!* Jock thought.

The judge brought the testimony to an end and stood to leave the courtroom. The guards had Jock ready to go when something delayed them. For a moment, he stood next to Blagovest Trifonov.

'I'm sorry,' said Jock, quietly looking the witness in the eye. He wanted to convey that he was truly sad that a young man had died, that his friends had lost a mate, that his parents would suffer the loss forever. He could imagine what his own parents and friends would have felt had it been Jock who was killed that night.

Blagovest did not respond. Tanya Alakusheva remembers thinking that the young man must have heard what Jock said and chose not to respond. She has never forgotten the Australian's words. *That's a confession if ever there was one,* she thought. *He's obviously eaten up with remorse. At least he has the decency to apologise. But what possessed him to thrust that knife into the body of another young man right up to the hilt?*

Jock recalls on the trip back to the Remand Centre one of the guards asked him in English why he had committed this crime given that he seemed like a nice boy.

'I was defending two guys,' answered Jock.

'You were defending Gypsies. Gypsies are monkeys,' the guard said, pointing to a Roma prisoner also in the van. 'White man cannot be friends with black man.'

. . .

21 February 2008

Aksenia did not want to answer the telephone. Her son would have turned twenty-one today. His friends wanted to let her know they were thinking of him, but she could not be comforted. Nothing would bring Andrei back, but she wanted the man who did this to her baby put away for life.

Oblivious to the significance of the date, Dinko requested that his client be brought before a judge to give his version of events. He knew that once they were given access to the police statements and expert reports, Jock could be accused of having been influenced by what others had said. He wanted to be able to show that his client had not changed his story.

Tanya Alakusheva said the request was unjustified. With only seven days of the allotted investigation period remaining, such testimony would 'delay and hinder the course of the investigation'. She rejected the request.

Thoughts of Andrei haunted Jock. He could no longer lie on his stomach, because when he did so he could hear his heart beating. The soft thuds that had once been the comforting countdown to sleep now served as a drum-roll soundtrack to images of a knife penetrating another person's heart. His knife! It couldn't have been. It must have been. He couldn't bear it.

. . .

27 February 2008

Tanya Alakusheva presented all the witness statements and the expert reports that she had collected to Antoan Zahariev and the dead youth's parents. Aksenia Monova spent three and a half hours reviewing the material with the investigator; Hristo Monov spent ten minutes on it.

Aksenia gasped as she looked at the photographs showing where her son had fallen. She could see the outline of his body in the large amount of blood on the road. Drops of blood were on concrete pavers. By the time police photographed the scene, the blood had frozen, and it glistened. Yet rather than being repelled by these images, Aksenia would keep returning to them. On several occasions during the trial she would successfully request permission to review the court file and any additional evidence in it. She was a notary, after all, trained in the law. Evidence mattered.

Hristo stared at a photograph of Jock's jacket. The killer had obviously worn two pairs of trousers so he could discard the outside pair. He had chosen a jacket with an orange lining so he could turn it inside out and avoid being identified in CCTV recordings. Clearly, this was a carefully planned execution.

The next day Jock was handcuffed and taken once again to Police Station No. 3. Alakusheva presented the evidence file to him and Dinko. It was all in Bulgarian. Dinko would have to arrange to have it translated at Simon's expense. Once Jock and Dinko had gone, the investigator went downtown to submit her detailed report to the prosecutor.

Alakusheva drew on material from various statements without identifying from which statement each detail had come. She made no reference to the unidentified men as having been described as Gypsies. She said one of those men was chased but she did not describe the attack near the metro that the Sheraton workers had described. She also made no reference to Jock's calling out 'Don't attack', 'Go away' and 'Get back', which some of Andrei's friends had heard. She determined that there had been no physical contact between Andrei's friends and the unidentified men.

Although the psychiatric panel's assessment of Jock's character suggested he was not violent by nature, the investigator appeared to dismiss Jock's version of events out of hand. The only reference she made to the panel's report was to note that it indicated Jock was fit to understand the charges and stand trial.

. . .

While Jock waited to hear back from his lawyer, he had to deal with the vagaries of life in prison. An Albanian had moved into the cell he now shared with the Russians, Vasia and Sasha, and he kept stealing the food that Sasha's mother and Jock's Samokov friends brought in, even though it was shared among the four of them. The angrier Jock became, the more aggressive the Albanian was. Once he king-hit the Australian in the face and backed off only when one of the Russians hurled a Bible at him.

The attacks continued. Each time, Jock would scream out in English because his limited Bulgarian vocabulary would vanish in the panic. He begged the guards to move either the Albanian or him, but they refused. He was locked up with a madman. The other detainees and Jock took it in turns to sleep so that someone was always on guard. Eventually one of the Russians stole some sleeping pills the guards kept for drug addicts in withdrawal, and they drugged the Albanian one night.

After reviewing the file, Dinko went to see Jock. 'Police haven't interviewed any Gypsies,' he said. Jock's heart sank.

'But there's a bit of evidence suggesting Roma were at the scene that night,' Dinko added, almost as an afterthought.

'Is that all?' exclaimed Jock. Having heard some of the testimony in court, he knew that proving the Gypsies were there was not going to be easy; still, he had hoped some witnesses might have seen them.

Dinko shrugged. 'We will have to see what the prosecutor makes of it,' he said.

CHAPTER 17

12 March 2008

In springtime, Sofia is full of roadside stalls selling *martenitsas*, pairs of red-and-white tassels. As folklore has it, by wearing a martenitsa you are asking Baba Marta, Grannie March, to bring on spring and good fortune. The minute you see a stork or a blossom, you take off the charm and hang it in a tree.

There was no change in Jock's fortunes when Prosecutor Parvoleta Nikova submitted her indictment. According to her, Andrei's group had had a verbal, but not physical, exchange with two 'unidentified individuals' of 'Roma origin' near Bulbank. When the argument was over, the youths had walked across the square to the traffic lights. Blagovest stopped at the kiosk to buy cigarettes. Tony 'the Tall' Yordanov, Andrei, Kristian and Alexander were the last to reach the intersection. Passing some of the youths as he crossed Stamboliyski, Jock had run towards the kiosk, where the rest of the group was gathering. Anton 'Tony' Doychev had shouted at him to come back, but he did not. The youths had scattered as Jock penetrated the group, fiercely swinging a knife at anyone who came near him. To defend themselves and to scare Jock, some of the youths had thrown stones at his feet.

Like the investigator, Nikova argued that Jock's killing of Andrei was premeditated murder, motivated by disrespect for Bulgarian society. According to her, this was confirmed by the type of knife he used, the location of the wounds, the force Jock used to inflict the wounds, and his shouting 'No fascism' and then, 'provocatively', 'C'mon, c'mon' at the group of 'astonished' Bulgarians, who in her version had asked, 'What are you doing; what is this knife?' Using selected pieces of the witness statements, she depicted a frenzied attack on a group of innocent youths.

Nikova alleged that, unprovoked, Jock had stabbed Antoan Zahariev and Andrei Monov 'immediately one after another', in one 'continuous' action. This suggested a ferocious and deliberate attack.

Nikova said the independent witness accounts supported her version of events. She made no mention of the skirmish near the metro that the workers at the Sheraton had described. Other than her description of Jock crossing Stamboliyski and running through a group of youths, the prosecutor did not outline where in the square the incident had taken place. This suggests she believed that the lead-up to both stabbings and the stabbings themselves took place in one location near the traffic lights and the kiosk rather than in a number of locations extending across the square.

Nevertheless, Nikova was very clear on one point: the surveillance cameras outside the Ministry of Health would not have filmed the incident.

· · ·

17 March 2008

When Maria Grozeva heard that her colleague Associate Professor Stanislav Hristov had been arrested, charged with breaching the rules on organ transplantation, the forensic doctor knew she was in for a rough ride.

Grozeva and the panel of experts she headed had spent some eight months investigating autopsy files after an official complaint was lodged about the harvesting of body parts in Bulgaria. It was alleged that forensic doctors were paid privately for every corpse they stripped of tissues and bones, and that the practice was jeopardising criminal trials by compromising and even destroying evidence. A Bulgarian company called Tissue Bank Osteocentre Bulgaria was paying the doctors while they were working in their official roles performing forensic autopsies. Osteocentre was linked to an American company called Osteotech, which used harvested material to make products like gels for tissue regeneration and adhesive for dentures.

At that time corpses of murder victims were highly sought after because they were less likely to be aged or diseased.

It was alleged that some corpses had been harvested before an autopsy took place and might have been cremated without the required permission from a prosecutor. To harvest the parts, the forensic doctors had to scrub the corpses with a solution that destroyed blood, bacteria and other potentially vital evidence. They were allegedly also taking body parts without running all the tests required to check for infection. As well as the integrity of the evidence, the practice potentially endangered the lives of people using the Osteotech products.

When questions were asked in parliament about the practice, the Ministry of Finance released data showing between 2003 and September 2006, Osteocentre Bulgaria had exported more than seventeen tonnes of body parts to the United States and the Netherlands—a huge amount for a population of little more than seven million. According to the prosecution, there had been ninety-eight cases of improper harvesting; a further 500 cases were still under investigation. Also, according to the prosecution, Hristov had personally been involved in many of the cases under scrutiny and had made money from illegal harvesting.

If he was found guilty, Hristov faced a prison sentence of three to five years. At his two bail hearings, he protested his innocence, claiming that the allegations were motivated by professional jealousy. Bail was at first denied, then granted on appeal. The prosecution request that Hristov be stood down from his position during the ongoing investigation was denied.

Hristov's fall from grace was very public. Newspaper coverage of the scandal was lurid. Headlines included: 'Number 1 Forensic Doctor Has Been Selling Organs,' 'They inserted PVC pipes in the bodies of the deceased, exporting tissues to the USA,' 'The Dirty Business with Dead Bodies' and 'Super Arrest'.

Not long after Hristov's arrest, Maria Grozeva's work came under scrutiny. When Hristov's mentor queried her autopsy results in a high-profile murder case, she launched a defamation action against him. When he later committed suicide, Hristov claimed Grozeva had driven his mentor to despair, whereupon she launched legal action against Hristov.

Although he was still under investigation, Hristov continued acting as the expert pathologist in the Palfreeman case. In a year's time the two doctors who worked with him on Andrei Monov's autopsy would also be charged. Like Hristov, they would be allowed to testify at Jock's trial.

. . .

19 March 2008

Jock was not aware of the controversy surrounding such a key expert witness in his trial. His thoughts were elsewhere. Simon had told Jock about the mass he had attended in a Catholic Church in Sofia. Jock wrote to the church and asked if an English-speaking priest would visit him. He also wanted a Bible. 'Eventually I would like to take the Eucarist [sic] again,' he wrote, 'but I don't know if the police will allow it.'

Meanwhile, the Interior Ministry was in turmoil. The minister, Rumen Petkov, resigned amidst allegations that he had had dealings with the notorious alleged gangsters known as the Galevi Brothers. Petkov was replaced by the Monovs' friend, Mihail Mikov.

. . .

24 March 2008

Public attention soon returned to the incident in St Nedelya Square. The prosecution case was featured prominently in the popular daily *24 Hours*, which headlined its story 'Three Only Just Survive Jock's Knife: The trial against the Australian butcher Palfreeman goes to court'. The newspaper carried a detailed interview with Parvoleta Nikova, in which she asserted that Jock was guilty as charged and should get life imprisonment.

The story named Anton 'Tony' Doychev despite the court's assurances that his identity would not be revealed in the lead-up to the trial. According to the paper, the prosecution had concluded that 'not one, but four people could have died at the hands of the Australian Jock Palfreeman who had been raging through the centre of the capital with a knife'. Nikova was quoted as saying the hit to Antoan Zahariev was aimed at 'vital organs' and that had he not stumbled, he would have suffered 'the same fate as Andrei'. She said Jock was motivated only by the desire to 'stab flesh'.

The prosecutor was quoted explaining her lack of interest in interviewing Lindsay Welsh: 'From [Grayham's] statement it is clear that she [Lindsay] didn't even understand that Jock had killed a man. That's why it is pointless to question her.'

Asked what Palfreeman had said about the incident, the prosecutor was quoted as saying: 'He has not confessed. He says he rushed [towards the youths] after he saw Andrei's group was fighting with other individuals, without specifying whether they were Roma or not. So far we have questioned 49 witnesses on the case and none has given evidence that they saw such a thing.'

In the full statement Jock had given a month before, he had mentioned an attack on two men he thought were Gypsies. Independent witnesses had referred to the bashing. Some of Andrei's friends had referred to an altercation with Roma. Indeed Nikova had referred to an exchange with individuals of 'Roma origin' in her indictment. The prosecutor's comment swept all of those facts aside.

Jock's lawyer, Dinko Kanchev, knew he had grounds to formally challenge Parvoleta Nikova's involvement in the case. In his view, she had just broken one of the cardinal rules of a fair trial, the presumption of innocence. But he decided against it. *What's the point*, he thought. *The damage has been done.*

CHAPTER 18

1 April 2008

Simon and Helen Palfreeman flew into Sofia. Unaware exactly when the trial would begin, they brought a suit and tie for Jock, as well as letters from family members. They were staying in the apartment that Simon had found on his first trip to Sofia.

Simon took Helen on a tour of the city, explaining the history of the country through its monuments and architecture. He had felt useless at home for the past month; now he felt he was getting something done. Some of Jock's Samokov friends met the couple for a simple but traditional dinner of sausage and Shopska salad, made of tomatoes, cucumber and feta. They had taken Simon under their wing and he was clearly fond of them.

When Simon took her to visit Jock, Helen was shocked by the primitive conditions in the prison and by the sight of her stepson behind a glass barrier. After six weeks of mulling over what had happened, Jock had a vast amount to tell his father. It all poured out in a torrent, leaving Simon flustered and upset.

Back in the apartment, Helen tried to get him to focus on the tasks ahead rather than stew over how Jock was coping. When Dinko had given Simon a copy of the evidence file, he said there seemed to be a lot missing, including the recording from the CCTV camera outside the Ministry of Health. An expert had analysed the images recorded by the cameras in the metro and by the traffic camera on Maria Louisa Boulevard. There had been aggressive behaviour commensurate with the throwing of rocks and pavers that Jock had described well before a figure could be seen falling on the road. Simon presumed this figure must have been Andrei. The expert's report included some fuzzy freeze-frames from those recordings, but not the recordings themselves.

Simon fretted over whom to trust with the translations. Galina was the only person who came to mind, but Simon thought she might be prohibited from taking on the job. Dinko assured him that the court would not be bothered by such an arrangement, and she agreed to take it on. Day after day, Galina sat in the apartment going through the huge stack of photocopied documents with Simon and Helen. Not knowing when the trial would start, they were anxious to get through it all quickly. Galina would translate aloud while Helen typed, running a tape recorder at the same time. Simon would then replay the tapes to check that Helen had transcribed Galina's words accurately. It was a slow process. Adding to the difficulties, some of the pages had not been copied well and some words were unintelligible.

Trying to get the job done as quickly and cheaply as possible Simon resorted to skimming over statements and reports that seemed to offer little by way of corroboration. When Jock found out that his father was taking short cuts, he took Simon to task, arguing that they needed to have every shred of evidence laid out in front of them. Jock was almost totally dependent on his father. For such an independent young man, it was not a pleasant feeling.

One morning Galina picked up Viktor Georgiev's statement from the pile. As she translated one sentence at a time, often stopping to search for the right phrasing in English, Simon and Helen moved closer to her, hanging on every word. Here was confirmation of Jock's story. According to this security guard, Jock had been surrounded and beaten near the subway. Only then had he brought out the knife. He had subsequently been attacked near the kiosk.

Suddenly, it was all making sense. In the first attack Viktor Georgiev might well have mistaken the Gypsy for Jock, who could have blended into the scrum as he bent over the man. When Simon told Jock about the witness, Jock felt a wave of relief. He was not going insane—the bashing had really happened as he remembered it.

Over the next few weeks the documents yielded further corroboration of Jock's story. But there was no clue to the identity of the Gypsy. Galina was not surprised. If police did not look for the man, it was most unlikely that he would come forward. No Gypsy would voluntarily tangle with the Bulgarian police and justice system.

As he walked through St Nedelya Square trying to retrace Jock's steps, Simon suspected there was more than the identity of the Gypsy missing from the file. The area between the Ministry of Health and the subway had not been established as a crime scene. Nor had the rocks and concrete pavers been retained as evidence. Possible blood and DNA evidence had been lost. Members of Andrei's group had not been searched for weapons. Apart from Jock, only Andrei's corpse and Antoan had been tested for alcohol or drugs. This had all the hallmarks of a botched investigation.

Every weekday, Simon went to see his son and together they analysed the evidence. Part of Jock was annoyed that the Gypsy had not come forward. Had the shoe been on the other foot, he was certain he would have told someone. On the other hand, perhaps the man did not even know Jock was in trouble.

'Surely there were more independent witnesses!' Jock said, grilling Simon about the translations. The investigator had not even identified who were the bodyguards who kept the youths away from him.

Jock was angry that the prosecution did not seem to have taken anything he said into account. 'It's like they decided right from the start I was out to kill people,' he said. He thought that had made them ignore the assault on the Roma.

Simon tried to reassure him. 'I'm sure that's not the case,' he said. 'Even if you are right, the judge will look at the evidence on its merits.' Simon knew that no system is perfect—there had been miscarriages of justice in Australia—but he had grown up believing that ultimately the system will work and justice will prevail; there was no reason to doubt that would happen in this case.

Jock picked at a scab on his hand, an injury he had sustained when a guard pushed him against a wall. 'Dad,' he said. 'Where is the document describing what was in Andrei Monov's wallet?'

There was no mention of Andrei's money or his ID card—or his wallet, for that matter. Simon frowned.

'That's where his Levski Ultras membership card would be, if he had one,' Jock said. He thought the disappearance of the wallet was no accident. Simon shook his head, worried that his son was getting carried away with conspiracy theories. Part of him wondered if Jock's case might actually be strengthened by the absence of evidence. The wallet might not have contained anything linking Andrei to football hooliganism. The Ministry of Health CCTV camera might not have captured any of what happened, either. Or, worse, it might have suggested the group's behaviour was benign.

Galina had told Simon that it was a common practice in criminal trials here to hire Gypsies to play the victims. In Bulgarian there is even a word for a paid witness: *kosharevski*. But the Palfreemans would not hear of this.

Jock thought the idea was right out of a B-grade movie. But if they could find the Gypsies who were really there . . . He badgered his father to hire a private investigator to search for them. Simon did not know how to begin finding one, and feared that anyone he did find would probably double-cross him.

. . .

Sydney

Jock's mother, Mary Jane, had so far decided against travelling to Bulgaria. She wanted to keep life as normal as possible for her youngest son, Angus, who was just starting high school, and her middle son, Spencer, who was at university. Simon was keeping her abreast of developments in Sofia.

Mary Jane knew from long experience that if Jock thought something was unfair, he went at it like a bull in a china shop. He was impetuous and at times let his feelings overrule his judgement. But he did not have it in him to attack anyone without provocation, much less kill them.

Thoughts of how different things would be now if only Jock had remained in Australia tormented Mary Jane. She had not wanted her son to go off travelling; he had been far too young and, because of that, oblivious to danger. But Jock had saved the money to buy a ticket and nothing she said would have deterred him.

Night after night, Mary Jane returned to the copies of the forensic evidence Simon sent. She was a dentist, not a forensic doctor, but something about the description of the fatal wound struck her as odd. Also, there didn't seem to be any evidence tying Antoan Zahariev to either Jock or the knife he had carried, other than the forensic doctor's assertion that the wound could have been caused by the knife. *Why can't Simon see that this is fishy?* she thought. But Simon was in charge of Jock's legal affairs. She felt she had to stay out of it.

. . .

Vasia had told Jock that he would be moved to the main section of the prison once his trial began. Jock wanted to transfer sooner; anything had to be better than remand. In mid-April, his request was granted. After giving him a close crew cut, the authorities put him in the processing area. One young Gypsy who had just arrived thought the Australian was a skinhead. Another Roma told the new prisoner what the Australian had done. The Gypsy thanked Jock and gave him his camouflage baseball cap.

After a fortnight, guards led Jock to the foreigners' section, past the overcrowded section for Bulgarian nationals, past a sentry box and through one rusty metal gate after another. A couple of mangy cats darted among the broken beds and chairs lying in the yards. Corroded water pipes were held together with tape.

As Jock entered his cell in Group 13, his seven new cellmates stared at him. They all knew who he was—the Australian butcher, the guy who loved Gypsies, the guy who killed a Bulgarian. Jock was much younger than the others. A fat Iranian Swede named Mohammed broke the silence, leaning down from a top bunk to shake hands with him. The rickety iron bed frames were lashed together with discarded belts, cables and rope. They screeched and groaned every time a prisoner moved. Mohammed pointed to the bottom bunk. Jock nodded at him and placed the camouflage cap on the thin stained mattress.

The cell was about seven metres by nine metres, almost homely, with a power point and a TV. Sunlight streamed in through a small window that had three bars across it. Jock looked out hopefully, but the only view was of a vast brick wall. The window glass was smashed and held together with tape. There was a squat toilet, a sink and a table for eating and writing. As Jock threw the rest of his things under the bunk, cockroaches scuttled across the cracked concrete floor.

A twenty-eight-year-old Chechnyan prisoner named Murad remembers that day well. From what he had read in the newspapers, he had expected to see a terrifying Australian fighting machine. Jock struck him as anything but. He looked like a frightened little boy.

A heroin addict, Murad was in jail for stealing four bars of chocolate. He was no stranger to prison, but he knew just how Jock felt. Jock could tell Murad was sick with withdrawal symptoms. For the next few days he made him coffee every morning and brought it to his bunk. Murad never forgot that.

· · ·

By May the *martenitsas* no longer adorned the clothing of commuters rushing to get home. Now they were all blowing about in the trees. Jock's trial was scheduled to start soon. He would sit on his bunk flipping through the notebook of questions he wanted to ask witnesses. Note-taking was a habit he shared with his father and grandfather.

Jock wanted his lawyer to ask the court for a copy of the traffic-camera recordings from the fateful night. But Dinko said such a request would be regarded as 'exotic'. Among the photocopied freeze-frames in the CCTV expert's report was a shot that looked a bit like people running. Jock was confident the recordings would show how aggressive the young men with Andrei had been. He wanted desperately to know what had happened between when he was hit on the head and when he saw the men with truncheons. Jock respected Dinko but found his lack of pushiness infuriating, and often argued with him. Dinko's view seemed to be that this was how it works here.

The Palfreemans were already aware that the prosecutor was seeking a life sentence. But they had just been advised that Antoan Zahariev's and Andrei Monov's parents were seeking life without the possibility of parole. Under Bulgarian law, that punishment could be given only to a person over the age of twenty. Jock was just old enough to die in prison. The stakes in this trial could not be higher.

PART III
THE TRIAL

CHAPTER 19

21 May 2008

Palace of Justice, Sofia

Dinko butted out a cigarette and left his regular coffee shop for the court. Jock's trial was due to start at 9.30 a.m. Dinko knew all the Palfreemans would be nervous. Jock struck him as a sensitive young man, certain of his version of events and very different from the character the media had portrayed.

Judges were supposed to be assigned to cases on a random basis. The deputy head of the Sofia City Court was assigned to preside over Jock's trial. Judge Georgi Kolev was forty-one, young for a judge. He had studied law at the former Communist Police Academy and his wife was a notary like Aksenia Monova. His daughter was about the same age as Andrei Monov and was a law student at the New Bulgaria University, just as Andrei had been.

Helen Palfreeman was panting when she got to the top of the stairs at the Sofia Palace of Justice, but not from exertion. Her stomach was in a knot. Milling around outside the first-floor courtroom was a large group of Andrei Monov's friends, who were there both as witnesses and to support his parents. Helen walked past them and took a seat with the Australian consul David Chaplin and honorary consul Indiana Trifonova.

Chaplin would soon return to Canberra, but Australian diplomats from the embassies in Athens and London would continue to attend court and assist the family. Indiana would always be with them. A British military attaché would come to see Jock several times, and the Army monitored his case.

Jock was brought in, surrounded by cameras. He was wearing the suit Simon and Helen had brought from Australia. His crew cut had grown out and he had slicked back his hair because he hated the way it went curly. He had lost weight. He looked like a boy in a grown-up's outfit. Simon turned to Jock and straightened his tie, relieved that his son looked all right. Jock looked at his father, surprised. Simon had left the family home by the time Jock needed to learn how to knot a tie. Jock had taught himself after being punished for wearing his school uniform incorrectly.

When the judges entered, everyone stood, but the camera crews remained. Simon stood next to Jock, Galina and Dinko at the bar table. Jock briefly turned his head and saw his young Samokov friends as well as Tihomir, the former military captain who had written him a reference. Finally the cameras were shooed away and the hearing began.

The lawyers for the Monov parents and Antoan Zahariev asked the court to hear their damages claim at the same time as the criminal case. The defence objected. Given the complexity of the criminal case, Dinko said, each matter should be heard separately. His objection was overruled; the three victims were joined in proceedings as both private accusers and plaintiffs. The Monovs sought 200,000 *leva* each in damages and Anton Zahariev 50,000 *leva*. At the time this was the equivalent of about A$375,000 in total—a huge sum in Bulgaria.

Dinko then asked if the court would consider summonsing witnesses, such as Emil the taxi driver, who had been identified in the case documents but not interviewed. He also requested that the panel of experts who had assessed Jock's mental state be asked to testify as to whether his alleged actions were in keeping with his personality rather than simply whether Jock was fit to stand trial. Finally, Dinko asked if witnesses could remain in the courtroom after testifying so as to minimise discussion between them. Judge Kolev withheld his decision on all points.

In many ways the courtroom resembled one in Australia, with high ceilings and furniture made of dark wood. The judge sat with a young female assistant at an elevated bench. Next to them sat three lay judges, two men and a woman, who would assist the judge in reaching a verdict.

The various parties taking part in the proceedings sat at the front of the courtroom, before the bench. To the left of the bench, Aksenia and Hristo Monov sat at a small bar table next to a lectern with their lawyers and Antoan's lawyer. Sitting with them was the female prosecutor, who was filling in for Parvoleta Nikova while she attended to other cases.

Witnesses were called to a microphone set up in the centre of this front area, directly in front of the bench and at the end of the aisle that separated the two sets of seats for spectators. The defence bar table was to the right of the bench and opposite the prosecutor's table. Next to it was another lectern, which Dinko used.

Jock stood with his father and Galina between the witness microphone and the defence lectern. The court microphones were unreliable, and Galina needed to be near the witness to hear properly.

Space was tight. The discomfort of all concerned was almost palpable. The grieving parents were only a few metres from the Palfreemans.

To Simon's dismay, the Monovs were the first witnesses called. In Australia, victim impact statements are heard in a criminal trial only after the jury has delivered its verdict and as part of the sentencing phase. Simon tried to put out of his head the thought that an account of what the grieving parents had endured would colour the whole trial. One of the Monovs' lawyers requested that the parents' statement be heard behind closed doors owing to its personal nature. No one objected.

When everyone but the defence, the prosecution, the judges and the panel had gone, Aksenia moved to the witness microphone. Papers ruffled; feet shuffled; no one wanted to stare grief in the face.

Jock looked fleetingly at Aksenia. *If Mrs Monova honestly believes I killed their son in cold blood, just looking at me must be excruciating for her*, he thought. Then he remembered what was at stake. *This trial isn't about them*, he reasoned. *It's about the allegations levelled at me.* He looked straight ahead. He had to be tough. Simon had said he shouldn't take part in questioning the Monovs. To do so would be insensitive, he argued. But Jock decided he had to examine those accusing him of murder. *This is my trial, not theirs.*

Aksenia began to speak. Andrei had been her only child, she said. He had always been a cheerful boy who had never caused any problems at home or at school. She spoke glowingly of his early years and of his decision to study law as she had done. Then she described the last time she had seen her son, setting off for a night out with friends. Her account of her growing alarm when he did not come home and her battle to find out if Andrei had been at St Nedelya Square was heartbreaking. She finished by saying that when her father heard that his treasured grandson had been murdered, he had lost the will to live.

Questioned by the lawyers, Aksenia told the court that, yes, her son supported the Levski football club, but his team affiliation did not dominate his worldview. Indeed, she said, some of his friends, and even his father, had been supporters of the Levski's rival team, CSKA. No, Andrei had not drunk alcohol at home, though he might have done so when out with friends. She had never seen him behaving aggressively nor heard any complaints about him.

The father of her son's alleged killer stood and faced her. They were so close they could hear each other breathe. Aksenia stared at the judge. Simon began by gently expressing both his and his son's sorrow for her loss. Aksenia's face flushed slightly. Simon asked if her son had ever been in trouble at school or university for having expressed racist views. 'I have no information about my son breaking rules at school,' she said.

Simon pushed a little further, asking her if Andrei had it in for Gypsies. 'No,' Aksenia replied. 'I have not noticed my son having a different or negative attitude towards people who are different from us or are part of a minority group.'

When Aksenia stood down, Hristo took her place. He spoke more assertively than his wife, and some of the tension in the room lifted. He described his last conversation with Andrei, in which they had discussed a Turkish family Hristo was helping after their child had been murdered. Andrei had expressed sympathy for the family. 'At about 14.00 he left,' added Hristo. 'And the next time we met, it was at Boyana Cemetery.'

Hristo told the court he had never seen his son under the influence of alcohol or drugs. He said that 'as a psychologist with twenty-five years' experience' he knew the characteristics of his son's various groups of friends and had never been concerned that any of them might have a bad influence on him. Moreover, he said, Andrei's friends belonged 'to the real elite of Bulgarian youth'.

'With regard to their educational status, they have all graduated from high schools and study at universities,' he added. 'With regard to their social status, they all have many opportunities, so it is not surprising that some of his friends are studying in Europe and America.'

Asked about Andrei's political leanings, Hristo said his son was 'right-wing conservative', but not an extreme nationalist, though for Andrei, 'Bulgaria was the most superior and sacred [country]'. He did not think his son discriminated against anyone on the basis of ethnicity or sexuality. Andrei believed in 'Bulgaria for all Bulgarians'.

Jock interrupted, asking him to clarify what he meant by 'Bulgaria for Bulgarians'.

'I said Bulgaria for all Bulgarian citizens,' Hristo said carefully, making it clear that he meant to include all ethnic groups. There being no further questions, he resumed his place at the bar table with his wife.

Spectators were allowed back into the courtroom, which filled quickly. Andrei Monov's friends sat in the rows behind the civil claimants. Jock's friends and family, as well as the Australian consular staff, sat behind the defence. The experts were supposed to attend every session, and most were here today, jostling for seats among the well-wishers and reporters, standing along the back if they missed out.

Antoan Zahariev was called to testify. Jock felt strongly that he was anything but a victim. As part of the group that had attacked him, he was a witness. Jock believed he should not have been allowed to give what amounted to a victim impact statement.

Having read both of Antoan's police statements, Jock and his father noticed a subtle change in his recollections of that night. One week after the tragedy, he no longer referred to a dispute with strangers he thought were Gypsies. It was important that the judge hear the word 'Gypsy' now, they thought. Yet try as they might, the defence could not bring Antoan back to his original observations. 'I don't remember there being Gypsies, Roma or any other people before or after the incident,' he told the court. 'There was no exchange of blows between these boys and our group . . . I haven't said to anyone that I saw an exchange of blows.'

Dinko would be in charge of questioning for the defence throughout the trial. He asked the judge for permission to examine Antoan on the contradiction between what the young man was saying now and what he had told the investigator on the day of the tragedy, when he claimed there had been a fight between his friends and others who he thought had been Gypsies. The prosecutor objected, as did the lawyers for the Monovs and Antoan. The judge dismissed Dinko's request.

Under Bulgarian law at the time of the trial, any party could refuse to allow as evidence statements not made before a judge. Dinko had warned the Palfreemans that this might happen, but Simon was stunned nonetheless. He had understood that the prosecution's role here was to help the judge elicit the truth, not just to lock up his son. Why would the duty prosecutor deny access to any of the statements on which the prosecutor in charge, Parvoleta Nikova, had based her indictment?

When the defence tried to get Antoan to confirm that his friends shared a common interest in football, he became quite definite: 'There were no CSKA or Levski clothes or scarves . . . I don't remember us singing. None of our group carried a weapon . . . We wanted to have fun.' He said his desperate effort to escape from the defendant had scarred him psychologically as well as physically. 'After the incident I have a feeling of insecurity,' he explained. 'I became timid. For a long time after the incident I stayed at home and didn't want to go out.' Antoan Zahariev stood down, and the judge gave him permission to leave the courtroom.

A court official put her head out into the hall and called Martin Stoilov's name. Like Antoan, Martin denied that their group had been singing or chanting, although he did agree they were Levski fans. Of the moment when he and some others ran after the unknown men, he no longer said they had thought the strangers were looking for trouble. He said nothing about hearing Jock call out 'Get back, get back' before advancing on his friends.

Once again, Dinko asked the judge for permission to refer to what the young man had told the pre-trial judge. The civil claimants objected. But this time the prosecutor objected only to having the section about what Jock called out read aloud. Judge Kolev found no contradictions between what Martin had said before the trial and what he said in this hearing, but he did agree to read aloud Martin's earlier testimony on the ground that the witness might have suffered a memory lapse. 'They were waving their arms, if that can be accepted as an aggressive action,' the judge read. 'The defendant, when approaching, was shouting in bad Bulgarian, "Get back, get back."' But when asked what Jock had meant, Martin said: 'I can't remember why the defendant said the words "Get back".'

There were no further questions, and the judge gave Martin permission to leave. When the court door opened, Simon could see a group of young men just outside. 'Isn't there anything we can do to stop this?' he whispered to Dinko. The defence counsel approached the bench, and Judge Kolev promised to prevent further witnesses from leaving.

After lunch, Blagovest Trifonov gave evidence. Once again he described a chaotic situation in which Jock was swiping the knife at Tony 'the Tall' Yordanov. The defence wanted to get a picture of what Andrei had been doing when he was stabbed. Blagovest said Andrei and Jock had faced each other, one and a half metres apart. Andrei's arm had been raised when Jock stabbed him under the armpit 'with a quick short hit'. Blagovest identified the knife shown in court as the one he saw that night.

This time he said Andrei Monov and others had been singing the national battle song 'Shumi Maritsa' as they emerged from the metro; he denied they were chanting Levski slogans. When asked what Jock was wearing, he said nothing about braces. This time, he said the accused had been wearing a singlet and a jacket. Mystified by how the witness could have seen a singlet, Dinko asked the judge for permission to show him the photograph of Jock taken on his arrival at Police Station No. 3, in which he is clearly wearing his sweater. The prosecutor and the lawyers for the civil claimants both objected, but the judge overruled them. Blagovest conceded that when he saw the defendant, he had looked the same as he did in the photograph, but he insisted that his jacket had been open, exposing the singlet.

Simon turned to Blagovest's statement before the pre-trial judge, in which he said he had thrown a 'rock' at Jock after he stabbed Andrei. This time

Blagovest said he had broken up a brick and, along with friends, had thrown fist-sized pieces of it at Jock's chest. Simon felt dizzy. He suspected that he should have been pushing the witness harder to expose the contradictions in his testimony, but he was not even sure he fully understood what was going on. Within half an hour there were no more questions, and once again the judge let the witness leave the courtroom.

A court official called for Tony Yordanov. He strode in, his expression a strange mix of detachment and disdain. He told the court that he had not been drinking much on the night. According to a police incident report before the judge, this was unlikely. Tony then said he and Andrei had had an altercation with two people as they headed to the traffic lights.

'They were ordinary people,' said Tony when asked to describe them. 'They were middle-aged. I could not say if they belonged to a minority group or not. It all lasted about ten seconds. We exchanged words. I asked them if they wanted something from me and that was all. It seemed as if they were somewhat aggressive to Andrei and me. The tone of their voice was more aggressive. I thought that some of the people ahead of us had had an argument with them, because it made no sense why they would pass by me and say something to me.' Tony recalled that when the people saw they were outnumbered, they 'calmed down' and headed off towards the metro.

Simon tried to get the witness to describe how the group had chased after at least one of the men. 'There was no need for my friends to come and help,' Tony responded. 'When I was having the dialogue with these people, none of my friends came to help—for these ten to fifteen seconds that I am talking about. The [two men] left a little after the argument was over; they actually disappeared.'

As Galina translated what he said, Simon stared at the young man, astonished. In his statement to the investigator on the day of the tragedy, Tony had said he had exchanged words with a Roma man and then some of his friends ran after the man and he could hear shouts.

Before Simon could decide how best to take this further, Judge Kolev moved on to the matter of the knife. Simon had no idea how to steer the questioning back to the moment when Jock had said he intervened. Already handicapped by his lack of legal training, Simon also struggled to follow what was being said as he waited for Galina to translate. It was like boxing in the dark. Whatever Tony had once seen and heard close to the metro entrance no longer seemed to exist.

Tony now said that after the defendant swiped his knife at him, Tony threw two pavers at him. He added 'in self-defence', and later said, 'the two rocks missed'.

When the judge dismissed him, Tony left the courtroom and Kristian Dimov entered. He had been next to Tony when Jock was swinging his knife and, according to Tony, had got him out of harm's way.

Kristian said that although he and his friends had been drinking that night, no one was drunk. This contradicted the autopsy finding that his close friend Andrei had a blood alcohol concentration of 0.29 per cent; and Antoan a concentration of 0.18 per cent. Kristian agreed that most of them were Levski fans and said they 'might' have been 'loud', but he insisted that they had no physical contact with the strangers. He said Jock did not speak in Bulgarian, contrary to testimony that he had said 'C'mon, c'mon' and 'Get back' in Bulgarian.

Jock asked what they had been throwing at him. Kristian said that he had thrown 'some wood', but that Tony had not thrown anything. When Simon tried to clarify where Jock had been in relation to the group, the witness responded: 'I saw no one attacking the defendant from behind.'

The judge asked Kristian to remain in the courtroom while Emil Aleksiev was called. Emil said both that he had drunk a bit and that he had abstained from drinking because he had exams coming up. According to the young man, no one had drunk much. He saw Tony and Andrei exchanging words with some strangers twenty to fifty metres from the metro. When the strangers saw the rest of Andrei's group running towards them, they realised they were outnumbered and ran away.

Emil claimed that the first time he saw Jock was by the ticket booth, which is about halfway across the square, a metre north of the Nescafé billboard. Jock shouted 'No fascism' and the group of friends started to retreat.

Simon knew this version was at odds with Emil's earlier testimony that he saw Jock running from Stamboliyski Boulevard across the square shouting 'Don't attack, get back' in Bulgarian. But it was already too late to pull him up on this; the judge's line of questioning had changed again.

Emil talked of throwing concrete pavers at the defendant. He claimed they had somehow managed to break the pavers into small pieces. Since the trial transcript does not include questions asked, it is not clear if he meant this took place before or after Andrei was stabbed. Emil said that when he ran away, he thought Andrei must have returned to the fray without him. 'I saw silhouettes,' he added, describing what would be the final showdown. He concluded his testimony by denying that he had hit Jock with the pavers, that any of the group had attacked Jock from behind, or that anyone had attacked Lindsay.

Once all the witnesses had left the courtroom, Dinko again asked the judge to consider his request for further witnesses and material evidence. He wanted a court-appointed psychiatric panel to assess whether the actions of Andrei and his friends could be put down to group behaviour or mob mentality. He wanted the psychiatric panel that had examined Jock to sit in on the hearings and to be available for questioning about whether Jock's personality made it likely that he would commit the crime for which he had been indicted.

Dinko asked for a second opinion on the autopsy results. He wanted Lindsay to be summonsed, as well as the people who had been identified in witness statements but not interviewed. He wanted to see the traffic-camera and subway CCTV recordings that had been collected and to have them shown in court. Finally, he wanted the Ministry of Health's CCTV hard drive examined, to see if any video recorded on the night could be recovered.

The prosecutor objected to the additional psychological review of the group and of Jock, but the transcript does not record her reasons, if she gave any. She agreed to the second opinion on Jock's wounds, but not on the autopsy results, and said summonsing 'the girl' was unnecessary. She dismissed the request to have the Ministry of Health hard drive examined on the ground that it had been damaged in an electrical failure and she objected to showing the traffic-camera recordings, saying that at night visibility was too low for them to show anything.

Dinko pointed out that the prosecutor's objection to an examination of the Ministry of Health hard drive relied on a letter from the ministry that did not even resemble an official document. In other words, no one appointed by either the prosecution or the court had determined whether the hard drive was indeed damaged.

The lawyers for the civil claimants objected to any assessment of Andrei's group, claiming such an analysis would be too abstract to be meaningful. One of the lawyers argued that to ask what effect alcohol might have had on the actions of Andrei and his friends was in itself 'immoral'.

In the end Judge Kolev withheld his decision on whether to allow a viewing of the traffic-camera and subway CCTV recordings, but he did agree to ask the Interior Ministry to find out whether the Ministry of Health CCTV recording could be recovered. He agreed that Lindsay should be interviewed, but made no mention of the other witnesses. He ruled that, as there was no evidence thus far that the young men had all been football fans, the report requested was unnecessary. He said he would rule on whether to have an assessment of Jock's character and a second opinion of the autopsy after he had heard the initial expert testimony. The court would reconvene in seven weeks' time.

Simon looked at his son. It was almost six in the evening. They had been on their feet all day and were exhausted. Simon knew Jock would be cross about how much the witnesses had been allowed to say uncontested, but for the moment his overriding concern was with the way the judge had run his court. As Jock was led past the Monovs and out of the courtroom, the couple looked away. Simon stared at his notebook, but his eyes glazed over and he shoved it in his pocket. He put the folder of police witness statements in his backpack, then got up to leave. Helen approached him. Simon wanted to talk to Dinko. 'Maybe that can wait until tomorrow,' said Helen, who could see he was too tired to think straight.

The Monovs walked side by side through the media scrum outside. They did not hold hands or speak to each other. Aksenia politely asked a cameraman to move aside. Some of Andrei's friends shook hands with Hristo as they farewelled the couple. Outside the courthouse, the hounds of Sofia were sniffing around commuters who rushed to catch the tram that rattled along the boulevard to St Nedelya Square.

Jock's Samokov friends went to a nearby coffee shop to talk about what they had heard during the hearing. They found the denial by the witnesses that they had been swearing unlikely and suspicious.

Galina had found the first day of the trial disturbing. She did not claim to know what really happened that night, but after translating all the witness statements and the expert reports, she believed that Jock had been outnumbered in the square and that if Andrei Monov and his friends had wanted to get away from him, they could have done so. She found Hristo Monov's assertion that his son's friends were part of 'the real elite of Bulgarian youth' unnerving. It struck her that they had every reason now to lie in court—they would not want anyone to think that they had contributed to their friend's death, let alone be accused of an indictable offence.

The next day Simon went to see Jock, who was talking a mile a minute. He still wanted to hire a private detective—this time to find more witnesses and get hold of the Ministry of Health CCTV recording, which Jock was convinced had been purposely removed.

Simon shut his eyes. There was very little he could do for now. He and Helen had to return home.

. . .

Jock's days were punctuated by roll calls. Guards came through at 6.30 and 8.30 in the morning and then at 8.30 at night when the cells were locked down. Prisoners were allowed an hour a day in the exercise yard. Many dressed up for the occasion to show off a cap, a T-shirt or a pair of sunglasses as they would have done on a night out in their civilian life. Jock was not interested in what was known as the fashion parade; he missed doing exercise. He had loved pushing his body to its limit during rowing and Army training; it had given him a break from mulling over the problems of the world. But there was nothing to do here and fights were commonplace. By now just walking to the yard was exhausting and made him even hungrier. Jock soon stopped going. The foreign prisoners were not allowed to eat in the mess hall with the Bulgarian prisoners. Food was brought to them in their cells. It was never enough.

In Jock's cell, lock-down was the signal to bring out the cooking equipment and any food that visitors had brought. Jock now shared the cell with the Iranian Swede Mohammed, the Chechnyan, Murad, and Glenn, a Dane picked up at the Romanian border for tax evasion who had been raped and beaten in remand. The four men got on well and became firm friends. Everything was shared, including the literal pain of cooking. To boil water they had made an element from razor blades separated by matches and held together with metal twine whose ends they shoved in a power point. Electric shocks were an inevitable hazard of any cell-made meal.

The power was cut off at 10.30 every night. They would sit around a candle, telling stories in a mixture of broken languages. Sometimes they made music by banging tin plates, stomping their feet, blowing into empty bottles and singing. 'Hey, mister, can you give me some bread? If you have Viceroy you can have bread,' went one chorus, referring to the cigarettes sold in the canteen, which were a form of currency among the prisoners—'If you have Viceroy, you can have anything!'

. . .

23 May 2008

Father Petko Valov wrote to the court seeking permission to visit Jock in prison. He explained that Jock wanted to receive the Eucharist and that this would involve hearing his confession. Permission was granted.

In a remarkably frank interview for this book, the priest recalled that the first time he visited Jock prison officials warned him that the Australian was dangerous. According to Father Petko Jock wept as he talked of the horror he felt that a life had been lost. Jock did not say if he remembered stabbing anyone. He only said that everything had happened very quickly and he had been scared. He was upset that the court did not seem to take into account his version and that people called out 'murderer' to him.

Father Petko would continue seeing Jock regularly and would eventually hear his confession. He found Jock's open nature inspiring, but he feared Aksenia Monova's standing as a notary in Sofia's small legal fraternity would make it difficult for the prisoner to get a fair hearing.

CHAPTER 20

July 2008
Newcastle

Helen was cleaning up around Simon, who sat at the kitchen table reading the English-language Bulgarian news website. Their flight back to Sofia via London was already booked. They would stay in the same apartment complex, whose manager had agreed to store pots and pans, crockery and cutlery for them. They set off on the three-day journey to Bulgaria still assuming that, even accounting for trial delays, this ordeal would be over by the end of the year.

. . .

Sydney

Jock's mother was at a loss to know how to help her son, other than to stay clear of members of the media. Then her parish priest put her in touch with some Benedictine nuns in Tsarev Brod, a village about 300 kilometres east of Sofia. Most of the nuns from their abbey had fled in the dying days of the Third Reich. When the Communist Party came to power, those who remained were sent to labour camps. When the Bulgarian sisters were finally allowed to return, they had to hand over half the abbey to the state to house a women's psychiatric hospital. Today an unnerving cacophony of shrieks accompanies the ten nuns as they make medicinal ointments from the marigolds they grow in their garden.

The elderly German abbess, Mother Beate, and Sister Maria, a young Filipina, travelled seven hours by bus to visit Jock. They were struck by his positive attitude and his conviction that he had been right to help someone in trouble. The nuns resolved to make the long trip to Sofia as often as they could, particularly on hearing days, and left a set of rosary beads for Jock, which he keeps in his pocket to this day.

. . .

9 July 2008
Sofia Palace of Justice

More of Andrei Monov's friends were waiting outside the courtroom to give their evidence. They looked across at a young man with long hair who was waiting alone. It was Anton 'Tony' Doychev. He knew they hated him. When the court official called for him, he was shaking. He felt like a dead man walking.

For the most part, Tony repeated what he had already told Chief Investigating Officer Alakusheva and the pre-trial judge. He struggled to describe what he had seen and heard while loading his mobile phone with credit: 'The shouting could be heard but at some point it stopped. The people were already at the intersection, at the kiosk. I am not sure how many, but I think there were ten of them.' Tony then explained what had happened just before Jock ran across Stamboliyski Boulevard: 'He asked me . . . if the people had attacked someone. I told him I didn't see them attacking anyone . . . Jock went to cross the street. I don't know why. Perhaps it seemed to him that the people had attacked someone.'

Again Tony said that he did not see Jock carrying a weapon. But this time he agreed that he had heard someone shouting 'C'mon'. He did not know who shouted this, but it might have been Jock. He repeated that he later saw someone kicking Lindsay: 'When Jock was held to the ground, I heard swearing. Lindsay was kicked in the waist, in the back, and she fell to the ground.'

The lawyers for the Monovs and Antoan wanted to know more about the moments leading up to Jock's dash across the street to the square. 'I tried to stop Jock when he started to go. I shouted at him "Come back",' said

Tony, adding that he had seen neither Jock attacking the group nor the group attacking him. Lengthy discussion ensued about how long it took to load credit into a phone. Tony was not making much sense. At some point he told Judge Kolev quite adamantly: 'I didn't see an attack.' But since the transcript does not record the questions asked, it is not possible to know whether Tony was referring here to an attack on Roma or to the attack which the group members claimed the defendant launched against them.

The prosecutor changed tack, requesting that the court hear the section of Tony's statement dated 15 January 2008, which she said 'describes the establishment they were in before that and Jock's actions when he went into the group'.

'No objection,' responded the lawyers representing the civil claimants.

'I object,' said Dinko, who asked that the transcript of what the witness had said before a judge be read instead.

Simon could see that Dinko was doing exactly what the other side had done in the last hearing. Dinko wanted to prevent Tony's more complete description of his political discussion with Jock in the bar from being used as evidence, because it would play into the prosecutor's argument that Jock was on some sort of ideologically driven mission to tackle Bulgarian fascists. The judge overruled the prosecutor's request.

When Dinko questioned Tony about the youths, the young man said very little. Despite protests from the prosecution and civil claimants, Dinko was allowed to read aloud the section of Tony's police statement where he described the group coming out of the metro. Tony's response was hesitant: 'It was a long time ago and I can't remember what exactly the chants were. The chanting was about football, they were shouting. I can't remember what exactly . . . When they held Jock to the ground, I think they shouted *chorbar* at him . . . I don't know if the boys were under the influence of alcohol.' Tony was finding it hard to get his words out. He could sense the bereaved parents standing to one side of him; he could sense some of the young men who had been there that night behind him. He just hoped Jock had seen what he thought he saw.

Now it was Nikolai Rabadzhiev's turn. He had told the investigator that he had met Andrei for the first time that night and that he had passed two

Roma in the square as he walked to the traffic lights. Now he doubted they had been Gypsies, saying it had been too dark to tell. When Dinko asked to read from his police statement to highlight the inconsistency, the prosecutor and civil claimants objected and the judge denied the request.

Nikolai had also told the investigator that he had seen 'people' chase Jock before Andrei Monov fell to the ground. It appears that the defence did not try to draw this detail from him in court. If that is the case, it might have been because the expert CCTV report did not describe such a chase. However, it would become evident much later that the CCTV report had left out many details visible in the video images. For whatever reason, the defence lost a major opportunity to establish that Jock had feared for his life, a central element of its argument that he had been acting in self-defence.

Anton Petrov was called to testify. He had also been with the group on the night of the incident. During the investigation he had told the police investigator that he had heard someone calling out 'George'. Now he claimed he had heard 'John or Jock'. Anton had previously said he saw a skirmish in front of the kiosk and went towards it, but in court he said he ran away, scared. When asked why the others did not do the same, Anton said that the man with the knife had them 'jammed at the kiosk': 'I can't say how many people were wedged there,' Anton added. 'But I think there were more than five people being pushed by just one.' The suggestion that he had trapped this large group echoed a detail in Martin Stoilov's pre-trial statement to a judge, a detail he had not mentioned to the investigator.

'Do they think I am Superman?' Jock whispered to his father incredulously. He remembers asking the witness what was blocking their escape, but his question was ruled inadmissible.

Judge Kolev adjourned the next court for two and a half months, and ordered that a number of witnesses, including Viktor Georgiev, be subpoenaed to testify. Jock's shoulders relaxed momentarily. He could see his father breathe a little more easily, too. They were pinning their hopes on the testimony of the security guard at the Sheraton car park. Nevertheless they feared the media reporting of the incident might colour his recollection of events and that he would be afraid to say exactly what he had seen.

. . .

The next day Australia's honorary consul in Sofia, Indiana Trifonova, met up with the Palfreemans for coffee. She had brought with her the daily newspapers and gave them a rundown of the main stories. Simon wanted to stay abreast of events in Bulgaria, so he could better understand both how his son's trial was being covered in Bulgaria and the environment in which it was being heard.

He looked up as Trifonova read a headline referring to Roma. The European Court of Human Rights had formally asked for a stay of the proposed demolition of the Roma ghetto at Vuzrazhdane. The town's deputy mayor had responded, lamenting that this was the second time the council's plans had been thwarted and that it was losing credibility with its residents, who wanted the Gypsies out of their neighbourhood.

Simon mulled over this as he and Helen caught a taxi to the airport. *Gypsies were clearly outcasts in Sofia, as they were in many European cities. But would middle-class university students bash them up without provocation?*

. . .

Hristo Monov was made deputy head of the Child Protection Agency, a government organisation. The promotion meant he now had an even more prominent platform from which to comment on issues ranging from parenting and child abuse to teenage drinking and violence.

. . .

Burgas, Bulgaria

In late July the European Union announced it was freezing hundreds of millions of euros of funding to Bulgaria owing to financial mismanagement and widespread corruption. The move was unprecedented and devastating. At the same time, Eurobarometer survey results suggested that Bulgarian public confidence in the judiciary was the lowest in the EU.

The news would come as no surprise to investigative journalist Assen Yordanoff. For several years he had been researching the link between the judiciary and organised crime, in particular a gang headed by Svetlozar Lolov, who operated out of Burgas, where Yordanoff was based. It was part of a larger investigation that would see him win the Leipzig media award for journalistic bravery established in Germany after the Berlin wall came down. It would involve a key player in Jock's case.

Dubbed 'The Rice Baron' in the early 1990s, Lolov was accused of smuggling huge quantities of rice into the European Union using fraudulent customs papers. On his payroll was a local man named Rangel Stanchev. One night the journalist saw Stanchev standing and talking on his mobile phone outside Yordanoff's house. After a while Stanchev got into a black BMW with four men, circled the block and cruised past the house.

Having been brutally attacked during a previous corruption investigation, Yordanoff complained to the head of the Burgas police. Commissar Milen Dimitrov warned Stanchev to stay away from the journalist, but he was not able to prove that the incident represented an attempt on Yordanoff's life.

The reporter alleges that a few days later, he was walking home when Stanchev pulled up alongside him, beeped his horn and hollered out abuse. Sitting next to Stanchev was a thin blonde woman whom Yordanoff later recognised as none other than Prosecutor Parvoleta Nikova.

In an interview for this book, Burgas senior prosecutor Angel Georgiev confirmed that Nikova had been dating Stanchev. 'I've known her for long time,' said Georgiev. 'And I know that she has been in close relationship with him for many years.' At this stage Nikova's private life did not concern Georgiev. But that would soon change.

. . .

The prison was hot, unbearably hot. And this wasn't even a particularly hot summer. Fights broke out all the time in the overcrowded Bulgarian section and now the violence was spilling into the foreigners' section, where boredom reigned supreme. Prisoners facing trial were not allowed to work and trials could take years. In any event there were not enough jobs for all the convicted prisoners.

Jock knew prison was changing him. He was becoming more erratic. He had developed a nervous laugh and his eyes twitched. The random way in which rules were applied almost made him explode with rage. One day he watched as the guards knifed their way through all the food that his Samokov friends had brought him on visit day, slashing tomatoes and salami to pieces and upending a bag of sugar over it all. Jock shouted so much he nearly lost his voice.

Another day, a prisoner hurled a cup of boiling water at him. When Jock talked it over with him later, the man said he had just snapped. A brawl erupted in a cell near Jock's after a prisoner threw out the remains of an onion. The guards did nothing. He could hear the shouting and shuddered. But it was not just the random attacks by frustrated prisoners that worried him.

Rumours darted about the prison. Some were the stuff of petty intrigue. Others were more insidious. Jock had heard that someone connected to Andrei's group of friends had offered a large sum of money to any prisoner who killed him. He assumed that offer extended to guards. On one occasion he had found himself alone in the gym with a guard, who purposely tried to provoke him. Jock knew that if he had hit him, the guard would have drawn a weapon and claimed this was justified.

Jock had also heard witnesses in his favour were being targeted. *That's why Tony was so nervous in court,* he thought. *That's why the Sheraton workers aren't turning up!* Jock knew he had no proof that anything untoward was afoot but the thought messed with his mind. *Am I becoming paranoid?* He couldn't tell. What he did know was that the struggle to survive was slowing his review of the court documents, and that his next hearing date was not far away.

· · ·

25 September 2008
Sofia Palace of Justice
When his name was called out, Alexander Donev entered the courtroom. He would be the last of the group to testify. Alexander nodded at his friends who were sitting there. Hristo Monov was standing at the front of the courtroom and turned around to see him.

Alexander said Andrei was the last to leave the restaurant on the night of the incident, since he was settling the bill. He did not appear drunk. According to his testimony, as the group of twenty or twenty-five headed for the Solo Disco Club, Alexander was a little ahead of Andrei. Waiting at the traffic lights on Stamboliyski, he heard a 'quarrel' behind him, which lasted for about one minute, and went back to see what had happened. He was told that two guys had said some offensive words.

Alexander located the quarrel close to the metro. He said he and his friends had started returning to Stamboliyski when he heard shouting. He turned around and saw a man, presumably Jock, brandishing a knife ten to fifteen metres from them. He saw Jock go to attack someone but was not sure who that was or if that person was hit by the knife. Then he saw Jock go for the same person again and this time the knife went close to the group member's chest. Alexander tried to kick the knife from Jock's hand but missed. Jock then brandished the knife at Alexander; it came within centimetres of him. Scared, Alexander ran away and then shouted to his friends to be careful as the attacker had a knife. He said the next thing he remembered was Kristian shouting, 'Come quickly! Andrei has been stabbed.'

Presumably in response to questions about whether he and his friends had provoked Jock, Alexander said: 'I don't remember if anyone else was trying to kick the defendant when I tried to kick the knife from his hand. I don't remember anyone throwing rocks at the defendant.' Dinko tried to get Alexander to say again what he had told the police investigator on 28 December about the altercation earlier on. 'I didn't tell anyone that Andrei had argued with Gypsies,' Alexander said indignantly. Once again Dinko tried to have sections of the original statement read aloud. The prosecutor joined the civil claimants objecting to any reading. Once again the judge overruled the defence request and dismissed the witness.

The court official called Mladen Nikolov. Although Mladen no longer worked at the kiosk in St Nedelya Square, the thought that someone had died next to it had stayed with him. The prospect of appearing in court unnerved him.

Mladen told the court what he had seen that night from the window of the small kiosk. A group of youths had run across the square towards the metro, and a few minutes later fifteen to twenty of them had walked back, 'laughing loudly and talking'. Pressed to describe the youths, Mladen said they had been chaotic and looked drunk. Two of them had stumbled against the kiosk.

Repeating what he had told the investigator, Mladen said there had been two groups in the square that night. The big group had been near the traffic lights and, when they all turned to face the metro, one of its members had taken 'a big paver' and thrown it at someone. A fight had broken out between two groups, with one man in the smaller group trying unsuccessfully to push the bigger group back.

Mladen tried to answer Jock's many questions. No, he could not be sure if Jock was the man in question. No, he did not see a weapon. He found Jock's examination unsettling. It was as if the defendant didn't like his answers; at one stage Jock even blurted out, 'You're not telling everything.'

Jock thought the witness seemed honest but confused. He wanted Mladen to specify where people were in relation to each other, but the twenty-six-year-old either could not remember or had not taken in such detail. Significantly he did remember seeing someone throw a paver that was twenty-five centimetres wide and eight centimetres thick; 'the person who threw this rock, this paver, did that with both hands,' he said. Jock wondered if that could have been Andrei Monov: *Were his arms raised as he held the paver, about to throw it when I was waving the knife around? Did the knife enter his armpit area then? Could that be what happened?*

Jock could see that the witness was getting annoyed by the questions and the seeming attack on his integrity. Jock knew how he felt. He also knew his father had been hoping for more solid evidence of a violent attack on him. Yet given that Jock had been on his own, Mladen's description of the smaller group did seem to add weight to the defence argument that, when the melee moved from the metro to the kiosk and the Ministry of Health, young men had been both in front of and behind Jock, throwing rocks at him from both directions.

Viktor Georgiev failed to appear, but his offsider at the Sheraton that night, Lyubomir Tomov, was the last witness of the afternoon.

Acutely aware that everyone was staring at him, the car park attendant repeated the account he had previously given, starting with the group coming out of the metro chanting Levski songs. Although he did not belong to any of the Levski fan clubs, Lyubomir went to the team's matches, so he knew the chants well.

Lyubomir said he had not looked at Jock's face, but he had an approximate idea of his height. He said Jock had been pushed to the ground and five members of the group had kicked and punched him. Jock pulled the knife out after he was attacked and as the youths were walking away. Aksenia Monova leaned forward and frowned. She was sure she recognised Lyubomir and decided the young man must have it in for her son.

. . .

Jock got permission to attend Bulgarian language classes. With him was an illiterate Bulgarian Gypsy. Jock helped him trace out the Cyrillic letters. One day the Gypsy revealed that he knew of a drug addict named Borislava who had seen what had happened in the square. He told Jock where she could usually be found. Jock passed on the details to his lawyer. Borislava might well be the women to whom the Sheraton car park attendant, Nikolai Kotev, had referred in his police statement, and the woman whom police had not identified during the investigation.

Dinko asked the court to search for a drug addict or prostitute who might be called Borislava. The court in turn asked police how many Borislavas they had on record. On 8 January 2009, police would respond that there were thirty-six, but with that the search seems to have stopped.

. . .

13 October 2008
Sofia Palace of Justice
The court heard from one police officer after another. Their names blurred together in Jock's mind. As they described it, the crime scene on their arrival was chaotic. One officer said he had repeatedly called for an

ambulance for the boy bleeding to death. It took twenty to twenty-seven minutes to arrive, during which time the group members were trying to 'lynch the perpetrator'. He neither saw nor heard anything about Gypsies. Another officer said members of the group had tried to push aside the arresting officer to get at the suspect.

Jock recalls the prosecutor putting only one question to the police officers. She asked Nikolai Apostolov what the suspect had said in the vehicle. The transcript records only the officer's response: 'He said the incident was racially based. He was saying that there are fascists here—Nazis. He repeated that.'

It was the testimony from Asen Stoychev that most struck Simon. This officer described how members of the group were pushing and shoving police, trying to prevent them from loading the suspect into the van and then hitting the sides of the van, prompting police to drive away as fast as possible. He recalled that Lindsay was behaving 'inadequately' and seemed to be in shock. But under questioning, Stoychev went much further than in his original statement. Now he said that at the scene he had picked up two very different versions of what had transpired.

One version came from the youth holding Andrei's head, who told him that they had been 'walking' when suddenly someone with a knife had 'come at them'. Other group members told Stoychev that the group had had an 'altercation' with people from 'the minority' and the defendant had tried to stop it, after which they attacked him and he had 'defended himself'. The officer added that passers-by and security guards from the Sheraton had told him the same thing.

The hearing over, Simon headed to St Nedelya Square on his way to the market. He turned up his coat collar against the wind. Chestnuts flew across the cracked pavement as he walked past the Ministry of Health entrance. Court had gone well and Simon was elated. Stoychev's testimony supported what had been said in witness statements by the officers due to appear in court the next day. *Surely police won't change their account of what happened*, he thought.

. . .

14 October 2008

One after another, officers Viktor Lyubenov, Petar Katsarov and Krassimira Stoyadinova pledged to tell the truth. One after another, they said the injured boys' friends had told them there had been some sort of altercation and the foreigner had pulled a knife, stabbing two boys. Originally these officers had told the police investigator that when they arrived at the scene, colleagues told them the boys had been fighting with Gypsies and a foreigner had intervened to help the Roma, but each time the defence tried to bring them back to their earlier account, they said they did not know why Jock had run into the group. Each time, Dinko Kanchev asked to have the relevant section of their statements to the investigator read aloud. Each time, the judge accepted the prosecutor's and civil claimants' objection and overruled the request.

Simon was floored. The ground seemed to be shifting under him, and he could get no traction. When Jock later ranted to him about police corruption, Simon said the judge would surely see through any attempt to sanitise the group's involvement.

His son would have none of that. No, Jock said, the whole system was rotten to the core. Simon tried to calm him: 'That is going too far.' He wanted to sound confident, but something in Simon was changing. 'Let the system play out,' he urged Jock. Deep down he was terrified. What if his son was right?

Before returning to Australia, Simon and Helen had dinner with Jock's Bulgarian friends at a downtown restaurant. Later, as they waited for the tram back to their apartment, Helen watched a young couple embracing. The well-built man was holding a half-empty beer bottle, and they both looked a little drunk.

When the tram arrived, Helen nabbed a seat while Simon stood beside her, holding onto the ceiling straps. The lovers had also boarded and stood near them as the tram moved off. Simon watched the young man, who suddenly left his girlfriend and moved towards a thin young Gypsy boy who was sitting by himself at the back. Just as the tram reached the next stop, the young man kicked the boy in the head and jumped off the tram.

Simon was shocked and grabbed Helen's shoulder, asking her if she had seen the attack. She had not. Then the Gypsy staggered past Helen's seat on his way to the front of the tram. He tripped, fell to the floor and then jumped to his feet, clutching the side of his head. His eyes watering, the boy looked around furtively, like a dog that had been kicked and feared being kicked again, and slunk back to the rear. The other passengers paid no attention.

Simon picked up the boy's baseball cap, which had fallen to the floor, and went to the back seat to give it to him. The boy thanked Simon with a hand movement, a shake of the head and a few unintelligible words. Upset that he had not tried to intervene, Simon returned to Helen's side, and the tram rattled on its way as if nothing had happened.

'Jock's right about one thing,' Helen said later. 'If you are a Gypsy in Bulgaria, this is the kind of treatment you can expect—anyone can attack you with impunity, because no one gives a toss.' But the knife Jock had carried still worried her.

. . .

Sofia Central Prison

Budimir Kujovic moved into Group 13. He was accused of drug running, not an unusual charge in this prison population. But there were allegations that Budimir had received protection from police and state authorities. Among those implicated was the former Interior Minister, Rumen Petkov. Such controversy made the Serbian prisoner someone with whom to be reckoned. Budimir was marking out his territory, and anyone who was not in it was vulnerable. Jock had no intention of linking his fortunes to this man. If convicted, both of them faced long sentences. So the first time Budimir picked a quarrel, Jock thumped him, believing he needed to set the ground rules early.

Jock was also coming into conflict with prison authorities. He badgered them to let some prisoners make a vegetable garden; he tried to get things fixed in the cells; he refused to follow orders he believed were outside prison regulations; he insisted on rights outlined in the regulations, like the right to a certain level of sustenance. Prisoners told him he was wasting his time, but they went to him for advice when they felt they had been treated unjustly. Some told him horrific stories about Bulgarian lawyers taking their money and not turning up at court, or about having drugs planted on them at the border.

There was an outbreak of tuberculosis in the prison. The authorities wanted to give all prisoners a blood test for the disease, but Jock refused to see the doctor: the possibility of infected needles filled him with horror. Chronic funding shortages ensured that medical care in the jail was primitive. He had heard prisoners screaming in pain after having teeth extracted without anaesthesia. He had seen a Turkish prisoner dying of cancer because he could not afford to pay the prison for treatment.

The more injustices and abuses Jock saw, the more determined he became to stand up against them. His cellmates warned that that would get him into trouble, but Jock was not listening.

CHAPTER 21

12 November 2008

It was the day before Jock's twenty-second birthday. The nuns made a cake for him with fruit from their garden and carried it carefully into Sofia with them. They packed little candles to decorate it and some big ones that he could use to read by at night. It wasn't much, but it was all they could afford. When they got to the prison, the guards told them only store-bought cakes were allowed. Jock couldn't have their cake. He was only allowed to have the candles.

Jock grinned when he saw the sisters from the other side of the barrier. They picked up the intercom telephone receivers to talk to him and broke into a rendition of 'Happy Birthday' in English. His grin widened. The song alone was a wonderful present.

But Jock's joy was short-lived. Prisoners are not allowed to have mobile telephones. For that reason there is a roaring trade in them. Soon after the nuns' visit, guards found one on Jock. He was sent to the isolation cells, on a top floor of the prison. At this time of the year it was bitterly cold there. Prisoners call the area Pamporovo, after the ski resort in southern Bulgaria. Because of overcrowding in the prison, isolation does not necessarily mean being completely alone. Up to four men can be crammed into each tiny, windowless cell. They are allowed out for an hour each day, but only with each other. And Jock was due to face court again in a week.

. . .

4 December 2008

Sofia Palace of Justice

Jock was released from isolation in time for the Thursday hearing. But as he sat with his father Judge Kolev announced that court was adjourned because one of the three lay judges was abroad, and the trial could not continue without him. Simon had travelled for several days to get here from Sydney and would now have to return home with the case no further advanced. The next hearing would be in almost three months' time.

That afternoon Jock shouted at Simon when he came to visit. He was frustrated, angry, confused, depressed. *At least Dad seems to understand what I'm going through a bit better now,* Jock thought. He felt like a deaf, dumb, blind quadriplegic in here.

Being allowed to attend Bulgarian lessons had helped—he could understand and speak Bulgarian better now. He could follow a bit of the news on TV. When he had phone credit, he could stand in line for an hour or more and try to call one of the ten numbers allowed him—those of his lawyer, the Australian honorary consul and his Samokov friends among them. But he knew his English was becoming rusty from disuse. In jail, he was forced to reduce every idea to simple words in a mixture of languages, to converse with prisoners and guards. Letters arrived, but he feared many did not get through. His brother Spencer, his grandfather, his grandfather's partner, his aunt, his Samokov friends and mates from Sydney had come to see him. He was luckier than most of the other foreign prisoners, many of whom got no visitors. But weeks would go by with no word from anyone.

The night before he left Sofia Simon received an email informing him that Jock's school friend Louis Simpson had been diagnosed with diffused gastric cancer, rare in someone so young and already at stage four. On the way to the airport he went to the prison to say goodbye and give Jock the bad news. Jock was devastated. In the coming weeks he could not sleep. The four walls around him seemed to be contracting. More than ever before he felt trapped and useless. There was nothing he could do to help his friend. Once again Jock was left waiting for his father to return.

. . .

Sofia

28 December 2008

Three days after Christmas, a young bTV reporter pulled her cameraman closer to her side. There was something creepy about the youths marching from the First English High School, which Andrei Monov had attended, to St Nedelya Square. It was the anniversary of Andrei's death. They carried Bulgarian flags and wore hoodies, many covering their faces or turning their backs when cameras were pointed at them. They wore black armbands bearing the silhouette of Andrei, his arms outstretched. They looked like skinheads.

Hristo Monov addressed the crowd at the makeshift memorial that was still on Stamboliyski Boulevard. The reporter asked him about the youths marching. 'They don't want to forgive the evil,' he told her. 'And they don't want evil to blacken their lives.'

But this march went beyond an expression of shared grief. The reporter was not alone in finding it unsettling. After hearing an account of the march on the radio, a popular blogger named Magdalina Guenova raised questions about it on her site. 'I want to know why Andrei Monov is turning into a nationalist icon. I'm not familiar with the case as a whole or the results of the investigation. The who and why, or whether it was unprovoked, or a case of self-defence; whether Andrei was a football fan and a good student as well as having some other exotic political views. Besides, it's irrelevant in this case and I'm very sad about the boy, his family and the whole sick society. I just don't think it's normal for a procession "against violence" to turn into a procession of revenge.'

The blogger went on to argue that the courts were the proper place for such cases; the state should not tolerate such extremist displays by so-called patriots. 'Behind Andrei's portrait there were [the same] people who threw bombs during the [annual] gay pride parade, which could have killed some other young . . . man. Are the boy's parents happy about this fact? Do they want to have an "eye for an eye, a tooth for a tooth" situation? Do most of the people who took part in the procession care about Andrei and did they know him? Or do they just rattle the sabre and want blood?'

. . .

During the Christmas break, Jock's mother brought Jock's fourteen-year-old brother, Angus, to Bulgaria. Not only was it an emotional time for Mary Jane, it was the first time the brothers had seen each other in three years. The honorary consul arranged for the family to sit together in a small room rather than be separated by the usual iron mesh. Jock was already in the room with a guard when Mary Jane and Angus entered. The teenager stood back stiffly, not knowing what to do. Jock understood. 'Angie, come here—they won't stop you,' he said gently. Angus ran into his big brother's arms and clung to him, not wanting to let go. Mary Jane struggled to stay composed.

CHAPTER 22

February 2009
Newcastle

I first contacted Simon in June 2008, after receiving a call from Jock's friend Ash. For several weeks, he was reluctant to talk with me. Jock had been urging him to get in touch with the media but Dinko said that would not be in his interest. Simon felt responsible for whatever happened to his son—damned if he did something, damned if he did not. But he was growing desperate and in August that year he agreed to meet me. I flew to Newcastle and spent an evening in the Palfreemans' small rented townhouse where Simon and Helen tried to explain the case to me. Sea air nudged its way under the front door; their dog Rosie barked at it, wanting to go on her nightly walk, but there would be no time for that. Although their account of what they had been through was confusing, the Palfreemans struck me as intelligent and earnest. I had no idea whether Jock was guilty as charged, guilty of something else or innocent. But the court documents Simon showed me were intriguing. If he agreed to take part, I knew I had a story.

My liaison in Bulgaria then rang Hristo Monov on my behalf to ask if he and his wife would take part in an interview. 'I will not speak to anyone coming from a country that produces a monster like Jock Palfreeman,' Hristo said before hanging up. The liaison tried Antoan Zahariev's lawyer, who said his client would not take part either. But Prosecutor Parvoleta

Nikova agreed to meet me. By the end of February I was on my way to Sofia for the first time, to film a half-hour documentary for the Australian Broadcasting Corporation's *Foreign Correspondent* program.

During this and other visits to Sofia, I was impressed by the power of rumour. Whenever the Palfreeman case was raised, Bulgarians referred to the unsubstantiated allegation published in Sydney's *Daily Telegraph* that Jock had been responsible for a knife attack in Sydney. It seemed not to matter to them that Jock had no police record. From the man on the street to members of the judiciary, people were convinced that Jock had done this kind of thing before. My job was to separate fact from fiction. Part of that involved seeing firsthand how the system operated; it also involved trying to understand what made Jock tick.

Thick snow covered the footpaths as I followed Simon to the prison. He had brought flannelette shirts, Vegemite and a CD of Gregorian chants from Australia, and fruit and vegetables from the market. Guards at the front gate poked at the food; they removed the packaging from other goods and stared at the tube of Vegemite, unsure what to make of it. We handed over our phones and went through a metal detector.

The visitors' area in the prison is a long rectangular room with a window onto a courtyard at one end. There is a row of eighteen stools bolted to the ground for visitors. Here, an iron mesh separates visitors from the prisoners who sit at a bench with handsets.

Jock was thin and pale. His hands were shaking as he gripped the mesh barrier in the visit room. He was anxious about how guards would react to the camera. The guards were not sure what to do either and for ten minutes let Simon and Jock sit together. They hugged. At first Jock stiffened—this was not part of the prison routine. But soon his hug became firm.

Simon wanted to discuss the upcoming court proceedings. But Jock was not interested in teasing out what they should ask witnesses. He ranted about injustices endured by his cellmates in their trials.

'Calm down,' Simon urged ineffectively. Jock wanted his father to bring in toilet paper, lots of it—the prison refused to give them any. He also wanted toilet cleaner. The toilet in his cell was filthy—indeed, it might never have been cleaned. A big lump of plaster had fallen on another cellmate's head. The decaying building was dangerous as well as unhygienic.

'In the past Jock always tried to lighten the situation, at least to start off,' Simon told me as he slumped in the back seat of a taxi afterwards. 'He'd laugh; he'd make me laugh. But this trip he's finding that harder. He is losing the ability to see things through and he looks sick. What disturbs me most, though, is that mentally he doesn't seem to be as strong as he has been for the past year. It's not just being in prison, but being in prison waiting for justice to be done. After one year we are no closer to a resolution than we were six months ago. Jock still hasn't been able to give his testimony. One of the key witnesses can't be found. I am afraid that Jock's resolve could wane.' Simon paused for a moment.

'Each time I come he seems to be more disoriented in time; he is more and more focused on day-to-day things. He acknowledges he has an institutionalised mentality. He gets very concerned about other prisoners and fights on their behalf any number of battles they are having with their cases or with the prison. It is increasingly difficult to get him back and focused on the important issue for me, which is to get him out of there.

'It's very hard as a father to sit back on the other side of that iron barrier and watch him hurting like that and not be able to do anything about it. Partly because I know he's relying on me so much, I feel inadequate.'

'My father has a very high moral standard,' Jock told me when I saw him alone. 'He's very principled. I guess his faith that people will do the right thing clouded his understanding of the situation that this is not a place where you can just believe that people will do the right thing for the sake of doing the right thing. It's not what happens here. There's nothing my father can do, and this is what would infuriate him.'

In this strained situation, father and son were learning more about each other than they would in the normal course of events. It was too early to know if such insights would improve or damage their relationship.

· · ·

25 February 2009

Sofia Palace of Justice

Prosecutor Parvoleta Nikova was now taking part in the court proceedings. She stood near the Monovs wearing a long crimson robe. For a second time, the lay judge who had been overseas failed to appear. Many of the witnesses also failed to turn up, among them Viktor Georgiev. Still there was no word on Lindsay Welsh or Grayham Saunders. The hearing was postponed; it was business as usual.

Before the judges stood to leave, Dinko again asked Judge Kolev for access to the traffic camera and subway CCTV recordings. He did not get a definitive response and became exasperated.

I wanted to approach Hristo Monov outside the courtroom, where all the other reporters and media crews were busy quizzing the participants. While I waited for a suitable moment, he stormed over to my cameraman and pushed his camera aside. His wife stood quietly nearby. I left her alone. I knew the couple must be finding the trial an agonising process.

. . .

Parvoleta Nikova agreed to be interviewed on camera. In response to my questions about why she had chosen to block examination of police witness statements, she said only that the Criminal Procedures Code allowed her to do so. She spoke with little intonation, eye contact or pause for reflection; it was as if she was rehearsing for a law exam.

According to Nikova, the defendant was guilty of even more than that with which she had charged him; he was guilty of trying to injure as many people as he could. 'I believe he should be given one of the heaviest penalties under our criminal code,' she said. 'As far as I am aware of the factual situation, depending on what the court decides, there [might easily have been] another victim from the group of Andrei Monov and Antoan Zahariev. But under some lucky circumstance this didn't happen.'

In response to my query about the alternative version of events provided by the two men working in the Sheraton car park, she said Viktor Georgiev and Lyubomir Tomov had been mistaken in their belief that they had seen the events leading up to the death. It was that simple.

When I put to her that Viktor and Lyubomir appeared to have described the very incident that Jock said had prompted him to run towards the group, Nikova returned to her central thesis: Bulgaria was a civilised European country, and Jock Palfreeman's behaviour was not civilised. She cited one section of the code after another as proof of Bulgaria's abhorrence of unethical and criminal conduct.

. . .

In the lead-up to Easter, Bulgarians celebrate *Zagovezni*, which is also known as Apology Day. This year it fell on the first of March, the same day people exchanged brightly coloured *martenitsa*s to farewell winter. Bonfires of tyres and wood burned in town squares and city streets across the country. While neighbours drank the grape brandy known as *rakia* and watched the flames, children asked their elders to forgive them for all that they had done wrong during the year.

A few days later, I accompanied Jock's Samokov friends Didi and Dobri to the general visit day. Prisoners were only allowed to see visitors twice a month. That day the visit room was full; children, wives and mothers all talked at once as they tried to pack in as much as possible during the 45 minutes allowed with their loved one. It was like a party and incredibly noisy. Few used the handsets; they just shouted through the mesh. Didi had brought Jock a *martenitsa* and asked him if there was anyone to whom he would apologise. 'Mr and Mrs Monov,' he said without hesitation. 'But I don't think they would listen.'

I then spoke to Jock alone. He was worried about his family, in particular Simon and Helen. 'Simon has Helen to look after him,' Jock said. 'But who will look after Helen?'

I asked Jock the question that I knew was playing on the minds of his father and stepmother: 'If you had your time again, would you have done the same thing that night?'

'Of course,' he exclaimed. 'I would always go to help someone!'

'Would you take a knife out again?'

'No,' he responded quietly. 'In all likelihood, without the knife I would have been beaten senseless or worse. But maybe that would have been better than Andrei dying and all this.'

. . .

25 March 2009
Sofia Palace of Justice

This time, the judge had scheduled two consecutive days of hearings. On the first day the lay judge once again failed to turn up and the hearing was cancelled. The next day he appeared and the hearing went ahead. There was still no sign of Viktor Georgiev.

But there was some good news. The Criminal Procedures Code that had previously allowed the prosecution and the victims to block the admission of police witness statements had been amended. Now the judge had to take into account only the victims' objections. Simon realised that this was unlikely to be the end of their problem, but at least the change acknowledged that it was absurd for a prosecutor to reject as evidence the very material she had relied upon to write her indictment.

The Sheraton car park attendant Nikolai Kotev was the first to give evidence. Since the court had previously been unable to locate him, the defence team was relieved to see him. But any flicker of hope for evidence in their favour quickly died. Nikolai had previously told the police investigator that he saw some of the boys trying to kick a man on the ground and three or four others trying to stop them. But when Dinko asked the witness about this memory, the guard went blank. 'I can't remember telling anyone that there was a boy who had fallen to the ground and they were kicking him,' he said. Now the only boy he could remember lying on the ground was Andrei. He recalled the blood as vividly as when he had given his original statement. The defence was flummoxed.

The judge asked if Nikolai had seen a Gypsy. 'After this thing happened there was a girl of Roma origin next to the police booth,' he said, referring to a small elevated platform in front of St Nedelya Church and near the Sheraton car park, from which police could observe traffic. 'This was later. When I first noticed the people across the road, I didn't see if there were Roma.'

Dinko asked to be allowed to read the section of Nikolai's witness statement that described the group attacking Jock on the ground. Before the judge could respond, he started reading it aloud. When Prosecutor Parvoleta Nikova objected, Dinko reminded the court that her consent was no longer necessary. When the civil claimants also objected, the judge overruled Dinko's request and dismissed the witness.

Emil Yankov was next. He was the taxi driver with whom Nikolai Kotev had been smoking in the car park that night. Police had failed to interview him during the investigation. The defence had urged the court to find him, even though they had no idea what he would say. But too much time had passed since the incident. Even though he had been facing the square, Emil testified that he saw nothing of the events leading up to the fatal stabbing. He said that when he crossed the road to the scene, the defendant was on the ground and everything around him was quiet, as though time stood still.

The defence was making no headway in its attempt to show what Jock had been up against and why he had continued to wave the knife. Emil did say that, as the suspect was being taken away, the youths had shaken the police van and caused problems. Jock tried to ask him more on this, but Emil's answers were brief.

The last witness that day was police officer Slaveiko Tsonkov. He described the situation when he had arrived at the crime scene. The prosecutor and counsel for the civil claimants had no questions.

Dinko Kanchev asked Tsonkov if he had been able to ascertain what caused the incident. 'The colleagues we met there were saying . . . that some Gypsy had been attacked by them and he rushed to free him from the beating,' he replied.

A murmur ran through the courtroom. Hristo Monov turned to his lawyer, and Andrei's friends whispered to each other. The Australian honorary consul translated for Helen, whose eyes widened. The witness was repeating what he had said in his original witness statement about what prompted Jock to run towards the youths. It was the same information that his fellow officers Krassimira Stoyadinova and Petar Katsarov had given the investigator.

Dinko then asked who exactly had said that. 'They are from other stations,' Tsonkov replied. 'And I don't know them.'

Once the witness had been dismissed, Dinko turned to Judge Kolev and asked that officers Stoyadinova and Katsarov be brought back for further questioning, given that what the court had just heard contradicted their testimony. Prosecutor Nikova objected immediately, arguing that there was no inconsistency in the witnesses' testimony. The civil claimants' lawyers shared her objection. Antoan Zahariev's lawyer added that Dinko's request was 'pointless and irrelevant' to the case.

Judge Kolev ruled that the defence request was unjustified, and that a search for the officers to whom Tsonkov had referred was also unjustified, given that the witness could not identify them.

Simon stared ahead as Galina translated the judge's decision. This was a turning point for him. Since reading the witness statements of the police officers from Police Station No. 3 who had spoken to group members at the scene, Simon had been asking himself questions that seemed naïve now that three of those officers had changed their accounts. *Why didn't the investigator chase up the first police at the scene? Why was the fact that they were from a different station seen as making that impossible?*

Simon accepted that Antoan's lawyer was trying to protect his client from being charged with assault, but he could not understand why the judge was seemingly unwilling to gather and hear all the evidence.

Dinko ploughed on stoically, reminding Judge Kolev that the defendant would not be able to give his testimony until all eyewitnesses had been heard, and that many were simply failing to appear. He requested that Viktor Georgiev be forcibly brought to court and, if he failed to provide an excuse for his absence, that he be fined 500 *leva*—more than A$300, a large sum for an ordinary Bulgarian. The judge agreed.

. . .

Sofia

Viktor Georgiev was listening to the midday news on the radio. There was something about the incident at St Nedelya Square. He heard his name mentioned. Apparently he and one of his former colleagues at the Sheraton had failed to appear in court that day. Viktor was stunned. He had made his statement a year before and since then he had not been contacted about the case. He had certainly not received a subpoena. He was still on the same mobile phone number that he had given the investigator. Someone was now renting the address he had given, but the place still belonged to his family. Viktor was angry. He was neither a suspect nor a victim. *Why was his name being bandied about in public like this?*

. . .

18 April 2009

The news was full of stories about two youths being stabbed to death outside the Solo Disco Club, which is on the street that runs along one side of the Palace of Justice, Positano Street. Solo is the same nightclub to which Andrei Monov and his group had been heading. The incident received considerable media attention. One of the dead was the goalkeeper of Bulgaria's national ice hockey team. But the public's concern was more that this was yet another downtown stabbing involving young people.

The alleged attacker was the son of a member of the ruling Socialist Party in a town not far from Sofia. It seemed he and his friends had been entertaining foreigners when someone took offence because they were speaking in English. The suspect, Iliyan Todorov, faced charges of double murder with hooligan intent.

. . .

24 April 2009
Sofia Palace of Justice

Once again the Sheraton guard Viktor Georgiev did not appear in court. Jock's friend Grayham Saunders was the only witness to give evidence that Friday. In preparation for the hearing he had shaved off his mohawk.

One of the Monovs' lawyers wanted to know more about the knife. Why had he bought it, and for what had he used it? Grayham stuck close to his police witness statement, saying that he had bought the knife on impulse to use in his kitchen. He added that in 2008, not long before going to Madjare for the Christmas holidays, he had read about a woman being attacked by dogs in the Bulgarian countryside. It had struck him then that he might also need a knife when out in the mountains.

When the trial resumed on Monday, there was still no sign of Viktor Georgiev and no word about Lindsay Welsh, so Judge Kolev cancelled the hearing. Simon and Jock looked at each other, disappointed. Then Kolev dropped a bombshell. He had decided the defence could not have copies of the traffic-camera and metro CCTV recordings, but he would let interested parties examine them right now in a smaller courtroom on the first floor, without the judges present.

Simon and Jock's relief at this news withered as the designated room filled with people. Andrei's parents and friends were there. A court technician put a laptop on a desk and started to play a DVD. There was no soundtrack. They all stood around the table, jostling to see the grainy, blurred images. Behind them, spectators wandered in and out of the room.

Simon insisted that the technician play the entire DVD rather than skipping straight to the timeframe in which the incident occurred. They watched seemingly endless shots of traffic and people crossing at the lights on Stamboliyski Boulevard. Then two figures approached the kiosk—Tony Doychev and someone in white clothes, who he assumed was Lindsay. A third figure crossed Stamboliyski and joined them; Simon thought it could be Jock. The quality of the recording was so poor that no one could be positively identified. Nevertheless, their ghostly presence was captivating. Within seconds the Jock figure ran back across the road towards the Happy restaurant with Tony, closely followed by Lindsay. *Jock does have a flight instinct*, thought Simon, relieved.

When a large group of more clearly defined figures emerged from Serdica metro, everyone in the room started to pay close attention. Simon took notes as they watched the young men and women traversing the square from right to left of frame. He was frustrated that the technician seemed unable to play the images in slow motion, much less zoom in on key moments so that Simon could compare the images with the CCTV expert's report.

As the last members of the group stood waiting at the lights to cross Stamboliyski, a lone figure, walking in the opposite direction, passed them seemingly without stopping. Two of the youths at the lights then turned and started following this figure to the right of frame, back towards the metro. Another figure started crossing Maria Louisa from near the Sheraton as though heading to the square and gesticulated at the figure being followed, as if to warn him. Simon figured that both the man being followed and the one gesticulating were the Gypsies.

Simon squinted to see what was happening; Aksenia Monova was visibly agitated. Suddenly, the two youths were joined by the rest of the group members. Together they ran after the men Simon assumed were the Gypsies, as though a signal had been sounded. Some came from as far away as the Happy restaurant on Stamboliyski Boulevard. Filling the frame from left to right, they headed towards the metro and disappeared behind a big billboard advertising Nescafé. Jock felt as if a truck had hit him. *That is it*, he thought. *I wasn't imagining things!*

Simon burned with indignation. Tony 'the Tall' Yordanov, in particular, had told the court this did not happen, and the court had accepted his story.

About twenty seconds later, a new figure came into view and ran across Stamboliyski, past the kiosk and along the front of the Ministry of Health building until it too disappeared behind the billboard. Simon felt chilled to the bone. The figure had to be Jock.

One and a half minutes passed. During this time none of the figures were in shot. Then two youths appeared from behind the billboard and ran towards the kiosk. More time passed. The rest of the group walked towards the pedestrian lights on Stamboliyski, some of them looking over their shoulders. A single figure was walking quickly behind them, as though pressing them towards the intersection of Stamboliyski and Maria Louisa. Simon assumed this was Jock and strained to see if he was carrying a knife, but he could not make out any details. No one was running away from Jock, but Simon felt anxious. *Why was he moving so far across the square after them?*

When they all reached the corner, Simon could see some of the youths start bending over as though to pick up objects from the ground; then they looked as if they were throwing them. After a short time, the swirl of activity moved away from the corner and closer to the tree between the pharmacy and the Ministry of Health entrance. This was about the limit of the camera's range, but at the blurry edges of the confused activity, some figures could be seen bending and throwing, running towards and away from a central point. One of those figures moved towards the centre and then went back to Stamboliyski, where he fell on the road. That figure could only have been Andrei Monov.

Simon could feel Aksenia Monova straining to watch her son's last moments, angry with him for being in her way. He appreciated that this was her child they were staring at so clinically. But he too had to know the truth.

The ambulance came into view about eight minutes after Andrei fell to the ground, much faster than the young men had remembered. As the stretcher was lifted into the ambulance, Andrei's face was clearly visible, as were his right arm and leg, which flopped over the side.

Simon felt upset. This was a horrible experience for everyone. It was also a frustrating one; this was not a good way of studying such potentially important evidence. He worried that he might have missed moments of it in this viewing. But the CCTV recording had clarified a lot. The youths had clearly rushed after someone before Jock intervened, later some of them did appear to have been throwing things at Jock and then far from trying to escape from Jock, Andrei was running towards him.

The video also showed that there were several witnesses who had not given statements. When the camera swung away from the action and towards the Sheraton, two, maybe three men and a woman could be seen watching. The woman might have been the Roma prostitute. Simon assumed the men were some of the workers at the Sheraton who had already given statements. What happened behind the billboard and closer to the metro was missing from this footage, but the witnesses working across the road at the Sheraton would have seen it all. *If only Viktor Georgiev would turn up*, Simon thought.

When everyone returned to the courtroom, the defence submitted that there were clearly more witnesses to the incident than had been interviewed and requested that attempts be made to locate the unknown female onlooker.

By now the defence had also discovered that the Ministry of Health CCTV cameras were monitored at night by a doctor. Dinko asked that the doctor on duty in the early hours of 28 December 2007 be identified and summonsed to give evidence as both a potential eyewitness and as someone who might shed light on what had been filmed that night. The judge agreed.

. . .

April 2009

Through the Old Boys' network at his alma mater, Riverview, Simon had got in touch with Julian McMahon, a criminal defence barrister in Melbourne with a reputation for helping free of charge young Australians in trouble abroad. He agreed to look through the case file. McMahon brought in another Melbourne barrister, Peter Morrissey SC, and they engaged Ruth Shann, a junior barrister who agreed to go through all the translated witness statements that Simon provided, and try to establish who stood where and what they saw.

Ruth drew up a huge flow chart showing where the evidence intersected with Jock's version of events. Right away, she could see many gaps in the police investigation. She could also see that at this stage the defence had no trump card. Recovering the 'deleted' CCTV recording from the Ministry of Health entrance and getting Viktor Georgiev to court seemed to be their only chance.

The team decided that the best tack was to fight the charges as they would have done in Victoria, but using Bulgarian legal principles. Even though Ruth had gone through the local legal code carefully, she was acutely aware of her unfamiliarity with the way that code worked in practice. When Simon returned to Newcastle at the end of April, Ruth set about tutoring him over the phone in how best to draw information from witnesses, but she felt unnervingly like a beginner herself.

. . .

Sofia

Behind the scenes, the mystery of Viktor Georgiev's whereabouts had deepened. Police had already lodged enquiries with the private security firm that had employed Viktor, the National Social Security Institute, the Interior Ministry, Border Control and prisons across Bulgaria. On 24 April

2009 police assigned to the Ministry of Justice wrote to the court stating that Viktor Georgiev could not be brought forcibly to court because he could not be found.

On 12 May, a police officer dialled the number Viktor had given in his witness statement. Viktor answered. The next day he turned up at a police station and received a subpoena. He was told he now owed a fine for previously failing to appear.

CHAPTER 23

27 May 2009

Sofia Palace of Justice

Simon flipped through his notepad nervously. Not knowing from one hearing to another which witnesses would turn up made it even harder to prepare his questions. When Viktor Georgiev's name was called out, Simon looked over his shoulder at the public seating area. A young man stood up. Simon caught Jock's eye and nodded at him. His son exhaled. *Finally.*

Viktor stared at the defendant. He looked different now, with longer hair and a suit. But he looked surprisingly well, given that he had been in prison for eighteen months. Viktor's gaze turned to the man and woman also standing at the front. He figured they were the dead man's parents and felt for them.

The former security guard at the Sheraton was not nervous about speaking in this very public forum. He began his testimony confidently, but when he got to the part where the group of youths attacked the defendant, he started to feel anxious. Viktor was acutely aware of how hard it would be for the Monovs to hear what had taken place during the last minutes of their son's life. Asked why the group had pushed the foreigner to the ground and beaten him, Viktor said it was inappropriate for him to speculate.

Viktor's account was very similar to what he had previously told Chief Investigating Officer Tanya Alakusheva. He said by the time the Sheraton workers crossed the road the defendant had been twice attacked by the group of Levski fans—once near the metro and once in front of the kiosk. In the attacks at the kiosk, the defendant's head had been hit by something and he had fallen to the ground. Viktor recalled that, as he and his colleagues crossed the road, a car had stopped on an unspecified boulevard and a man had got out to intervene in the fight. By the time Viktor arrived at the square, this man was holding the foreigner on the ground. The defence assumed he was one of the still-unidentified bodyguards to whom other witnesses had referred.

Viktor said he had run thirty or so metres across Maria Louisa. His view of the scene was probably impaired as he concentrated on crossing the boulevard. From Viktor's testimony, it appears that it was during those few seconds that Andrei Monov was stabbed, stumbled to Stamboliyski and fell on the road.

Prosecutor Parvoleta Nikova asked the witness if he knew any of the people in the group personally. Viktor said he didn't. He bristled a little when one of the lawyers for the civil claimants asked him why he had not phoned police straight away. The young man prided himself on doing the right thing and had contacted hotel security, fearing the man being attacked at the metro was a guest. 'I can't answer your question why we didn't call the police immediately,' he answered. 'Maybe it was our mistake.'

Simon was pleased the witness had made it clear that his son had produced a knife only after the first attack had begun and as he was getting up from the ground. The defence thought Viktor most likely did not notice Jock running across the square alone, as his attention would have been focused on the bashing under way. For that reason he might easily have decided that the person being chased was the same person he saw rise from the melee holding a knife. Simon wanted to make it clear that Viktor had indeed seen Jock attacked well before Andrei was stabbed. Using 'boy' to mean 'young man', Viktor replied confidently: 'There were two occasions when the youths were beating the boy—one at the metro, the other at Stamboliyski Boulevard.' Judge Kolev sought further clarification. Viktor's response was unwavering: 'These were two incidents with one and the same person.'

Simon then wanted to know if the youths had surrounded Jock when they attacked him at the kiosk. At one point Viktor said that they had him surrounded as they moved from the metro towards the kiosk, where they remained around him. He could not remember if they hit the defendant from behind. Simon asked if Jock had somehow trapped the group near the kiosk. Viktor said he did not think so.

The prosecutor finished by asking him if he had understood what the defendant had been saying. 'I speak and understand English,' he responded. 'And I heard the boy shouting some swear words . . .' He made no mention of Jock calling out 'No fascism.'

Judge Kolev then turned to Viktor and waived the fine that had been imposed upon him. Viktor left the courtroom, relieved it was over. The Palfreemans had no idea why it had taken so long for him to turn up. By now Simon, like Jock, suspected foul play. Mystery only increased their suspicions.

The Palfreemans were not the only ones jumping at shadows. The Monovs also suspected foul play. At some stage they had requested that the Sheraton car park attendant who had been working with Viktor that night be brought back to court to answer more questions. The prosecutor now asked Lyubomir Tomov if he had known people who were in the group that night. He said he knew no one there. The Monovs' lawyer then asked him if he knew Andrei. 'I don't know Andrei Monov,' Lyubomir responded. 'I have never been his classmate.'

Aksenia Monova stood and questioned him further. She was convinced his testimony was motivated by a pre-existing dislike of her son. 'I live in Lozenets,' he answered steadily. 'I have seen Andrei Monov around, but I don't know him.' The judge dismissed Lyubomir, but Aksenia's lawyer would not let the matter go. He requested that a friend of Andrei's, Vasil Valkov, be summonsed to testify about the relationship between Andrei and Lyubomir—'that is,' he added, 'that they knew each other and were on bad terms with each other.' The prosecutor supported calling the proposed witness, but Dinko objected, saying Lyubomir had already said he did not know Andrei. The judge dismissed Aksenia's lawyer's request.

. . .

The trial was adjourned for a month. But Simon and Helen did not return to Australia just yet. Iliyan's cousin, Sonja, was getting married and they had been invited. It would be a chance to see Jock's Samokov friends under happier circumstances and to thank them again for bringing him food in their absence. The Palfreemans joined the convoy of guests driving behind the groom as he headed to Sonja's place. According to tradition, the groom had to break into his bride's house to take her away from her parents. The guests stood on the footpath urging him on. It was wonderful theatre. After the Orthodox ceremony, folk dancing and drinking at the reception continued long into the night. Simon and Helen were touched that Sonja had included them in the festivities.

. . .

Jock was relieved to be back in the Block. He did not much like being away from it now. He had made good friends there. They accepted him as he was. They knew his story and believed him.

Court just made Jock angry. After more than a year of hearing what the hooligans who'd attacked him had to say, he longed to give the court his side of the story. He was wound up like a spring each hearing day, anticipating the moment when he could speak.

. . .

Eighteen months after the incident, Lindsay Welsh's statement had finally arrived in Sofia and copies of it had been distributed to the appropriate parties. Describing herself as a landscape gardener, Lindsay said that in the bar Jock had talked to Tony (Anton 'Tony' Doychev) about music and that the evening had been 'fine'. She recalled that, as they had been walking to another bar, she had heard shouting coming from the subway. Tony told Jock and her that it came from football hooligans. Tony said he had been beaten up by such people in the past, just because of his clothes.

Shortly after that, Jock said 'someone's being beaten up' and ran 'towards the crowd'. She did not see him carrying a knife at any time. The next thing she saw was what appeared to be the group chasing Jock; then they disappeared from view.

Lindsay said she took off across Stamboliyski to find Jock. Her next recollection was of Jock kneeling on the footpath with his hands in the air. Rocks lay all around him. She was worried about what had happened to him. Then a youth with dark hair had kicked her in the stomach with a blow that threw her backwards to the ground. Tony pulled her away just as she thought the youth was about to stomp on her head. Tony said they had to get out of there because it was dangerous. Lindsay was scared. When she saw police arriving, she assumed they would help Jock.

The detail about Jock having been chased dovetailed with what Nikolai Rabadzhiev and Viktor Georgiev had said took place near the kiosk. It is possible also that she was talking about Jock being chased near the subway, which Viktor Georgiev and Lyubomir Tomov described. But it would be much easier to fit all the pieces together if the recordings from the Ministry of Health could be recovered.

· · ·

2 July 2009

Dr Georgi Angelov was at work in the Ministry of Health building. He was sixty-eight and planned to retire later that year after a career spent mostly as an army doctor. While his title was duty doctor, he was not at the Ministry of Health to care for patients. Angelov was on standby in case of any kind of crisis with medical implications, such as an earthquake or an outbreak of disease. His job was to decide whether and when the Health Minister needed to be notified and emergency services called in. On overnight shifts, after the security guards left, he also kept an eye on the bank of CCTV screens and changed over the recording tapes when they ran out of space. He believed the tapes were kept until all of them were full. That had always seemed to him to be a long time. Once full, they were erased and reused.

That morning Angelov had been instructed to give evidence in a murder trial. As he walked to the Palace of Justice, he thought about what he had read of the case. He presumed he was a witness for the prosecution.

Angelov told the court that on the night in question he had been the only person in the Ministry of Health building. The security guards had gone at 10 p.m., leaving the alarm on. He was on the mezzanine floor, overlooking St Nedelya Square and the Sheraton hotel. There was a bank of CCTV monitors there and, although Angelov was not required to watch them constantly, he did look at them every so often. 'It is very quiet at night,' he said, 'and suddenly there was an uproar. It wasn't loud talking, but rather an uproar—people were shouting and some were screaming in fear.' He told the court the noise was coming from the corner of Stamboliyski and Maria Louisa boulevards, but he couldn't see anything on the screens. Angelov opened the window and looked out to see what was going on. All he could see was 'a young girl with white or very light clothes, a knee-length coat, trousers and fair hair' shouting something. Just as suddenly as the uproar had started, it stopped. The girl called out, 'Jock, Jock', but there was no response. She then headed down to the subway and out of his view.

It was not until later in the day that Angelov learned that a murder had been committed in the square. No one had come to interview him about what had happened, but that day someone had been in touch with the doctor who took over from him on the next shift.

The usually mild-mannered doctor was irritated by the defence's line of questioning. 'I couldn't see people from where I was,' he said. But the defence team was not satisfied. It seemed to be preoccupied with the CCTV recordings. In response to Simon's questions, Angelov confirmed that there were two stationary cameras attached to the entrance of the building. 'One of them points at Bulbank, towards the metro,' he said. 'I saw a young girl. The cameras covered the whole pavement in front [of the Ministry of Health] . . . The range of the camera is almost to the entrance of the subway.'

The defence seemed to be suggesting that Angelov had not been paying attention that night or that he had been away from the control room at the time of the melee, only returning as it ended. Or perhaps he had fallen asleep. 'It's not my job to monitor the cameras,' he protested.

Jock told Angelov that he had been pushed against the ministry door and was banging on it for help. Surely the doctor had heard the noise. 'I did not hear anything banging against the doors of the ministry,' Angelov said.

'There was no one at the entrance of the ministry. Moreover, I neither heard nor saw anyone.' For Angelov, this question proved that Jock was untruthful. St Nedelya Square was very quiet at that time of night and you could hear everything outside, even footsteps.

Jock asked what had happened to the recordings that were made that night. The doctor said that as far as he knew, nothing relevant had been recorded. 'If there had been a person [at the door], he would have been in the footage, because there is another camera inside that monitors and records twenty-four hours a day.' The Ministry of Health had not mentioned this camera in its correspondence with the investigator and prosecutor. Yet it must have been recording through the glass doors. Rather than ask what had happened to its tapes, the defence wanted to know whether police had talked to Angelov about the incident. It was intent on establishing whether police had questioned all possible witnesses: 'I heard about it, but I wasn't present when they looked at the footage the next day,' Angelov said.

This was a bombshell. According to the Ministry of Health, all relevant recordings had been erased after the investigator failed to retrieve them before they were automatically erased in the scheduled tape recycling process: no one had seen them because there was none to see. The defence pressed him for details about exactly who had come to see the footage. 'I can't say and I don't know who looked at the footage,' responded Angelov. Was it police who had come? 'I don't know if police came the next day,' he replied.

Angelovs' testimony had raised more questions that it answered. Who had come to enquire about the recordings on the day of the tragedy? Had they watched the material and, if so, what did they see? What, if anything, had they done with the recording? It now appeared the camera would have captured a far greater area than the Ministry of Health had advised the investigator and the prosecutor. It seemed much more likely now that the camera would have captured the area between the subway and Bulbank that the traffic camera had missed. The Ministry of Health had never said anything about the camera that filmed the entrance from inside the building. What had happened to that recording and to that hard drive?

The next witness that day was Jock. Guards moved him the metre from his father's side to the witness microphone and stood in the aisle behind him as he addressed the bench. Simon's heart was in his throat. He knew his son was angry that witnesses had been allowed to change with impunity their accounts of what had happened, that the hearings had dragged on for so long and that he had been unable to do more than ask a few questions. He hoped against hope that Jock would be restrained. As his son spoke, Simon relaxed. Sure, Jock rambled and jumped from point to point in a way that sometimes made him hard to follow. But he was telling his story at last, and doing so in a measured voice. Jock's grandfather Tony, his brother Spencer and his Samokov friends were all there to hear it. The Monovs sat at the civil claimants' bar table, at once listening intently to see if Jock contradicted his earlier police statements and appalled by the audacity of his claims.

Simon and Jock had argued some time before about whether Jock should refer to the men whom the youths had attacked as Gypsies. Simon feared this might put the court offside. Jock had disagreed, but now he went along with his father's wishes. He said he had run across the square when he saw the youths chasing 'someone', whom they pushed to the ground. He had gone around the group to get to the man. By the time he reached him, most of the youths were also there, some beating the man.

'I pushed two or three of them in order to get in,' said Jock. 'I knelt, took him by the shoulder to check if he would react, and asked him in Bulgarian if he was OK. He didn't respond. His eyes were closed. I stood up and pushed aside the boy who was closest to me. At first they were shocked, then they started coming at me.' At this point, Jock said, he was between them and the man on the ground. 'I took out the knife, raised it in the air very high above my head and with my left hand I gestured at them to pull back, shouting in Bulgarian, "Get back, get back, back off." They started to retreat. Some of them tried to come close to me, but one . . . grabbed his friends and pulled them aside.'

Jock described how the youths had backed away as he slowly walked towards them. 'When there was enough distance between me and them, I went back to the man on the ground to check on him,' he said. 'And then all—not all, *some*—of the group came at me when I had my back turned to them. I turned around quickly, waved the knife from left to right and said "Get back."'

Jock said that, as he began to retreat, the whole group had surrounded him, trying to kick and punch him. 'Then they threw rocks, white pavers. All of them were hitting me. Most of them I blocked with my left arm raised in front of my face. I held the knife in the air and, every time someone would come to attack me, I would wave the knife from left to right, but not to hurt them, only to scare them away. I was constantly going in circles because every time I had my back to one of them, they would attack me. Then someone hit me, I fell on the ground, propped on my elbow. They began to kick me, to hit me. Then the police came.'

Dinko asked Jock for more detail about the attack on him once the melee had moved away from the metro and closer to the kiosk.

'While I was waving the knife, I was turning around the whole time because they had me surrounded,' Jock responded, speaking faster now. 'And when my back was turned to one of them, then I was attacked. Then I would turn around to this man and wave the knife; the man would jump back and then I would immediately have to turn around again, because I was being attacked from behind in the same way by someone else. And this just went on and on. The only time they stopped doing that was when one of them would come at me and they would make way for him.' Jock said the youths picked up pavers and lunged at him. He raised his arms above his head to demonstrate how the youths had then thrown the pavers. 'I can't remember how many times I was hit, but it was a lot. I can't remember. My arm was the only obstacle for the . . . pavers.' In response to questioning by Antoan's lawyer, Jock said his left arm still hurt and he still had no sensation in two fingers.

Prosecutor Nikova asked the defendant why he had come to Bulgaria and why he had a knife in his pocket. He said he had wanted to see a white Christmas and his Samokov friends. He took the knife, he added, because he had been attacked several times before while walking in Bulgaria. He described the attack on Simo, the Gypsy he had met at a concert.

The prosecutor asked Jock to describe the moment when he first saw the man who was beaten. Jock said it was when the man was 'near the kiosk with the group'. How close did Jock get to him? 'Some of the boys from the group grabbed him and shook him, swearing and shouting at him . . . I was closest to him—I touched him—when I knelt on the ground.'

Antoan's lawyer asked when Jock last saw 'the boy' he claimed had been attacked. Jock said it was when he returned to check on him, at which point Jock was attacked from behind. As to the stabbings, 'No one from the group was stabbed with my knife,' Jock said. 'When the police came, I saw blood on the knife and said, "Shit, where was I stabbed?" because when I was on the ground, I saw that the knife was about a metre away from me and some of the men were coming and trying to pick it up. The people who were bodyguards were pushing and stopping them, preventing them from taking the knife. While I was defending myself, I can't remember if the knife was with me the whole time, because I was distracted. When I was on my stomach, the knife wasn't on me and the people were fighting around me and spitting at me, still trying to attack me.' Jock told Antoan's lawyer that he could not remember what had happened immediately after he was hit on the head.

The lawyer asked him why Jock had seen fit to rush towards the group in the first place. 'When the conflict with the group began, I could just as well have let them beat the man on the ground,' said Jock. Well, said the lawyer, since he was outnumbered, why had he persisted? 'I stayed [there] because there were twenty people who were beating one on the ground.'

The lawyer turned to the attack on the defendant. 'I wasn't attacked by all the twenty people—there wasn't enough space. They attacked me by taking turns, they were kind of swapping places with one another,' said Jock, who was struggling to describe what he had told his father was like a rolling rugby maul. 'The ones behind me threw rocks; those in front of me were trying to kick or hit me. The distance between me and them was about half a metre and, when they tried to hit or kick me, I waved the knife from left to right.' He made a horizontal movement with his hand backwards and forwards.

Antoan's lawyer asked what skills Jock had learned in the Army. Did he have knife and close-combat training? Jock listed all the topics covered in the first weeks of basic training: First Aid, Chemical and Nuclear Attacks, Radioactive Attacks, Gas Attacks, Shooting, Discipline, Marching, Weapon Maintenance, Push-ups. 'Close-contact fighting and knife fighting were not included. Knives were prohibited on the base,' he said.

Jock's father began his questioning. It was a surreal experience for both of them. Simon asked Jock what it had felt like when he was knocked to the ground. 'The best way to describe it is like when you step on the front brake of the motorbike,' Jock replied, 'when it is pressed too hard and when you rise from the seat—at that moment [you think] everything's over. Just everything's finished—my life is finished.' He paused. 'This is the body's reaction to the fear of death. I don't know, I just thought I was dead.'

Trying to establish that Jock's actions were premeditated, the prosecutor asked him to return to the moment when he first moved away from his friends at the Happy restaurant's garden. 'I watched the group coming out of the metro before heading towards them,' he said. 'I don't know how long I watched it.' The prosecutor alluded to Tony's comments that he had not seen anything and that he had tried to stop Jock running off. 'Tony did not try to stop me before I went,' Jock said bluntly. 'He was looking at his phone.' As far as Jock was concerned Anton 'Tony' Doychev had not seen what had been going on because he was preoccupied with loading credit onto a mobile. It did not cross Jock's mind that the Bulgarian's testimony could be interpreted in any other way.

The questioning over, Jock moved closer to his father. Having finally said his piece in court, he felt flat. He had expected a more probing examination. He took a breath and tried to focus on the rest of the hearing.

A forensic expert was called to discuss the blood alcohol report. Despite the testimonies of some group members that no one had drunk much, neither the Monovs nor their counsel contested the estimation that Andrei had a blood alcohol concentration of 0.29 per cent when he died.

That was it for the day. All in all, Simon thought, it had been a good day for the defence. He left the courthouse to debrief with Dinko in a nearby coffee shop, his backpack bobbing through the city crowd.

. . .

5 July 2009

In the Bulgarian national elections, the Bulgarian Socialist Party lost power and Interior Minister Mihail Mikov went to the opposition benches. Jock dared to wonder whether the change of government might augur well for him. By now he was sure that the Monovs had close ties to the Socialist Party, as well as to the Interior Ministry. His father objected every time he used the word 'corruption' in reference to the investigation and trial. Was he blind? Jock wondered.

. . .

16 July 2009
Sofia Palace of Justice

Hristo Monov paced at the front of the courtroom. Today the experts who had written the psychological profile of Jock were to present a second report; this one responded to the defence request for a profile of Jock. Hristo was ready for them.

In their new report, the psychiatric panel had described Jock as 'harmoniously structured', 'extroverted', 'socially mature' and 'spontaneous, but with good intra-psychic control'. The three experts said he was 'not apt to dominate and not aggressive'. They found he was motivated by a 'strong desire to fight for social justice' and to defend people who had suffered from discriminatory behaviour. His value system and social orientation evidently came from his extended family, in particular from his grandfathers. Jock's paternal grandfather had been a political scientist and his maternal one a combat Army doctor during World War II. On the question of what had motivated him that night, they concluded that Jock had seen violence being done to someone from a minority group. When he rushed to help that 'weak' person, he found that his arrival did not stop the attack. 'Surprised by that and facing the group alone, he immediately switched to "awe-inspiring" behaviour.' This was certainly not the picture that Hristo Monov, who prided himself as being an expert in psychology, had of the defendant.

The prosecutor had no questions. Instead, the Monovs' lawyer wanted to know when the examination of the defendant occurred and how long it had taken. Forensic psychiatrist Boris Shtarbanov, the head of the panel, explained that they had seen Jock three times and had spent 'hours' with him, but he could not specify how many.

It was now Hristo's turn. 'How many items are there in Buss-Durkee?' he asked Lilyana Behar, the forensic psychologist. The Buss-Durkee Hostility Inventory is a set of seventy-five true/false questions designed to measure hostility levels. 'I think that there are seven scales,' responded Behar, clearly irritated. 'I have passed my exam in medical psychology and I have no intention of sitting the exam for a second time.'

Hristo persisted. His questions now suggested that her testing had been impaired because of the need for translation. 'In psychology there is one test,' Behar said firmly. 'The test doesn't think; that is the psychologist's job.' The statements put to the subject had been very simple, she said. They were unlikely to be confused in translation. Where there was inconsistency, she asked follow-up questions. Hristo asked to see the notes Behar had taken during the examination. She said she would be happy to produce the chart she had constructed from the test, which showed no extremes, but she was not accustomed to producing her notes.

From the psychologist's responses, it appears that Hristo was insinuating that the panel had not undertaken tests that might have shown that the defendant's sociopathic tendencies arose from his upbringing. Behar said she had not run a test to measure Jock's value system. Her picture of that came from what he had told them about his family and his life. She had ascertained that he was particularly influenced by the values of his grandfathers. She said they had not discussed whether he had a warm relationship with his parents.

Shtarbanov was frustrated by what he regarded as Hristo's arrogance and intervened. He reminded the court that the panel's conclusion had not rested solely on the psychological testing but had also been firmly rooted in psychiatric observation and experience. 'Since 1962 I haven't seen anyone in a Bulgarian court asking for the original notes of people who are examining someone for the purpose of making a psychological expert report,' he added.

'My request concerns the principles of objectivity and scientific methodologies,' exclaimed Hristo. 'There are no grounds for accepting this report.'

As the court took in this outburst, Dinko asked the panel if the defendant was motivated by anti-establishment attitudes. 'No,' said Shtarbanov firmly, adding that the experts saw no sign that Jock was 'unwilling to conform to social requirements and regulations'.

Shtarbanov said that he was choosing his words carefully, mindful of Hristo Monov's feelings. He then explained that, as head of the expert panel, he had agreed with Behar's use of the disputed personality test in Bulgarian because of her familiarity with it. He also said the panel had agreed unanimously in their assessment of the defendant's responses to the testing. The judge accepted the report and overruled the request for notes.

Now it was the turn of the panel of two psychologists and a psychiatrist that the court had appointed at the request of the defence. Its task had been to assess whether Andrei Monov and his cohorts had exhibited the characteristics of a group of football fans on the night. The experts had not interviewed any of the members of the group, but on the basis of court documents, they decided there was no evidence of this. They said football fans were bonded by the shared experience of watching a match. The group walking from one club to another that night was a diverse one, brought together by a desire to celebrate the coming new year.

Simon was clearly perplexed. 'But what about the witness who called Jock and his friend *chorbar*?' he asked, referring to the insulting term for a fan from a rival team which Anton 'Tony' Doychev had testified to hearing. One expert said she had not seen that reference. Another interjected, saying that, irrespective of what the youths had said or sung, football allegiance was not the defining characteristic of the group that night.

The examination of this panel over, Judge Kolev said the trial would resume in two months' time.

CHAPTER 24

9 September 2009

Newcastle, Australia

Reading the BBC News website, Simon frowned. The British Secretary of State for Justice, Jack Straw, had announced a Royal pardon for Michael Shields, the young Liverpool soccer fan found guilty of attempted murder in Bulgaria and later transferred to the United Kingdom. It was the first time a British citizen had been granted a Royal pardon after being convicted abroad.

Shields claimed he had not been present at the crime scene; another man publicly confessed to the crime but later retracted his confession. Although Simon could see some similarities to Jock's case, he had carefully avoided discussing the Shields case in Bulgaria because of the strength of public feeling about it. He felt sure that the news of the pardon would work against Jock's interests by increasing Bulgarians' determination that foreigners should not be allowed to get away with murder.

At the end of September, Simon, Helen and Simon's eighty-three-year-old mother, Barbara, flew to London. Geri joined them on the flight to Sofia. Simon was exhausted, but he caught a taxi straight to the prison. '*Blagodaria*,' he mumbled politely as he paid the driver. 'Thank you.'

When he entered the visitors area, his son looked up and grinned. 'Welcome to my home,' Jock said, bursting into laughter. Simon's tensed-up shoulders relaxed. It was all right.

. . .

On 28 September, Maria Grozeva finally took the witness stand. The forensic doctor had grown increasingly concerned about the way the trial was being conducted. She believed there was real doubt that the defendant had inflicted the fatal wound on Andrei Monov, but her role as a court-appointed expert was strictly to answer questions put to her.

Given that Jock claimed to have been under attack, the court wanted to know more about the injuries he had sustained that night. Grozeva said the only injury evident was the one at his elbow, which he had received when he fell to the ground. Under examination from Dinko, she agreed that the defendant could have received the injury while trying to defend himself against concrete pavers being thrown at him. 'He wore coarse clothing,' she explained. 'The injury might have been received from a blow and not just from a fall to the ground.'

Yet when Simon pressed her about any further injuries, Grozeva said simply that Jock had not complained of any when she examined him. She had not seen the trickles of blood on his trousers described by another expert, and she thought the pins and needles he had experienced in his left hand could have been caused by the handcuffs.

After Grozeva testified, Dinko put it to the judge that the traffic-camera and subway CCTV recordings cast doubt on the prosecutor's version of events. However, given the low resolution and poor quality of the recordings, it would be helpful to find out if someone had been monitoring the cameras at the time and seen what had happened. If such a person could be located, they might at the very least shed more light on what the figures were doing and what had happened out of the traffic camera's range.

Dinko asked if the court could track down this person and have him or her testify. He also asked if the CCTV expert could be re-examined after the operator gave testimony, and repeated his request for the computer on which the Ministry of Health CCTV recordings had been stored, including the hard drive.

. . .

29 October 2009

The surveillance-camera operator from Sofia Police Headquarters appeared
in court the next hearing day. Nadezhda Peycheva said that she was able
to operate the traffic cameras individually if need be. However, as she
monitored many screens, she did not follow every camera all the time.
When she got a call from police to say that there had been an incident at
St Nedelya Square, she had looked at the relevant screen and seen some
twenty youths running around opposite the Sheraton hotel. Then she had
seen a man on the ground with youths surrounding him. The youths
appeared to be shouting at him. After that, some sort of security guard
intervened. She had tried to zoom in on the action. A blonde woman in
a white hooded jacket started fussing over the man on the ground, and
then police arrived. At that point she had rewound the tape to see what
had started the brawl.

Peycheva said there was a blind spot for twenty metres in front of the
metro, making it impossible for her to see the area in which she surmised
the drama had begun. But she had seen a group of twenty boys and girls
running in a confused manner and then a large object thrown on the road,
which broke into pieces; a man had then run in and picked something up.
She said she had phoned police immediately so they could go and collect
the object.

Simon sighed. If the broken concrete pavers and tiles thrown that night
had been tested, they might have helped demonstrate the extent to which
Jock had been under attack. With no other experts to give evidence, the
court adjourned early. Dinko told the Palfreemans that a letter had been
tabled from the Ministry of Health in response to the court's request for
everything to do with the computer, including the hard drive. The letter
said the video cassettes and technical equipment had not been kept when
the surveillance system was replaced.

Simon and Helen flew home, knowing that in less than a fortnight
they would again have to endure the long, cramped flight to Sofia. Simon
was finding the trips to and from Australia harder and harder to make.
Not knowing what would happen to his son, he dreaded leaving Jock. He
dreaded the journey and the jet lag. He dreaded returning to a trial he now

suspected was farcical. He still felt for the Monovs, but he hated watching the way Hristo Monov conducted himself in court. He just hoped that the judge would see through what the defence considered to be lies, and that the failure to collect critical evidence would favour, not harm, his son.

Meanwhile, Judge Georgi Kolev's career was rocketing ahead. He was promoted from deputy head of the Sofia City Court to head of the court. This would not be the end of his rise through the ranks of the Bulgarian judicial system.

. . .

9 November 2009

One of the forensic doctors who had examined Antoan Zahariev with Associate Professor Maria Grozeva had failed to appear several times. Finally he did, and examination of their joint report could proceed. Grozeva told the court that Antoan's level of intoxication helped explain why he had not realised immediately that he had been cut. She also said that whoever cut him had most probably been beside him at the time, but that it was impossible to gauge the speed of the thrust because both of them were in motion. This was in keeping with Simon's own understanding of knife wounds. In response to questions from Dinko, Grozeva said it was impossible to identify which weapon had caused Antoan's wound.

While Grozeva gave her testimony, two of the forensic doctors who had performed the autopsy waited anxiously just outside the courtroom. They were due to testify next. But their colleague had not turned up and was not answering his phone.

Associate Professor Stanislav Hristov, still under investigation in relation to the body parts scandal, had just been arrested again, this time for drink driving. His blood alcohol concentration had been 0.26 per cent, well over the legal limit. If he was found guilty, Hristov could be sentenced to a year in jail. Without Hristov present, the two other forensic doctors who had performed the autopsy with him were unable to testify, and the trial was postponed yet again. After the hearing Maria Grozeva passed by Dinko in the courthouse and mentioned her concerns about Hristov's autopsy report to him. Dinko was intrigued. But for the moment his concern was with the interruption to the trial.

Four days later, it was 13 November, Jock's twenty-third birthday. By now Simon had made more than twenty trips to and from Australia. He had spent more than 480 hours flying more than 380,000 kilometres, or nine times the circumference of the earth. He could not face another flight. Helen and he decided to remain in Europe for a month.

. . .

18 November 2009

Simon arrived at the courthouse early for the last day of hearings. He wanted to make sure the defence team had seats. This final session was held in a small room, where the parties sat at tables in a U formation. The judges and the jury panel were in the middle, sitting at a table on the same level as everyone else; the prosecutor and civil claimants were one side and the defence opposite them. There was less formality here. Spectators sat alongside the victims and the defence because there was very little standing room.

Simon and Helen had spent many months researching knife wounds, and Simon had with him the current editions of two classic texts: Knight's *Forensic Pathology* and *The Encyclopedia of Forensic Sciences*, which warned against making assertions about the force of a knife thrust. Hristo Monov had drawn on his area of expertise to contest the psychological evidence. Now it was Simon's turn to draw on his background in pathology.

Associate Professor Stanislav Hristov was first on the witness stand. It appears from the court transcript that neither the prosecution nor the civil claimants asked him anything. The defence does not appear to have raised any questions about Hristov's suitability as a witness; the Palfreemans were unaware that he had been arrested for more than drink driving. But Simon and Dinko had a list of questions about Hristov's report.

In the report Hristov had said that the perpetrator had delivered the blow to Andrei with considerable force. This suggested a deliberate, premeditated act of murder. The defence wanted to show that doctors could not measure how much force had been used to inflict a wound. Even if they could, a forcible blow was not necessarily at odds with Jock's claim that he had swiped the knife from left to right in self-defence.

Hristov insisted that his report was accurate. He said the lacerations in the corner of the wound suggested that the knife had only one 'cutting edge'. As there was no sign of additional lacerations, which would have indicated that either the body or the blade had moved, the perpetrator's blow must have been 'sudden and forceful'.

Citing passages from the medical textbooks, Dinko suggested that the kinetic energy produced as the body and the knife came together depended on a range of factors, such as the sharpness of the knife tip and the movement both of the arm yielding the knife and of Andrei's body. Hristov both agreed that the resulting kinetic force was what mattered and continued to argue that this depended on the force of the blow. Dinko put to the doctor that an unimpeded sharp-tipped knife moved through a body like a knife through butter—even with minimal force propelling it. Someone who moved into the path of a knife moving from side to side could still suffer a catastrophic wound.

Visibly irritated, Hristov said the most significant factor in the kinetic energy was the speed of the blow. Dinko then asked if it was possible that the victim might actually have fallen or been pushed towards the moving knife. Even more irritated, Hristov replied that of course it was possible, but if that had happened, he would have expected to find damage such as bruising around the wound, caused by the hilt of the knife. There had been no such damage. 'The blow was a quick, strong, sharp thrust and withdrawal of the weapon [took place] without causing any displacement,' Hristov said.

Dinko changed tack and asked the doctor about the nearly identical smooth cuts on Andrei's seventh and eighth ribs that had bothered Maria Grozeva. Surely this indicated that the wound was caused by a double-edged blade rather than, as Hristov had concluded, a blade, 'with a single cutting edge'. Simon looked at Dinko astonished. They had not discussed this before the hearing. Hristov replied: 'The injuries can lead to the conclusion that somewhere at the beginning of the blade in question there were well-pronounced cutting edges.' When Dinko pressed further about this, Hristov said the tip of the blade found at the scene technically had a double edge.

To demonstrate that Andrei had not been standing absolutely still, Dinko drew the witness's attention to the traffic-camera recording, which he said showed Andrei moving towards Jock just before he was stabbed. The lawyer reminded Hristov that the stab wound was below Andrei's armpit. Didn't this suggest either that Andrei had raised his arm defensively or that he was in the act of gesturing at Jock, possibly even throwing something at him? Surely someone fleeing wouldn't have his arms raised?

Hristov said for such a wound to have been inflicted, Andrei's left arm could have been slightly backwards, forwards or slightly up; there only needed to be a slight angling of the shoulder.

Turning to Andrei Monov's 0.29 per cent blood alcohol content, Dinko asked how such a high level of intoxication might have influenced Andrei's behaviour. The defence lawyer wanted to develop an alternative scenario from the concerted and vicious attack described by the prosecutor, one that put more responsibility for what happened on the shoulders of the victim. Hristov responded that such an analysis would have to be done in conjunction with a psychiatrist and a psychologist, adding that the same blood alcohol level could cause different aberrations in behaviour in different individuals.

Simon felt that the forensic doctor had not yet explained how the force and strength of the blow could be measured. He then suggested to Hristov that surely a strong blow, driving the blade in to the hilt, would have resulted in bruising. But Hristov said that that did not necessarily follow. It all depended on the angle of the knife as it entered the body, as well as the thickness of clothing.

Simon questioned the forensic doctor's measurement of the wound canal (twelve to thirteen centimetres), which he regarded as uncannily similar in length to that of the blade (12.3 centimetres). He put it to Hristov that, given the complex interplay of the victim's posture and the movement of his rib cage, heart and lungs, the wound canal might reasonably be expected to be longer or shorter than the blade. 'These are the ABCs of forensic medicine,' Hristov retorted, clearly resenting what he perceived as a put-down from a fellow pathologist. Simon was flustered. Was he asking the right questions? Was he making his point with the court? He feared not.

Dinko then addressed the judges, saying Hristov's testimony had raised more questions than it answered. He requested that a second panel of forensic experts reassess the depth of the wound canal and try to gauge what role the victim's extreme level of intoxication might have played in his wounding. He wanted this panel to include a psychologist and a psychiatrist.

'For the first time, some double-edged [characteristic] of the weapon was mentioned,' Dinko added. 'So far, in the reports that we have at our disposal, the knife has been described as having one cutting edge. But the fact that we have two adjacent ribs with identical cuts leads us to the conclusion that the knife had two edges. This issue calls for clarification.'

Dinko also said it was important for the defence to have the opportunity to test whether the blow could have been caused in a manner other than that described by the witness and friend of the victim, Martin Stoilov, whose account had been referenced in the pathology reports.

Prosecutor Parvoleta Nikova objected immediately, saying the existing reports were complete; there was nothing to add. Hristov had already testified that the victim's blood alcohol level was irrelevant, as the same level could affect different people in different ways.

Judge Kolev overruled Dinko's request, saying that Hristov had answered the questions regarding the wound canal and double rib cuts. As for the question about alcohol levels, everything that should have been looked at had been.

Simon stared at the judge in disbelief. Jock was smouldering with rage. But nothing they said now would make any difference. So they said nothing.

While Hristov had been testifying, Yordan Dalukov sat at the back of the small courtroom. As a research associate at the Institute of Forensic Science and Criminology in Sofia, his specialty was analysing CCTV recordings. That morning he had spoken to the court technician and been surprised to learn that the court had no capacity to play on a big screen the recordings from the traffic and metro cameras that he intended to present. He had wanted everyone to watch as he analysed the sequence of events captured in the recordings. As he mulled over how he could possibly achieve this with no equipment but a laptop computer, a terrible cry came from one side of the courtroom. He started and looked up. Everyone else stared, too. A court official had just entered the room, carrying the jacket Andrei Monov had worn. It needed to be formally identified as material evidence. Aksenia Monova was trying to get around the horseshoe of tables to get closer to it. 'Look at the blood!' she screamed. 'Look at the blood!'

Aksenia had seldom showed any emotion during the hearings, but now she shrieked in agony. Her cry pierced Simon's heart. Jock too was moved. His indignation with the civil claimants' power to steer the questioning and contest the admissibility of evidence had sometimes caused him to forget how much the Monovs were suffering.

Judge Kolev nodded towards the jacket, which lay on the evidence table, and an assistant picked it up and took it out of the courtroom.

Aksenia's emotion subsided, and the technician now placed a court laptop on the evidence table. The defence team, the civil claimants, some of the young people who had been at the incident, and a few general spectators closed in on the expert who sat at the table describing what he saw on the screen. Kolev could not see through the jostling crowd, and, according to Simon, only one of the lay judges went over to watch Dalukov's presentation. The noise in the room was so loud that only those very close to the screen could hear the expert. Neither the prosecutor nor the Monovs asked him anything. But Simon had many questions about the timing of events, and he kept notes as Dalukov spoke.

Dalukov pointed out the group emerging from the metro with their arms in the air. They appeared to be either singing or chanting. Some of them seemed to exchange words with two people whom they chased out of view of the traffic camera. Simon asked how many people were chasing after the two figures. 'Twelve,' Dalukov replied.

As the questioning continued, Simon grew increasingly anxious about the fact that the stenographer was not typing at all. Indeed, he recalls that at one point she rose and moved away from her table.

Simon was again struck by how much more evidence there was in this recording than in the series of still frames in the expert report provided to the court. He very much wanted the opportunity to review the video in a quiet and orderly manner. He could not be sure that any of those present were seeing all that the recordings revealed.

Distressed that the judge was not even looking at the screen, Simon leaned across to Dinko and asked him to complain that the stenographer had failed to record the discussion. He recalls being taken aback when the typist then asked Dinko what had been said. The judge gave her permission to include some of what Dinko had told her. *Jock's right*, Simon thought. *This is a circus.*

The official transcript of Dalukov's testimony is just twelve lines long. It is the most striking example of the incompleteness of the court transcripts. Even if the bench had been able to hear Dalukov clearly and see the small laptop screen, and even if their recall of what they had seen and heard was accurate, a full record of questions asked and testimony given in these proceedings would be crucial to any future appeal to a higher court.

As Dalukov was leaving the courtroom he was approached by the court technician, who was there to ensure there were no hitches with the DVD. 'You should have said that you could see the defendant stab Andrei Monov,' the assistant whispered to him, clearly annoyed. 'I could see it.'

Dalukov looked at the man, as if surprised by the request. 'It's not my job to give the prosecutor proof that does not exist,' he replied.

Later Dalukov reflected on what he had seen. In the moments before someone had fallen on Stamboliyski, he had seen what he assumed was the defendant in the middle of a melee between the kiosk and the Ministry of Health entrance. Members of the group had been coming at him, withdrawing and then returning towards him. It had been like a dance, with them trying to scare him and him trying to scare them back. Just before the figure he assumed was Andrei Monov fell on the road, Dalukov had seen two figures facing each other, both moving. But he had not been able to tell if there was any contact between them.

For all their lack of clarity, the surveillance-camera recordings were the final and most objective witnesses to the incident. Dalukov believed this would not be the last time a court would seek his views about them.

. . .

Night after night, Simon wrote and rewrote the summary he would present to the court. Simon now believed every part of his son's story. In his view, the sequence of events shown in the CCTV images matched the independent witnesses' accounts, and both sets of evidence corroborated Jock's version. Parts of the statements by Andrei's friends also backed up his story. Those who had changed their account of what happened were clearly unreliable witnesses.

Simon took the advice of the Australian consular staff and got copies made of Jock's passport photographs and a form ready for him to sign. If the judge acquitted his son, Simon wanted to get him out of the country fast.

CHAPTER 25

2 December 2009

Sofia, Bulgaria

Helen and Simon took the same tram they always did. Helen had a seat and watched Simon as he stood, hanging on to the rail with one hand while he flipped through his notepad with the other. They were both anxious. At the courthouse, they saw the nuns, along with Geri, Ash Hart, and Dobri and Sonja, two of Jock's Samokov friends. At dinner the night before, Simon had told Ash that he thought in a worst case scenario Jock might get eight to ten years. He had already served two, so Simon could live with six more. Jock acknowledged that he bore some responsibility for the tragedy, since he had drawn a knife.

In a blaze of camera flashes, Jock was escorted from the holding cell to the courtroom, his hands shackled behind him. His hair was slicked back, and he wore his suit and a red tie. He was tired and tense.

Dinko approached his client at the bar table, said a few words, then straightened the young man's tie. Simon was surprised: Dinko had never previously shown Jock any sign of affection. He turned to his son and also adjusted Jock's tie. The camera crews were shooed away and a hush came over the courtroom. Prosecutor Parvoleta Nikova approached the bench first. Recapping what she had written in the indictment, she said Anton 'Tony' Doychev's testimony confirmed that the defendant had clearly been out to kill. According to her, Doychev had seen a group of some twenty youths standing at the lights as though about to cross the road. The defendant had then run towards them with murderous intent, brandishing his knife 'ferociously and chaotically' and shouting 'No fascism.'

The prosecutor said it was clear from the testimonies of the Sheraton workers, including Viktor Georgiev, that Andrei Monov had already been stabbed by the time they started watching the melee. She did not refer to the chase that was evident in the traffic-camera recording. Again her summary suggested that the events played out in just one part of the square.

Nikova argued that Jock had not been provoked; instead, fuelled by talk of fascists, he wanted to show off. She said the attack on Andrei Monov and Antoan Zahariev and the attempted attack on Tony 'the Tall' Yordanov had been 'well planned' and 'aimed at vital organs'. She concluded that the group had thrown rocks only in response to the attack on Andrei Monov and Antoan Zahariev, an understandable attempt to stop the violence and protect their friends.

Hristo Monov slowly approached the bench. Less than one metre now separated the two fathers, both, in their own ways, fighting for their sons. 'Many times in my professional career I have had to stand before people who had suffered from the same thing that happened to me,' the psychologist said, addressing the judges. 'And I always found a way to explain their grief and to help them. I have no words to describe my grief. On the 28th of December 2007 my life just ended. Thanks to my friends, some of whom are here in this room, thanks to the solidarity of the normal part of Bulgarian society, my wife and I found the strength to go on with our lives. I realise the great responsibility which rests with you, but I ask you to prevent any other parents from experiencing what my wife and I have gone through.'

Hristo's voice became more strident. 'Not for a moment did the one who killed my son repent; not for a moment did he feel guilty for having committed a sin. This man is a sociopath, and no matter when he leaves prison he will do the same again because this is [what gives] meaning to his life.'

Simon had his head down, trying to hear Galina's translation. 'But there is one other man who cannot be punished by the laws,' she said quietly. 'And that is Simon Palfreeman. His son is his creation; he was formed in his family and became a murderer.' Hristo turned to Simon. 'Whatever happens, whatever his sentence, you will receive the most horrific verdict—a son a murderer! And no matter what kind of campaign you organise—whether you order Australian TV to make films disgracing our country, in which your son's friends take part—you will still be the father of a murderer.

'And there's no need to choose my son's name to have a campaign in support of your son,' Hristo added, referring to a rally some of Jock's friends had held outside Parliament House in Canberra several days before.

Hristo then turned to Dinko Kanchev. 'And you, mister,' he thundered, pointing a finger at the lawyer, who fidgeted with his moustache. 'Upon you too the shame will hang, because you have disrespected the memory of my son. Where do you see fascists among these people?' he continued, waving his arms in the direction of Andrei's friends. 'In many years to come, you will meet them in the street and I don't know how you're going to look them in the eye.' Hristo turned back to the bench. 'My plea is that not a single [other] parent go through this.' He sat down.

Aksenia Monova's footsteps were audible as she approached the bench. No one whispered. No one coughed. As the victim's mother faced the judges, the courtroom was silent. 'The defendant is a young man who comes to a foreign country, who comes to Sofia without identity papers. He doesn't have a passport; he doesn't have a mobile phone, which is common for all young people. He carries a thirty-centimetre knife and a screwdriver, which are among the items seized from him,' she said. 'For me this undoubtedly goes to his intent to do evil to other people.

'It took him just one blow to turn a healthy boy into a corpse. How many bruises did my son have on his face . . .' Aksenia did not finish her sentence, paused, and tried to regain her composure. 'Hasn't the defence seen the bloody pictures in the [forensic] album—how the heart was cut? This is a blow from a professional killer. This is not an accidental blow. This is not a blow inflicted during a skirmish or a fall. This is the deliberate blow of a professional killer.' She looked down. 'For me Andrei was the most beloved person. He made my life worthwhile. It's brutal to lose your only child. You all have loved ones, and I hope none of you will experience this.' She returned grim-faced to her seat.

Antoan Zahariev's lawyer repeated the prosecutor's arguments: Jock had approached the group of boys rather than the other way around; Jock had carried the knife, and this knife had inflicted the wounds. Ignoring evidence presented in the trial, the lawyer said it was by sheer luck that the other boys had survived, given that one of them had been 'stabbed in the back with a thirty-centimetre-long blade'.

One of the Monovs' lawyers gave a final summation of their case: 'The drama that unfolded did not start after midnight,' he said. 'It started the moment when the defendant bought this scary knife designed for murder.' He also said the autopsy report showed the blow was 'sudden and forceful', a 'murderous blow', not a defensive move.

The case against Jock had been summarised in just over half an hour. Now it was Dinko Kanchev's turn. Much to Simon's surprise, he came out swinging, accusing the media of 'purposefully' generating 'an extremely hostile' public perception of his client, from the morning of his arrest until now. He accused Prosecutor Parvoleta Nikova of feeding journalists with selected bits of evidence in a sustained effort to cast the suspect as guilty. He referred specifically to her interview with *24 Hours* on 24 March 2008, when she had 'eagerly' given a 'selective' interpretation of the evidence. This breached his client's right to be presumed innocent and proved that the police investigation ultimately under her command was 'one-sided and prejudiced'.

Dinko ramped up his attack, arguing that Nikova's actions were part of a wider campaign by the Prosecutor's Office to secure convictions in high-profile cases. Generating a media frenzy was one way of pressuring the court to rule in favour of the prosecution case, he said. Jock was as astonished as Simon. Dinko was taking a considerable risk here: after all, he would have to work with these people long after the trial ended.

The lawyer went on. Under Nikova's supervision, he said, police investigators had only ever sought evidence that would support the account given by Antoan Zahariev and his friends. Whether it had been done consciously or not, there had been 'significant and irreparable gaps in the investigation'. These included the failure to secure the crime scene all the way down to the metro, the failure or refusal to search for the two Roma men who were chased and the Roma woman who had been watching from the Sheraton car park, and the failure to locate those police who had been first at the scene and who had obtained the freshest accounts from the group. He reminded the court that, according to Bulgarian law, any doubt should be settled in favour of the defendant and his version of events.

Dinko's most scathing criticism of the investigation concerned the investigator's failure to secure the Ministry of Health CCTV recordings immediately. He said it was 'as if at that moment the investigating body had forgotten everything they had learnt' about investigative procedures. In his view, this failure was suspicious, given the on-duty doctor's testimony that some unnamed individual in fact examined the recordings that day, which in turn raised the question whether whoever did so had seen something that contradicted the prosecution's version of events.

Dinko then went through the evidence. The accounts of Andrei Monov's friends were 'unreliable', he said, 'quite contradictory and sometimes even downright false', so they were of no use in determining what happened, much less what motivated the defendant. According to Dinko, Antoan Zahariev had exhibited 'selective amnesia' in court. His claims that the defendant had approached the group with the knife already in his hand and that Jock had stabbed him in the back were both demonstrably false.

According to Dinko, while the disputed police witness statements might not be admissible as evidence, they were still part of the case file. They showed that Antoan, Alexander Donov and Nikolai Rabadzhiev had all lied in court when they said they had never referred to Roma or to a fight with Roma.

Dinko reminded the court of the 'valiant' declarations by the group members that Andrei Monov had not been under the influence of alcohol and the 'ridiculous' assertion that, alone and surrounded, the defendant had managed to trap fifteen people. He noted that one of the experts who insisted that Andrei's cohort did not act as a group of football fans had admitted that 'feelings of friendly solidarity between them' might have influenced their testimonies: had agreed, in other words, that they had been covering each other's backs.

Dinko concluded by saying that the CCTV recording, the testimony of neutral witnesses (Viktor Georgiev, Lyubomir Tomov and Mladen Nikolov), and the accounts of Jock's friends (Lindsay Welsh, Grayham Saunders and, to a certain extent, Anton 'Tony' Doychev) all described different stages or aspects of the incident. Taken together, however, they supported the account given by the defendant. The psychological report, most of which the prosecutor had chosen to ignore, suggested that the defendant was not a hooligan but rather had been motivated by 'the most normal human desire—to help two people who had been abused by a much larger group of youths'.

Simon then stood. Like Dinko, he spoke at length, his voice steady. According to him, there had been two incidents. First, the group of youths had assaulted an individual ten metres from the metro. Two minutes later, the same group had launched a second assault on an individual one hundred metres away, near the kiosk. This assault had started at least three minutes before Andrei Monov fell on the ground. He said the evidence also showed that Andrei Monov's group, bound together by a common love of the Levski football team, had lied to avoid responsibility for having started the violence that led to the death of their friend. The initial investigation of the incident had been flawed and biased; the prosecutor had consistently chosen to ignore evidence that supported Jock's version of events.

Simon went through the witness testimonies and the analysis of the CCTV recordings. According to Viktor Georgiev, during the second attack near the kiosk Jock had been knocked to the ground and was understand-ably terrified. The CCTV recording showed that Andrei Monov, far from running away from the melee, had moved towards it just before he fell to the ground.

Simon claimed that the forensic evidence cast further doubt on the prosecutor's allegations. 'The expert has stated that Zahariev's wound is consistent with a slash and a wound that could be accidentally received as many bodies are violently moving against each other. Zahariev's DNA is not on the knife. With the extreme sensitivity of DNA testing, the absence of Zahariev's blood has not been explained by the prosecution. The group was not searched for weapons. There is no definite proof that Jock's knife inflicted this wound and that it was not accidentally caused by one of Zahariev's friends.'

He reminded the court that it is commonly accepted among pathologists that it is impossible to determine precisely how much force was used to inflict a given knife wound, the direction in which the knife was travelling, or the position of the victim. 'The expert claims that there was little movement of the knife within the wound. This means that the knife could have gone in and out quickly. This is still compatible with a knife being swung from side to side in self-defence and Andrei Monov running into the blow.'

Simon turned to the testimonies of some group members, Antoan Zahariev's in particular. He argued that the changes made to their original statements suggested collusion with each other and with the investigator so as to cover up their own roles in a racially motivated attack and to prove the prosecutor's case.

Finally, Simon turned to his son. 'I am particularly proud of the way he has conducted himself throughout this trial, when so many witnesses were hostile and obviously lying,' he said. Simon had already spoken for longer than anyone else. He knew that he was testing the judges' patience. But he went on: 'Jock's motive originally was to help [the Roma man] and then to defend himself. This was an act that I can only describe as heroic. While as a parent I would have preferred that he stayed safe and did not get into trouble, as a human being I am proud that a young man would try to help another person despite the dangerous circumstances.' Jock looked at his father with admiration.

'What happened on that evening of 27 December 2007 was a tragedy,' Simon went on, speaking softly now. 'As I am also a parent, I can understand and respect the Monovs' grief, and I am sorry for their loss. As a family, we have also suffered. Jock has been in prison for almost two years. It would only make this tragedy worse if the truth of what happened that night was ignored and another young life lost.'

Simon stopped. His part was over. He shut his eyes as Jock got up and started to speak. *Please play it straight*, he thought.

Jock was reading from notes, but it was clear that he had written them himself. 'The charges against me are not just wrong, but they're horrible too,' he said. 'As if I actually wanted to kill Andrei and . . . Antoan. My only problem with these two strangers and the rest of the Levski hooligans was the immediate threat they posed to, and violence they inflicted on, the Roma man and me. I wasn't interested in causing any harm to the Levski hooligans. I just wanted to stop them [attacking] . . .'

Forty minutes into his address, one of the lawyers for the civil claimants tried to stop him speaking. But Jock continued, detailing the many times he had either witnessed an unprovoked attack in Bulgaria or been attacked himself, and the lack of police interest when time after time he had provided his contact details. 'These experiences and others have made me wary of going out at night,' he said. 'It was on impulse that I put Grayham's knife into my jacket as my friends were hurrying out for the night.'

By now the lawyers and Antoan Zahariev were laughing. Helen was not sure if they were mocking Jock himself or what he was saying, but she was angry that, after all the delays in the trial, he was being interrupted. 'A lawyer for the civil claimants asked me why I didn't run away when I saw the gang beating a man for the colour of his skin,' Jock continued. 'I haven't been that outraged for a long time. How can anyone who respects law and order or social order walk away from such an atrocious crime?'

Jock now turned to the Monovs. 'I am truly devastated by the death of Andrei Monov. I have nightmares when I hear my heart beating. I feel extremely sorry for Mrs Monova. The whole situation was totally unnecessary and should not have ended in death. There are no words to express what I feel about the loss Andrei Monov's parents must feel.'

Simon remembers Hristo calling out, 'Rubbish. I don't want to hear this!'

'I am not ashamed to say that I have cried many times, not for myself but, in all honesty, for Andrei,' Jock continued. 'In court I have to control my emotions so I can concentrate on the trial, but I am far from a cold-hearted person.'

Jock turned to Antoan Zahariev. 'I want all the people who were there that night to know that, although I am the one in handcuffs and on trial, they don't just share part of the responsibility, they are directly responsible,' he said. 'I'm annoyed by the arrogance of Antoan Zahariev, who took part in the attack on me and is now asking me for money. I know what happened that night, and all the Levski group also know what happened.'

Jock looked at the judges. 'I ask this court to find that I acted in self-defence, that I'm morally and legally innocent.'

Jock had spoken for more than an hour. Judge Kolev called for a two-hour break.

Dinko turned to the Palfreemans and said he was surprised that the other side had said so little. 'They were brief because they already know the outcome,' Jock said. But Simon dared to hope that the brevity augured well. Maybe the prosecutor knew her case was hollow.

In the holding cell Jock talked to a prisoner named Nikolai, who had just been sentenced to life even though the prosecution had only asked for twenty years. What's your bet on what you will get? asked the man in Bulgarian.

'Eighteen years, tops,' said Jock.

The break over, guards led Jock back to the courtroom. Everyone stood as the judges and panel entered. They remained standing as Judge Kolev read the verdict. Dobri had his arm around Ash. She felt his body stiffen. 'What is it?' she asked. But Dobri's English had vanished.

Jock Palfreeman was found guilty of murder and of attempting to murder more than one person with hooligan intent. The sentence was twenty years. Simon reached for his son and put his arm around him. Jock pushed his father away, frowning. He did not want anyone to think he needed help. In fact, it was probably Simon who most needed help at that moment.

The accused was to pay each of the Monovs 200,000 *leva* and Antoan Zahariev 50,000 *leva*. These were the full sums they had requested, and they accrued interest from the date of the incident. Jock also owed 31,905 *leva* (about A$20,000) in court costs.

As the guards shackled Jock and led him away, camera crews pushed into the courtroom and surrounded the defence team. Foreign reporters badgered Galina for details of the verdict and pressed Simon for his reaction. 'My son did what very few would do under the circumstances,' he began. 'To me he is a hero.' Helen stood next to Simon, looking at her feet.

The next day the Bulgarian newspapers covered the convictions of both Jock and Nikolai: two monsters dealt with in one day. Twenty-year-old Nikolai Arabadzhiev had confessed to hitting a friend on the head with a dumb-bell before stabbing him numerous times, then dismembering the corpse and hiding parts of it in the mountains.

When Viktor Georgiev heard about the verdict, it did not surprise him. The court had been asked to choose between two versions of what happened, one given by a lot of drunken youths who had gone too far and one by people watching from across the road who had nothing to do with the incident. In the end the court believed the youths and not the independent witnesses. Viktor had long thought justice was a joke in Bulgaria. A hangover from the Communist past. What had happened in St Nedelya Square was a tragedy for all concerned, but it was not his tragedy.

PART IV
THE FINAL VERDICT

CHAPTER 26

Dinko Kanchev lodged an appeal against the verdict on Jock's behalf. The prosecution and civil claimants appealed too. They were upset by what they regarded as the leniency of the sentence. The prosecution was still calling for life, the civil claimants for life without parole.

Jock's cellmate Murad could see that the verdict had hit Jock like a sledgehammer. The normally talkative Australian was now withdrawn. Murad felt he was talking to a shell. 'Jock was locked in the head, like he wasn't there,' the Chechnyan prisoner later recounted.

Just before Christmas 2009, Jock was caught with alcohol distilled in the prison and six illicit mobile telephones, some of which belonged to other prisoners. Jock knew he would be punished anyway, so he took the rap for all of them. The guards recorded that they had found only three. When they asked him for PINs, Jock presumed they had stolen the other phones. Once again he was sent to isolation.

This time he spent three weeks completely alone. It gave him a break from the cheek-by-jowl life in the Block, but by the end he was singing and talking to himself. When he returned to his cell, he talked so incessantly and incoherently that his fellow prisoners just stared at him. He could not follow a discussion, or make himself understood.

Soon afterwards, guards raided his cell and took his portable CD player. Jock shouted so much he could not speak for a week. He was sent back to isolation, officially for disobeying a guard's order. While he was there, guards claimed they found a knife in his belongings that remained under his bed in the Block. Jock went ballistic, and accused them of planting it. The allegation disappeared.

The isolation floor was crowded. Soon Jock was given a cellmate: the young Bulgarian he had met on the day of the verdict. Nikolai Arabadzhiev spoke English; he and Jock talked for hours about their cases and life in general. Nikolai played guitar and seemed like a gentle soul, consumed with remorse. Jock found it hard to believe he could have committed such an atrocious act.

During his four months in isolation, Jock also met a Bulgarian lifer named Stoyan, who used to stop outside the Australian's cell on his way back from time alone in the yard. The two would grab ten seconds of conversation before Stoyan was told to move on. It was just enough time for them to start hatching an audacious plan.

. . .

Simon read with some concern material posted on anarchist websites about Jock's case. It seemed that he was being used as an 'anti-fascist' icon in a global campaign against racism. He was already aware that rallies had been held in support of him outside the Bulgarian embassies in London, Vienna, Moscow and Paris. Jock was adamant that he did not think of himself as an anarchist, but he did correspond with anarchists and other political groups, including ones advocating prisoners' rights. Simon knew he welcomed their support but worried that being seen to be aligned with fringe groups was not in Jock's best interests now. Geri thought this was just an extension of his long-held interest in revolutionary politics. At times Jock seemed to believe he was a political prisoner who was being held hostage in Bulgaria. She wondered if the angry rhetoric was as much a way of avoiding thinking about Andrei's death and his role in it, as it was a reaction to the way the case had been handled by the police, the prosecutor and now the court.

. . .

The election of a new government had done Hristo Monov no favours. He lost his prestigious position as deputy head of the Child Protection Agency.

But he continued to lecture at Sofia University and to appear on television and in print as a psychologist specialising in youth crises.

· · ·

As the Palfreeman family waited for the official statement outlining the judge's reasons for his verdict, Simon became more and more distressed. Helen feared he was on the verge of a physical and nervous breakdown. Simon had always been intensely focused on the case. But now when he talked about it he almost raved, not finishing sentences and leaping from one concept to another. For the first time he was using the word 'corruption'. The man she knew, the calm, logical, rational Simon, was harder and harder to find.

· · ·

In early 2010, Geri started feeling breathless. Her doctor ordered some blood tests. The result was shocking. 'You need a bone marrow transplant,' she was told. She had myelodysplasia, a precursor to leukaemia. One by one, the specialist phoned her six brothers and sisters, looking for a match.

The only match was Simon.

Providing bone marrow for Geri required a trip to England and painful tests and procedures. But enduring all that made Simon feel better. He had not been able to help his son; at least he might be able to do something for his sister.

The treatment was a success; little by little, Geri rallied.

· · ·

Almost six months after the verdict, the defence received Judge Kolev and his assisting judge's undated statement of their reasonings. After poring over a translated copy of the document, the Palfreemans were even more confused.

The judges acknowledged Jock's clean criminal record, good character references, and sound psychological condition. They also found that Andrei Monov's heavy intoxication had been a mitigating factor in the crime. Nonetheless, they determined that Jock had deliberately attacked the group and not the other way around, and noted that it was just good luck that Antoan Zahariev had survived. In the absence of any other motive, they concluded that Jock had acted with hooligan intent—a desire to demonstrate his opposition to 'society and its rules' by showing 'brute force' and 'mockery' as well as depriving someone of 'the right to life'.

In the judges' view Andrei's companions had all been credible witnesses, and their testimony demonstrated that there had not been an attack on Roma or Jock. They dismissed the defence's argument that Antoan's credibility as a witness was compromised by his status as a civil claimant and said his evidence had been validated by the testimony of his cohort.

Yet the judges also accepted Viktor Georgiev and Lyubomir Tomov as credible witnesses, since they had no reason to lie and had been able to see and hear what happened. Viktor's testimony that he noticed someone lying on Stamboliyski as he crossed from the car park to the square was put down to timing: clearly, he and his fellow Sheraton staffer only saw members of Andrei's group throwing rocks at Jock after the fatal stabbing. The judges noted that the two independent witnesses had seen the group chasing a man across the square and beating him, but did not connect that fact with other elements of the incident.

Similarly, the judges made only passing reference to the CCTV material, describing the figures in it as unidentifiable. They said nothing about the large group of figures chasing two people. Nor did they mention the figures that appeared to be bending and throwing things before someone fell to the road.

Instead, the judges found that Jock's shouting 'No fascism' indicated he was on the offensive rather than defending himself, and that Antoan's asking Jock, 'Hey, you, what are you doing, what's with this knife' was further evidence that Jock had taken the group by surprise.

Drawing on Stanislav Hristov's testimony, the judges said the size of Andrei's and Antoan's wounds showed they had both been inflicted by the knife Jock carried. The fact that Andrei's wound canal matched the length of the knife showed that Jock had delivered the fatal blow forcefully. That force, combined with the location of the wounds in the chest area and the striking of the blows one after another, showed that he had intended to kill.

The 'hooligan' nature of Jock's crime showed that he knew no 'moral and ethical' boundaries and would pose a threat to society if released, the judges concluded. Prison, however, could correct his behaviour.

. . .

Throughout the trial Stanislav Hristov was facing serious charges relating to the body parts scandal. Despite this, Judge Kolev found no reason to question the credibility of this key witness.

It was not until five months after Jock was found guilty that the case against the forensic doctor was dropped. During this time Hristov had successfully appealed against the findings of Associate Professor Maria Grozeva's panel on the basis that her defamation action against him constituted a conflict of interest. The new panel set up to investigate his activities found there had been no irregularities. The drink driving charges against him remained. Eventually, in January 2011, Hristov was found guilty and sentenced to ten months' probation. He appealed and the matter has still not been finalised.

. . .

6 June 2010

Meanwhile, public attention would turn to one of the young men who had accused Jock of attacking Andrei Monov and his friends. A rally was planned to take place outside a detention centre for illegal immigrants, in protest against the harsh treatment of detainees. A group of men rushed onto a tram carrying students to the rally, attacked the students, and badly injured four of them. Police subsequently arrested six youths. Among them was Andrei Monov's friend Emil Aleksiev, who had been with him on the night he died and had testified at Jock's trial. He and his parents claimed he had been at home on the night in question, and publicly accused police of failing to follow correct procedures.

Bulgarian human rights groups published a formal complaint to government and European bodies about what they described as the increasing incidence of 'neo-Nazi' racist attacks in Sofia.

· · ·

On the other side of Bulgaria, Prosecutor Parvoleta Nikova's relationship with a suspected criminal was under scrutiny.

For months the police chief and senior prosecutor in Burgas had been investigating allegations that a businessman named Svetlozar Lolov was running a tax evasion racket using the building of apartments on the Black Sea as cover. Lolov's right-hand man was Rangel Stanchev. Tipped off about the investigation, Lolov had fled to Turkey; an Interpol warrant was later filed for his arrest. Stanchev stayed in Burgas. Unable to find him at home, police arrested him at the home of his girlfriend, Parvoleta Nikova.

According to senior prosecutor Angel Georgiev who had issued the arrest warrant, Stanchev suffered from diabetes, and when police began making a list of his several mobile phones, Nikova stuffed sweets into her lover's pocket. As he was taken away for questioning, he had a hyperglycaemic attack and had to be admitted to hospital. Owing to Stanchev's medical condition, he was held under house arrest rather than being taken into custody.

The senior prosecutor made an official complaint about Parvoleta Nikova's involvement with Stanchev. The police chief believed her case exemplified the rot in Bulgaria's judiciary. 'Morality and the law in Bulgaria have nothing in common,' Commissar Milen Dimitrov told me later. 'There are many people, police and prosecutors and all kinds, who use their legal knowledge to live an unethical life.'

· · ·

Forensic doctor Maria Grozeva had long harboured doubts about the integrity of her own profession. Her concerns went beyond the Palfreeman case. Grozeva had also worked on the Solo Disco Club case, in which a young man was accused of stabbing two other youths to death. At the trial, Grozeva testified that the wounds were not inflicted by the defendant's knife. This caused an uproar. According to Grozeva, she was warned that her life would be in danger if she did not withdraw her evidence. But she refused to bow to threats. In December 2011, the Sofia City Court would uphold Grozeva's evidence and acquit the defendant.

The victims' families would claim that the verdict reflected the influence of the defendant's father.

There was also discontent over the appointment of judges in Bulgaria. Almost one year after Judge Georgi Kolev found Jock guilty, he was elevated to head the Supreme Administrative Court, one of the two highest courts in Bulgaria (the other being the Supreme Court of Cassation). In an opinion piece for the newspaper *Dnevnik*, a prominent human-rights lawyer named Yonko Grozev argued that the appointment was an inside job. Noting that Kolev had no experience in the administrative area, he claimed that no one else had run for the position because Kolev was known to be close to the Interior Minister and that his selection was a foregone conclusion.

In an interview for this book, Grozev said Kolev's appointment exemplified a malaise within the Bulgarian judiciary that prevented the promotion of judges who wanted to clean up the system. According to him, the Supreme Judicial Council—which oversees the nation's prosecutors and judges—was a law unto itself, driven by tight networks of friendship and mutual favours.

Grozev was not alone in his concern. In February 2011, the European Commission's interim monitoring report on Bulgaria made note of 'one important appointment decision' in which 'the [Supreme Judicial] Council did not demonstrate the necessary commitment to accountability and transparency'. The commission decided to follow the Palfreeman appeal closely.

. . .

In Melbourne, Ruth Shann and her two senior colleagues were hard at work reviewing the trial transcripts and formulating a strategy for Jock's appeal. They believed the defence needed to highlight the flaws in the investigation and trial, demonstrate that Jock's account of events had not been given due weight, and focus on the inconsistencies in Judge Kolev's reasoning.

Jock's lawyer Dinko Kanchev had advised the Court of Appeal that his client would be requesting court-appointed experts to review the forensic evidence in the case, to give an opinion on the effect high blood alcohol levels would have had on Andrei Monov and his friends, and to go through the CCTV recordings with the judges.

. Dinko was hopeful that recent amendments to the Criminal Procedures Code would prevent civil claimants from blocking witness statements. He intended asking the court to re-examine five witnesses who had significantly changed their testimony during the trial.

If Jock's appeal was unsuccessful, he could take his case to the highest court in Bulgaria, the Supreme Court of Cassation. But this court would not review the evidence. Ruth Shann and her colleagues believed it was vital for Simon to establish the foundations of a potential appeal to the European Court of Human Rights in Strasbourg, France. The statistics gave at least some cause for hope: of 375 Bulgarian judgments delivered by the European Court, 343 had been found to demonstrate violations of the European Convention for the Protection of Human Rights and Fundamental Freedoms. Nevertheless the European Court would be a last resort. Even if it agreed to hear Jock's case, the court did not have the power to review evidence and could only make a finding on whether there had been due process. Whatever the finding, the European Court could not force Bulgaria to do anything.

. . .

Simon dreaded the appeal. It meant returning to the Sofia Palace of Justice, where he would be assisting Dinko once again as Jock's 'defender'. He hoped that a new court and new judges might view the evidence differently, but his faith in the system had taken a battering. Ruth's suggested strategy of hedging his bets made sense, he thought. He would try to get the best out of the Bulgarian appeal process while paving the way for an appeal to the European Court. Simon knew there was a long queue of cases waiting to be heard at Strasbourg and that it could take years for Jock's case to get near a panel of judges. But if all appeals failed in Bulgaria, he wanted to have the best possible shot at getting the case heard in the European Court. Jock had written to the European Commission about his situation. Simon decided to email the president of the prominent human rights group, the Bulgarian Helsinki Committee. Though not a lawyer, Dr Krassimir Kanev had special dispensation to represent Bulgarians at the European Court of Human Rights; he also understood how things worked in Bulgaria and might be a useful sounding board.

Kanev knew only what he had read in the newspapers about the Palfreeman case. He had gone to university with Hristo Monov, but had never met his son. He was familiar with Hristo's opinion pieces on Roma. He also had seen how the psychologist reacted to adverse publicity about Bulgaria. Not long before Andrei Monov died, the Bulgarian Helsinki Committee had helped a BBC crew expose the inhumane treatment of disabled orphans. When the documentary went to air in September 2007, Hristo had publicly condemned it as misleading and designed to show Bulgaria in a bad light.

When Simon arrived in Sofia, Kanev met with him and heard his account of the trial. Kanev was not surprised by the verdict. The court had been asked to choose between the son of a well-respected Bulgarian and a foreigner—moreover, a foreigner who claimed to have assisted a Gypsy. Although there was nothing to suggest the Monovs had actively influenced the verdict, Kanev knew that in Bulgaria, a word in the ear of someone who counted could help to tilt things one way or the other. The corridors of power were filled with networks of friends, friends of friends, extended family, and friends of family. The common wisdom was that connections were everything—in law, finance, the public service and politics.

Had Jock's claim been taken seriously, some of Andrei's group might have been charged with assault; Andrei himself might have been seen as bearing a portion of blame. Kanev wondered if there was more at play than grief and a thirst for revenge. In Bulgaria public image and family reputation are tremendously important. Andrei Monov was continually referred to as coming from a good family and as being the son of a well-known psychologist.

Kanev found Simon reasonable and as objective as could be expected. The case raised issues which already concerned him deeply, in particular the abuse of Roma. As he read through the court documents which Simon had left with the Bulgarian Helsinki Committee, Kanev resolved to find out as much as he could about what had happened and to make a public stand.

. . .

21 October 2010

On the first day of Jock's appeal, the prosecution, the civil claimants and the defence took it in turns to approach the bench of three judges, chaired by Judge Snezhana Dushkova. The judges refused the defence's request that the court review the alcohol, forensic and CCTV evidence, saying that the relevant experts had given sufficient testimony during the trial. However, they accepted the request to re-examine five witnesses. Simon looked at his son. Surely this was a positive step.

Krassimir Kanev took a different view. In failing to allow most of Jock Palfreeman's requests, he thought the Appeal Court might have breached Article 6 of the European Convention, which obliges national courts to be even-handed and to consider as much evidence from the defence as from the prosecution.

He would take a close interest in the next phase of the appeal, due to begin in three weeks. He was not the only one.

. . .

The Bulgarian Embassy in Canberra sent a letter to the Bulgarian government about how the first day of the appeal had been covered by Australian media. It noted that the embassy had received many calls of support from Australians for Jock. It also advised the government that someone had rung the embassy accusing Jock of a brutal attack in Sydney four years earlier.

The caller had been Sydney barrister, Jonathon Cohen. Very early one morning in 2006 a complete stranger had viciously attacked him while he was walking along Bondi Beach. Cohen's injuries had been horrific. Watching television coverage of the Palfreeman case years later, the barrister felt sure Jock was the attacker; he had the same voice, the same eyes and the same nose.

According to the case file before the appeal judges, the caller rang the embassy in Canberra several times, asking that the Bulgarian Court of Appeal uphold the sentence and offering to provide more information about the assault on him. 'He's ready to tell his story,' the embassy wrote to the government. 'Please notify us if this is of interest to you.'

The Bulgarian Ministry of Foreign Affairs marked the letter urgent and sent it to the Ministry of Justice, which attached a note saying that it was indeed relevant and sent it to Prosecutor Parvoleta Nikova.

. . .

11 November 2010

The courtroom was already filling up when Krassimir Kanev took a seat behind a representative from the European Commission.

Antoan Zahariev was the first witness to be called. He told the court that on the night in question he had passed two strangers as he crossed the road. Hearing a loud argument behind him, he had turned around and seen some of his friends clustered together. 'And the next thing I remember was that we were already walking more slowly towards the disco,' he said, not mentioning the chase. Antoan added that the following day some of his friends had told him the argument started when the strangers had said 'Death to Bulgarians'. 'I didn't see any physical fight,' he said.

Kanev listened intently. He seriously doubted that any Roma would have said 'Death to Bulgarians' as he walked alone at night near a group of Levski football fans. That phrase had been bandied about since mid-2007, when a furore erupted over media reports that a Gypsy had used it during clashes between Roma and skinheads. Kanev suspected the phrase was invented as an excuse for the violence.

Judge Dushkova told Antoan his account did not tally with what he had originally told police. She read out the relevant section of his witness statement, in which he had said his friends had been fighting with men he thought were Gypsies.

Antoan said he must have been mistaken. 'I was interviewed the day after the incident,' he explained. 'Maybe I was still in shock then.' Dushkova asked if he could still remember what had happened, given the amount of time that had elapsed. 'I declare that what I have said before the Court during questioning is the truth,' Antoan answered. 'No matter that it was at a significantly later point in time.'

Bearing in mind that only questions related to contradictions in witness statements were admissible, Dinko asked Antoan if police had told him what to say when they interviewed him a second time. 'I have not been prompted what to say,' he replied. 'I haven't been influenced in any way.'

Officer Petar Katsarov was then called. He now agreed that police who were first at the scene had told him there had been 'a quarrel between the group of injured boys and some Roma people'. He said he did not know what the row had been about, and no Roma were at the scene when he got there. This was closer to what he had told police originally, but very different from his testimony in the trial, which had made no mention of Roma.

The police officer had also said in his first statement that he had been told Jock had intervened to help a Roma in what was a 'fight'. When Dushkova read out the relevant section of the statement, Katsarov said he had forgotten those details but agreed they were accurate. Dinko then asked Katsarov for the names of the police officers who had told him what had happened, but he said he did not know them.

Kanev was bemused. The police officer had a credible excuse for the contradictions in his testimony. A lapse in time could cause memory loss. Antoan's excuse that shock had caused him to invent details and that time passing helped him realise his first impressions were a fantasy seemed unbelievable.

. . .

The next day Prosecutor Parvoleta Nikova forwarded the cable from the Bulgarian Embassy in Canberra to the Court of Appeal, where it became part of the court file.

Australian Department of Immigration and Citizenship records show that Jock had left Australia on New Year's Day 2006 and not returned. Cohen now agrees Jock could not have been the attacker. But the note from the embassy about his call would remain in the court file before the judges along with the allegation made by the two young Sydneysiders to the *Daily Telegraph* soon after Jock's arrest.

. . .

25 November 2010

Today Jock had a piece of paper on his suit pocket with '25' written on it to indicate the date. Television news reports frequently used file footage in stories about his trial. An Australian friend had remarked in a letter to Jock that this made it impossible to gauge whether he was currently healthy or not. The number was his way of letting her know when the video was taken.

Simon winced when he saw Jock's pocket. *What is Jock thinking?* he thought. As guards removed his son's handcuffs, Simon gently detached the paper and slid it under a folder.

Today it was Officer Krassimira Stoyadinova who took the witness stand. She now said that some of the youths at the scene had told her there had been 'some kind of quarrel', but she could not remember whether they had said it was with Roma. Judge Dushkova believed this contradicted what she had told the original investigator, so part of her witness statement was read aloud. The judge suggested that perhaps the contradiction was due to the passing of time. Stoyadinova agreed. She said the very first people she spoke with were fellow officers, who told her what they had heard. It was only when she later spoke to the youths that she found out what had actually happened.

Like Officer Katsarov, she said she did not know who the original officers were. Jock then asked her who had been tasked with finding the Roma. She said she did not know.

A court official opened the huge door and called out Officer Viktor Lyubenov's name. He testified that he had not been given a chance to explain himself fully in the trial. He now said that it was only later on and from 'rumours' that he had learned that the 'brawl had happened because there had been some Roma individuals'. He added that 'the accused had wanted to defend them and then the fighting and the stabbing took place'.

The prosecutor and lawyers for the civil claimants said nothing. But Dinko asked Lyubenov to clarify what he meant as what the officer had just told the court was not what he told the investigator. 'Rumours are one thing,' said Dinko. 'What is heard from colleagues is another thing.'

Lyubenov explained that he had heard this account 'from colleagues and crowd members who gathered later'. He knew neither the names of these colleagues nor whether any of the crowd members had been from the group of youths.

Alexander Donev had been due to appear, but his father told the court that he had a new job in Germany and did not have leave. He assured the court his son would attend the next hearing, which was now set for just before Christmas.

As Simon waited outside the jail to see his son, he was approached by Professor Boris Shtarbanov, the forensic psychiatrist who had examined Jock; he was on his way to visit another prisoner. 'You have a good son,' Shtarbanov said. Simon was glad of the affirmation from someone connected with the case. Interviewed for this book, Shtarbanov later said he was sure Andrei's friends had not been innocently going about their business that night, as they had all claimed.

. . .

As Jock lay in bed in his cell, he thought about the future. He tried to have a dream for every possible outcome. If the Court of Appeal overturned his conviction, he wanted to return to the British Army. If it reduced his sentence to five years, even ten, he wanted to earn enough money to be able to repay his father for what he had spent on the case. Jock dreamt of getting married and becoming a father. But when he thought about being in prison for twenty years, his soul shrivelled up.

Realistically, right now all I can do is try to change things here for the better, he thought. He wrote to the Bulgarian Helsinki Committee, requesting help in addressing problems raised by other prisoners. Krassimir Kanev was already concerned about the chronic overcrowding in Bulgarian prisons as well as the lack of food and resources. He wrote to the court requesting permission to visit Jock. Permission granted, the two talked for hours. They stayed in touch. Each time Kanev asked Jock to find out more about a particular case, Jock came through with the information. But still the weeks in jail dragged on.

. . .

22 December 2010

When court resumed, Sofia—and most of Europe—was in the grip of the worst snowstorm on record. Simon's flight from Sydney to London was redirected to Singapore and delayed by a day and a half. More bad weather forced his flight to Sofia to land at Burgas, 400 kilometres away. Simon tried to get a seat on another flight into Sofia, but all flights were cancelled, so he had to take a bus and endure another six-hour trip.

Meanwhile, the hearing went ahead without him. Alexander Donev took the witness stand. He told the court that he had heard a 'dispute' behind him as he crossed St Nedelya Square. He then qualified his use of the term 'dispute'; he had 'heard some shouts', he explained. Judge Dushkova asked Alexander if Andrei Monov had been involved. 'I couldn't say that I had seen Andrei having an altercation with anyone and I haven't heard of anything like that either.' The judge observed that what he had just said contained 'significant contradictions' to his original witness statement, in which he said he had seen Andrei Monov in 'an altercation' with Gypsies. She read aloud the relevant section. 'Obviously I have said what you read to me, but I can no longer remember whether I actually saw Andrei in this situation,' Alexander said. 'I don't exactly remember having seen Andrei taking part in the altercation. I read the statement when I signed it. This didn't strike me because I was in shock and I didn't pay attention.' The judge then read aloud from his trial testimony. Alexander said: 'Probably I got confused thinking [that] because he was injured, he must have taken part in the argument.' Possibly in response to further questioning, he added: 'I have not seen a physical fight or violence between the deceased and other individuals.'

Dinko asked for another adjournment to allow time for Simon to arrive. Asked if he wanted his father present, Jock said yes. 'My father has been present at the hearings almost thirty times and this is the first time that he could not come,' he explained. 'It's because of the snow. If this witness had appeared previously, the hearings would have concluded by now.' In light of Simon's past regular attendance in court, the panel agreed to delay hearing final statements until the following month.

Simon arrived in Sofia early that evening, unshaven and exhausted, only to be told that he would have to return to Australia and, in just three weeks' time, make the gruelling journey to Bulgaria all over again. Early the next morning he bought the ten kilograms of groceries Jock was allowed and delivered them to him on his way to the airport. Jock had been very concerned about his father. He knew the trips between Sydney and Sofia were draining Simon financially, physically and emotionally. When the familiar slightly built figure entered the visitors area, Jock felt a surge of gratitude and sympathy. After Jock's three years of detention, his and Simon's relationship was no longer that of child and father but of equals.

. . .

17 January 2011

By the time Simon returned and the snow had melted, the relationship had entered another stormy patch. The morning after he arrived in Sofia, Simon clicked open the *Sydney Morning Herald* website and saw an article on Jock's case. It quoted a letter Jock had written to a blog called 'Anarchist Solidarity', in which he complained that everything to do with his case was corrupt. The letter had been picked up by the Bulgarian English-language news service.

Simon was furious. *How could Jock show such bad judgement and timing?* he thought. Accusing the entire Bulgarian legal system of corruption would only raise the public's hackles. It also risked making the judges afraid to change the verdict or reduce the sentence lest they be accused of bowing to foreign criticism and letting a dangerous man off lightly. Simon certainly didn't want Jock to lose his characteristic exuberance, and yet still felt responsible for guiding his son. He wondered whether, if Jock had only been older, he might have understood his father's position.

By the time Simon reached the prison, he had calmed down. But Jock was agitated. He said he was sick of everyone getting away with calling him a bloodthirsty murderer without being called to account. He was sick of doing 'the right thing' to please his family. No one listened to him.

Putting this outburst down to a combination of anxiety and apprehension over the appeal, Simon could only hope his son would settle overnight and arrive in court with his self-control restored.

That day, the Supreme Judicial Council sacked the head of the Court of Appeal amid claims that he had behaved unethically in relation to a family member's business activities. The move followed complaints by the Interior Minister that the judge had wrongly acquitted criminals. Reading about the sacking, Simon was dismayed. *Not more chaos*, he thought, worried that the panel hearing Jock's case might now fear for their jobs and be reluctant to criticise Georgi Kolev's judgement, given the high position he now held.

Jock entered court in his suit but unshaven. As guards led him down the aisle, he smiled at his Bulgarian friends, thankful they had come. With his straggly red beard, he looked more like the Jock they had met five years ago. To the prosecution and the civil claimants he looked even more like a monster.

The prosecutor addressed the court. The sentence in this case needed to be increased to life, he said, to reform the defendant and to serve as a deterrent to others. He also argued that the trial judge had been wrong to take Andrei Monov's extreme level of intoxication as a mitigating factor. One of the Monovs' lawyers went further. He said 'the accepted factual circumstances' of the case remained unchanged despite the Appeal Court's re-examination of the five witnesses. According to him, a life sentence was not enough. The first court had declared that the defendant could not be reformed, so he should never be eligible for release.

Dressed in a black suit, Aksenia Monova approached the bench. 'Your Honours, you all have loved ones,' she began, her voice sounding strained. 'Andrei was the person to whom I was closest . . . Andrei was our only child; he grew up as a healthy, cheerful and educated young man. After he was murdered, our lives and the lives of our relatives became pointless, as if the blow inflicted by the defendant had caused a deadly wound to our souls.'

Aksenia said her pain had only been worsened by things that members of the defence had said in the public sphere. She cited the article in the *Sydney Morning Herald*, in which the defendant had been quoted as saying that 'a decision other than acquittal would be a proof of—I omit his expression—disrespect to law, ethics, society and justice'. Aksenia carefully avoided the word 'corruption', but she said such commentary was 'insulting and disrespectful' to the court and her family.

She went on, her voice rising in pitch: 'Throughout the trial, the defendant's position is "I am innocent from a moral and legal point of view." . . . Is it fair to attack young people who have gone out simply to see each other and to have fun during the New Year's holiday season with a thirty-centimetre knife? To claim that you have been brutally beaten and hit with stone pavers? That you even lost consciousness when, according to the medical experts' finding and from the photos attached to the file, you do not have a single scratch or bruising? Is it fair to direct multiple knife stabs at vital organs, and to inflict such a targeted, rare, extremely forceful blow to the most vulnerable part of the human body? To turn, with one blow of a professional in the worst sense [of the word], a young and healthy person into a corpse? Or to endanger the life and health of ten to fifteen people, by striking them with a thirty-centimetre knife? And this in the centre of Sofia—in the centre of the capital of a European country.'

The audience was transfixed. 'As a jurist and citizen of our country, I believe in justice,' she concluded. 'And I believe that the Court will impose a legitimate and fair sentence to isolate the defendant from society, and to protect society from him delivering justice as he thinks he should.'

Hristo then approached the bench. Hard as it was for him as a man who had lost his 'precious son', he said, he would speak as a professional, a psychologist with fifteen years' experience of both the victims and perpetrators of 'the most terrible things'. Pausing between sentences for maximum effect, Hristo said: 'The real question is: Can the killer be reformed? Please accept my firm opinion that he cannot.' In Hristo's professional opinion, Jock Palfreeman was a 'sociopath'. Hristo said one of the characteristics of a sociopath is to feel no remorse and cited Jock's request to have his hair cut for the bail hearing—his 'concern about his hairstyle'—as evidence that he had no insight into the enormity of his crime. Jock's two pairs of pants and his reversible jacket were evidence that he had prepared himself for murder.

'Apparently this blow which killed my son is the trademark of the murderer,' Hristo continued. He then drew the judges' attention to the report of an incident in 2004 published in the *Daily Telegraph*. 'This man is constantly lying, constantly ready to kill.'

As they had done during dozens of court hearings over the past three and a half years, the two fathers stood metres apart. Once again, Hristo claimed that Jock was the product of his family, 'a family which does not respect the highest human values . . . So now I understand the efforts of his father to defend him,' he added, turning to Simon.

'I have not seen such unprecedented pressure on the Bulgarian court in any other case,' Hristo continued. 'I believe that even now in the courtroom is the chairman of the Helsinki Committee, my classmate from the philosophy department, Krassimir Kanev, who doesn't dare to look me in the eye, because he knows very well the moral position which he defends and the blood money which the so-called famous Helsinki Committee will be collecting again.' Simon was astonished by the sheer audacity of this accusation. In fact, Kanev had already left the court room and so did not hear it.

Hristo then delivered a thinly veiled threat. 'Believe me, no matter when he gets out of jail, Jock Palfreeman will kill again. Pardon me for saying this, but anyone who gives a sentence other than life imprisonment without parole will be an accomplice to this murder. My son would have graduated in law by now. Given what kind of a person he was, he would have chosen the profession of magistrate.'

By contrast, Hristo described Jock's friends and supporters as belonging to an organisation that had sent letter bombs to embassies in Athens and Rome and been designated a threat second only to the terrorist group al-Qaeda.

The grieving father had gone too far. Jock started writing notes on the statement that, after much heated discussion, he and his father had agreed he would read.

Antoan Zahariev's lawyer now approached the bench. 'It has been proved . . . that there are several cuts in different parts of Zahariev's clothes, caused by the knife carried by the defendant, which suggests a few hits, one of which penetrated his body,' he said. 'Only by a fortunate coincidence was Zahariev spared from death. The size of the knife, the nature of the hits, the suddenness of their delivery, [and their] force and direction are proven beyond doubt.'

He dismissed the argument that Jock had acted in defence of another or in self-defence. 'First of all, there is no positive evidence of any brawl, fight, or altercation between the group of boys and any other group. It is all just in the realm of allegations, speculation and make-believe.' Even if there had been a verbal argument, he went on, that was no reason for murder. In any event, there was no evidence that Antoan or Andrei had provoked the defendant by 'word, gesture or act'.

It was Dinko Kanchev's turn. He said he would not get into arguments about political leanings of either his client or Andrei and his friends, because these were irrelevant to the events of the night. During an exhaustive summation of the evidence, he corrected Aksenia Monova's claim that there was not a scratch on Jock, reminding the court that forensic doctor Maria Grozeva had testified not only that he had injuries on his arm but that they were compatible with his having defended himself against an attack with paving stones.

Dinko argued that the appeal hearings had shown that two friends of Andrei Monov had lied during the trial and given implausible reasons for the contradictions in their statements. By contrast, the independent witnesses—Mladen Nikolov, Viktor Georgiev, Asen Stoychev, Slaveiko Tsonkov and Lyubomir Tomov—had given consistent accounts of what happened.

He said the investigator's failure to explore what caused the melee suggested they had set out to achieve a predetermined outcome. The failure to gather all the evidence should cast strong doubt on the prosecution's version of events, doubt that should incline the court in the defendant's favour.

Finally, Dinko said there was also reasonable doubt that the single-edged knife Jock had carried had dealt the fatal blow, since the nature of the wound suggested it had been inflicted by a double-edged knife. The fight had involved fifteen people, and Andrei Monov's blood could have got onto the knife at any point and in any number of ways. The knife bore neither Jock's fingerprints nor traces of his DNA, nor did it show any sign of having connected with Antoan Zahariev.

Dinko returned to his seat, and Simon stepped forward. Like Dinko, he emphasised Jock's right to a full and unbiased investigation and a fair trial. He outlined the evidence supporting Jock's claim that he did not run into the group wielding a knife, and described the group's aggression as seen in the CCTV recordings. He said the psychological report and the reference from Tihomir Pashev, the retired military captain, both proved that his son was not a murderer by nature. 'I am proud of how he behaved during the trial,' he concluded, 'in the face of so many witnesses who are obviously lying in an attempt to keep him in jail, to avoid responsibility for their own crimes, and of course to receive compensation.'

Now the guards led Jock towards the bench. Simon and Dinko both looked up at the ceiling and shut their eyes.

'I have never stolen in Russia with Baba Yaga,' Jock said, referring to the child-eating witch of Slavic folklore. Reading energetically from notes he had scribbled during the hearing, he continued: 'I have never had anything to do with pickpocketing by Dracula in Romania, and I don't know any terrorists . . . Until now the accusations against me have not been in the form of arguments, but have been [based on] intrigue, rumours, myths and legends.'

His friends winced; this approach was not going to help Jock's cause. Simon remained seated, spent; Hristo paced. One had done all he could; the other was still on the warpath.

Jock said Andrei's father spoke not as a professional psychologist but as 'a biased plaintiff' when he called him a sociopath. The only impartial account of his character, Jock added, was the independent psychological assessment, which showed he was 'not a sociopath, but just the opposite'.

'Mrs Monova said that we all have families, and we should think how we would feel if we lost a family member. She is right. Why didn't Andrei Monov and the rest of the Levski hooligans think about the families of the two Roma whom they attacked and tried to kill? Why didn't Andrei, Antoan and the group of fifteen people consider my family when they tried to break my skull with [concrete] pavers?'

After canvassing the flaws in the investigation and the evidence, and the contradictions in the testimony of Andrei's friends, he was done. 'I never thought that someone would die, other than the Roma who were attacked or me,' Jock concluded. 'We were the ones who were in danger and we were the ones who were attacked.' With that he returned to his father's side.

Judge Dushkova called a short break. Dinko explained to Simon and Jock that if there was to be an acquittal, the judges would announce it when the hearing resumed. If not, the court could take up to a month to announce its verdict. When the judges returned, they postponed their decision.

Outside the courtroom, Simon spoke to Australian and Bulgarian reporters. 'I feel for the Monovs, the fact that they've lost their son,' he said. 'But the reality is I've got a son, too, and I don't want to lose him.'

Two of Andrei's friends were interviewed by an Australian television crew. 'My friend was stabbed in the heart. You don't stab a person in the heart for self-defence,' said Ivailo Iliev, who had not been present during the incident. 'We don't bring knives with us when we walk on the streets. That's not what me and our friends would do.' Gabriela Videnova had not been in St Nedelya Square that night either but had attended the trial. 'I saw the knife,' she said. 'It's like made for murders and for killing people.'

When Simon and the Australian diplomat went to see Jock in prison the next morning, the young man was beaming, relieved to have aired his views publicly. Simon understood why he had chosen to ignore the statement they had worked on together and speak off the cuff. His words to the court had been honest and heartfelt. Simon would not have spoken like that, but he was proud of his son. Jock asked him to take his suit, since he would not need it anymore.

Several hours later, Simon was at Sofia airport, Jock's grubby jacket neatly folded away in his suitcase. Boarding the flight to London, Simon had the sense that he was taking a part of Jock home.

As the plane took off, Simon felt a weight lift from his shoulders. *No more court appearances*, he thought. *That's it. I've done my best. There's nothing more I can do.*

Dr Krassimir Kanev told me that Simon's polite and reasonable demeanour played better to a Bulgarian audience than Jock's assertiveness. But, he added, Jock had a much better understanding of the way justice operated in Bulgaria.

. . .

Back in Australia Simon threw himself into his work at the pathology laboratory. He spent long days there and came home exhausted. It stopped him thinking about Jock. But Helen was worried. Simon had changed. Now when they talked about the case, their discussion often resulted in an argument. Simon no longer disputed Jock's decision to take the knife out of his pocket to defend himself; Helen still did. Simon sounded increasingly like Jock; he now talked openly about 'corruption in the system'. He had lost his analytical approach to problem solving. Simon was at breaking point and deteriorating physically as well as emotionally. Helen was cross that Jock kept arguing with his father. Her stepson expected friends and family to do for him exactly what he would do for them and often did not seem to understand they were in fact already doing the best they could.

. . .

February 2011

As the Court of Appeal deliberated over the Palfreeman case, the media spotlight returned to Parvoleta Nikova.

She had run the case against Krassimir Georgiev who was known as Krassio the Black; the case was regarded as emblematic of the fight against corruption. Allegedly a powerbroker in some circles of the Bulgarian judiciary, Georgiev was accused of taking money from judicial officials in exchange for securing their positions or promotions. Unexpectedly Nikova reduced the charges from peddling influence to tax evasion. Ultimately he was acquitted.

In the meantime there were more revelations about Nikova's private life. The respected weekly newspaper *Kapital* reported that after investigating Nikova's relationship with a suspected criminal, the Supreme Judicial Council had decided the prosecutor had no case to answer. The Bulgarian internet daily Mediapool.bg reported that Nikova had told the council's ethics committee she had not known Rangel Stanchev was diabetic when she gave him the sweets. Nikova's superior, Nikolai Kokinov, was quoted in *24 Hours* as saying his prosecutors' private lives were their own business.

The Burgas police chief, who had helped launch the case against Nikova, never expected the investigation would amount to much. 'For the past twenty years the system has not been working,' Commissar Milen Dimitrov said in an interview for this book. 'The Supreme Judicial Council and the system . . . are a state outside the state. The state has no control over them. If we keep up the current pace of reform and of [addressing] corruption, it will be decades before we reach the European standard.' Indeed, that year Transparency International ranked Bulgaria as the most corrupt of all European member and candidate countries.

When I asked Nikova and the Prosecutor's Office for more information both declined to comment. The Supreme Judicial Council said it would respond to my questions about the investigation into Nikova, but by the time of publication had not done so.

Far from being damaged by her association with Rangel Stanchev, Parvoleta Nikova would be promoted to the role of prosecuting cases in Bulgaria's two highest courts: one of which was headed by the Monovs' friend, the other which was now headed by Judge Georgi Kolev.

. . .

14 February 2011

During an appearance on a TV crime show to talk about an unrelated case, Hristo Monov was asked about his experience with violent crime and with the legal system. He repeated his claim that Jock was a sociopath who should never be released from jail. Four days later an online site published an interview with Hristo in which he criticised successive governments for not doing enough to stop Roma crime. He then said police were the weakest link in the system and gave as an example the investigator's fifteen-hour delay in informing him of his son's death. As the discussion moved to the case involving his son, Hristo said he looked forward to the Court of Appeals' decision, which he had no reason to doubt would be just. In the meantime, he added, 'None of my family or of my son's friends have commented [about the case]. But the pressure from the other side [Jock's supporters] is immense. It is a pity that there are some voices in Bulgaria that have joined in.' Hristo then urged the authorities to investigate the

Bulgarian Helsinki Committee's finances, adding that some people would do anything for money.

. . .

21 February 2011

The Court of Appeal's decision was published online on the day Andrei Monov would have turned twenty-four; it upheld the verdict and the sentence. Jock found out when he turned on the TV news. Simon found out when a journalist phoned him at home. Both father and son were very upset. Despite their cynicism, they had dared to hope—Simon to a greater degree than Jock.

The appeal judges dismissed Jock's claim that he had acted in self-defence and to defend another person. They found that his actions were those of an attacker, not a rescuer, as evidenced by his use of a knife, his targeting of vital organs, and the fact that his victims were stabbed 'laterally' and 'in the back', with great force and speed. They concluded that Jock had intended to kill Andrei, and the only reason that Antoan and others survived was that they had managed to escape. The judges did not accept that the absence of Antoan Zahariev's DNA and of Jock's fingerprints on the knife cast doubt on his culpability. Because the wounds on the victims and the tears in their clothing matched the size of the knife, they argued, both wounds and rips must have been caused by that knife.

Unlike the first court, the appellate court accepted that some of Andrei Monov's group had fought with a Gypsy. Although the judges did not accept Antoan Zahariev's and Alexander Dimov's claims that shock accounted for the discrepancies in their testimonies, they maintained that the group members were reliable witnesses. They dismissed the defence argument that Antoan had a financial motive to lie. They found his allegation that Jock was the perpetrator remained consistent and his version of events was supported by the court's findings.

In contrast, the security guard at the Sheraton, Viktor Georgiev, was not in the judges' view a reliable witness. They dismissed his description of two brawls in different locations as unsupported by anyone else, including the defendant. They made no reference to the striking similarities between

Viktor's account and that of the car park attendant, Lyubomir Tomov, who had been with Viktor at the time of the incident. The judges regarded Lyubomir and the other independent witnesses as reliable, but said these witnesses had observed only the events that occurred after Andrei had been stabbed.

The judges took selected accounts of when witnesses first saw Jock as supporting the prosecutor's claim that Jock had run directly into the group when they were congregated at the kiosk. This seems extraordinary, given that the CCTV expert's report indicates that the figure presumed to be Jock ran across the road and the square only after the group had run across the square towards the metro. Again, contrary to the CCTV expert's evidence but in line with the prosecutor's indictment, the appeal judges determined that the group members threw dirt and stones only after Andrei was stabbed and in an attempt 'to defend themselves and to frighten the accused'.

As proof that the defendant had not been provoked and that he had run into a group of harmless youths, the judges cited Anton 'Tony' Doychev's testimony that when Jock asked him if someone was being attacked he had said he did not know and looked up from his mobile phone to see a group of twenty quiet youths who were about to cross the road.

Again, this interpretation is at odds with the CCTV images in which Jock seemed to run to something on the other side of the square. Tony's words might equally have meant that he looked up just before the youths ran across the square. Without the questions that prompted the responses, the court transcripts read like a stream of consciousness, into which almost anything can be read.

The judges found no evidence to support Jock's claim that he entered a group of fifteen youths to defend another person, and said his injuries were too slight to have been caused by an attack on him. They said the youths were not football hooligans and had no reason to lie. Despite being alone, they concluded, Jock could still have frightened the group—he was armed and had taken the youths by surprise.

The judges responded to defence complaints of procedural bias by saying that the court was not responsible for problems with the investigation. They did not reflect on whether such problems should weigh in Jock's favour; it simply was not their problem. They found that under the law at that time, the trial court was obliged to disallow examination of police witness statements.

Although the judges did not increase Jock's sentence, they said the first court had been wrong to cite Andrei's intoxication as a mitigating factor. Indeed, they concluded that Jock was even more dangerous than Judge Kolev had believed. In a stinging rebuke of Prosecutor Parvoleta Nikova, the judges said that if she had reviewed the material more thoroughly, Jock might have also been found guilty of the attempted murder of Tony 'the Tall' Yordanov.

All sides appealed the decision to the Supreme Court of Cassation, Bulgaria's ultimate court of appeal.

27 February 2011

Antoan Zahariev appeared on television station bTV in an interview about the case. He said the Monovs had given him permission to do so. The interviewer raised the allegation published in the *Daily Telegraph*. 'Yes, there was another case in Australia, as far as I know, an identical case to ours,' answered Antoan. 'Then he stabbed two people, but he was underage. In addition Australia has different rules and maybe he has struck some kind of a deal with the victims.'

The interviewer asked Antoan if the case had changed his life. 'It hasn't changed much,' he replied, 'except for the fact that at first I was a bit afraid, but then—time just heals.'

Eight days before the final appeal was to be heard, Levski fans at a football match unfurled a huge banner emblazoned with a portrait of Andrei, set off flares in the front row and chanted.

. . .

16 May 2011

Jock's wrists and ankles were shackled as guards brought him into court. It took fewer than three hours for the Supreme Court of Cassation to hear the final appeal. Simon was there as his defender and Dinko as his lawyer. The defence wanted a retrial, the prosecution wanted life and the victims still wanted life without parole. Once again Hristo accused the head of the Bulgarian Helsinki Committee of betrayal. This time Dr Krassimir Kanev was there; he stood and faced his former university companion.

A few weeks later, the Supreme Court of Cassation handed down its verdict in the case of Nikolai Arabadzhiev, Jock's cellmate from isolation, who had been convicted of murdering his friend and chopping up his body. He had originally been sentenced to life. The Court of Appeal reduced the sentence to twenty years, a decision which the higher court upheld.

At the end of July, the Supreme Court of Cassation decided on Jock's case. It upheld the verdict and the sentence. The court found no errors in the decisions of lower courts and no breaches of procedure that warranted a new trial or a different verdict. In response to specific complaints made on Jock's behalf, the judges said the defence had failed to explain why it wanted to re-examine the CCTV material and that the forensic evidence was self-explanatory and so did not require a second opinion. They found that there was no error in the appellate court's dismissal of Viktor Georgiev's evidence and that the loss of Ministry of Health CCTV footage was immaterial, as there was sufficient witness testimony. Rejecting the defence claim that no motive for an attack had been established, they asserted that the motive was hooliganism, a disrespect of society and its norms. Although they declared the psychiatric evidence irrelevant in that context, they drew on it to reject the request for a more severe sentence. Jock's clean police record and good character, they argued, meant twenty years would be long enough to reform him.

. . .

Jock was moved to Group 10, the section of the prison for foreigners who no longer faced court. Still one of the youngest prisoners, he had one of the longest sentences.

Convicted prisoners are allowed one day off their sentence for every two days they work or engage in formal study. Jock's grandfather, Tony, enrolled him in an arts degree by correspondence at an Australian university. The prison allowed him to do the course and the Palfreemans were led to believe that if he passed his subjects, Jock's sentence would be reduced. But in an interview for this book, the head of the prison said he had decided that only study offered by the prison would qualify as 'formal study'. The law governing how prison sentences are to be administered does not include such a stipulation. The prison was too poor to offer accredited courses.

It was six years now since Jock had left school, and he found the discipline of study, research and writing difficult. Prison conditions made it almost impossible. Because he had no access to the internet, he could not do independent research and had to rely on material sent by his university teachers. Lethargy and bouts of depression did not help.

Jock was lonely, too. By now many of his prison mates had moved on. Mohammed had been transferred to Sweden to serve the rest of his sentence. Vasia, Jock's friend from remand, had been moved to a low-security prison elsewhere in Bulgaria. Other friends had served their time and been released. That made him feel that part of him was free with them, but it also made his sense of confinement more acute.

Jock wrote an open letter to an insurrectionary anarchist online magazine, which published it. He thanked various anarchist groups for their support, including the Conspiracy of the Cells of Fire, members of which had been arrested after rioting in Greece. The CCF had included Jock in a list of people whom the organisation claimed were prisoners of the war against capitalism. Jock wrote that he had no contact with the CCF but admired the more aggressive form of protest that it promoted. In his view there was no point in talking about injustice if you do not act when you see an injustice, 'despite the real potential of death or capture'. He reiterated that he had done the right thing in going to the assistance of Roma and that he had known at the time this could get him into trouble. The Bulgarian authorities, he wrote, had 'officially kidnapped' him, denying him procedural fairness and delivering a wrongful conviction.

Tihomir Pashev and his youngest daughter continued to visit Jock. The former air force pilot and soldier knew that some Bulgarians would say it was unpatriotic not to side with the Monovs. But he was sure that Jock had not gone out that night intending to kill, and he was sticking by his friend. Still, he was angry with Jock. In defending a Gypsy, he had thrown away his future. Tihomir himself would not have rushed in to help that man. He also thought Jock had been foolish to take a knife into such a situation. But he was sure Jock had run in without thinking about what might happen, and though such impulsiveness exasperated him, he felt it made Jock less culpable.

Jock's other Samokov friends continued to see him, but their lives were changing and some were moving on. Didi had almost finished her engineering degree. Dobri was living in the United States. Sonja now had a son, and Iliyan would soon be a father.

The Monovs too were parents again: Aksenia and Hristo had adopted two little girls. These days, Aksenia would leave work and pick up her daughters from school. Hristo even appeared on television with the girls, arguing for stricter parental oversight of children.

Andrei's friend, Emil Aleksiev, still faced court, after being charged in relation to a brutal attack on some human rights protestors.

Bulgarians referred to the summer of 2011 as a *gypsy summer* because the hot weather dragged into autumn. Anti-Roma rioting broke out across the country after a driver linked to an alleged Gypsy crime boss was accused of running over and killing a young ethnic Bulgarian.

That December was especially cold. Levski fans marked the fourth anniversary of Andrei's death by unfurling a huge banner bearing a photograph of him at an indoor soccer match.

One month later, Hristo Monov took part in a panel discussion on a Bulgarian television station. The panel, made up of forensic experts, was asked to consider the role of psychiatric and psychological evidence in criminal trials. Hristo said the case involving his son showed such evidence could be misleading. According to him the experts who examined Jock based their conclusion that he was not aggressive on an outdated form of assessment. Hristo then broadened his attack to all the experts in his son's case and the courts that assigned them. 'At least as far as psychology and use of the tools of psychology are concerned,' he said, 'these people were not prepared.' He also claimed that judges needed to be better trained. 'In this particular case of Jock Palfreeman, we are talking about a proven sociopath,' he said.

Hristo said the judges had in front of them the only psychological profile of Jock required to lock him up for life: the unfounded allegation by two youths published in a Sydney newspaper soon after Jock was arrested and one made by a Sydney lawyer about an incident that took place when Jock was already abroad. 'This man, no matter when he will get released, will kill again. However, he only received twenty years. Let this be on the conscience of those who gave him twenty years.'

For Hristo the system had failed. He could not move on until Jock was locked up for life.

CHAPTER 27

While making a documentary about Jock's case for ABC's *Australian Story*, I started to worry that I might be too close to the facts and to the people involved. Seeking an expert but detached assessment, I approached Professor Dave Barclay, an internationally renowned forensic scientist based in Scotland, who had assisted police in many countries, including Australia. He agreed to go through the witness statements, expert reports and court transcripts I had gathered.

Barclay's initial reaction was that anyone carrying a knife was looking for trouble. Unlike Bulgaria, it was illegal to carry one in the United Kingdom where there had been a disturbing increase in the incidence of knife-related crimes. Barclay thought that even if Jock was not in fact looking for trouble, producing a knife had been an error in judgement. Jock had said he had hoped the youths would run away when they saw the knife. In Barclay's experience, drunken young men will run towards a weapon of any sort, determined to prove their superior might.

As he read the evidence, Barclay became increasingly disturbed by how much evidence was missing, particularly the CCTV recordings from the Ministry of Health. The forensic evidence was inconclusive and yet had been drawn on as proof of Jock's guilt. Worse still, the investigator, the prosecutor and the courts had made deliberate attempts to massage witness accounts so as to secure Jock's conviction. 'Every piece of evidence that was in favour of him was being ignored and had been ignored right from the crime scene and other pieces of evidence from the people themselves in the group, from independent witnesses and from Jock Palfreeman, they'd all been manipulated so they excluded the involvement of the Roma, they excluded any culpability by the group,' Barclay said. 'It became obvious that [Jock] was being railroaded completely.'

. . .

Many questions about this case remained unanswered. Now that the events of 28 December 2007 were no longer before the courts, I decided to return to Sofia. I hoped I could uncover more of the truth.

The first judge before whom Jock appeared had been bail judge Mimi Petrova. She told me his case was one of the few that had affected her emotionally. She was convinced that Jock was a racist who felt superior to Bulgarians. 'I compared some of his views with those of Hitler,' she explained. 'Yes, this case stayed with me because it's going to be very bad if we actually raise our children to hate certain nations or social groups. I even embrace Gypsies, although I can't deny the fact that most of the crimes [in Bulgaria] are committed by Gypsies.' Jock, she thought, regarded Bulgarians with the same disdain that people less tolerant than herself held for Gypsies.

The judge said she had found no evidence that the group of youths had attacked either Jock or a Gypsy. She repeatedly pointed out that no Roma had been found. Indeed, she believed he had made up the story about the Gypsy so as 'to have a good motive'. She was sure no Gypsy would have tangled with a crowd of youths: 'Roma in Bulgaria are fearful. They launch attacks in groups against people who are on their own. If you read the Bulgarian press, you'll see that they confront single women, single elderly people, but when they see a big group, there's no way they will confront it.' She was sure no Gypsy would have tangled with a crowd of youths. But she seemed to assume that if conflict arose between Roman and ethnic Bulgarians, it would have been the Roma who instigated it.

Even if there had been a Gypsy, Petrova said, Jock's running in to help would have been irrational. 'When you defend someone, don't you want first to know what's going on? Because the Roma [person] could have killed [someone]. Besides, there were no Roma.' She added that she did not know the Monovs, but she had understood that Andrei had been the least noisy of all the youths that night, whose only crime had been being a bit loud.

· · ·

Judge Georgi Kolev's analysis of what had motivated Jock was almost as perplexing as that of Judge Petrova. He had formed the view that Jock had wanted 'to take justice into his own hands'. After all, he had done so before. 'As far as I know, in Sydney he had a similar incident with the corresponding indigenous groups in Australia,' Kolev said, apparently confusing Jock's claim to have helped a Gypsy in St Nedelya Square with the unsubstantiated allegation that he had once been involved in a knife attack. But that still left unanswered the question of what had provoked Jock. 'Unfortunately, this was not established during the trial,' said Kolev. 'There could be only speculation as to why this happened. Since it was not established during the trial, it wasn't discussed.'

He saw no indication that Roma had been in the square that night, much less under attack. 'If it had been proved that such people were present, then [the case] would have been looked at in a whole new aspect,' he said. 'But there was no evidence for that.' This view ran counter to the appellate judges' finding that there was evidence of both. I reminded him of testimony from people working at the Sheraton that Jock had been caught up in a brutal bashing before he brought out his knife. 'There is no such independent witness that has said that he was attacked,' Judge Kolev said, then chuckled. 'It's not a secret; all that was filed during the trial is still there,' he said. 'It will be kept in the archive for the next ten years. If there is such evidence, it will be part of the trial [record]. You can look at it—you won't be denied access.'

· · ·

In the Sofia Palace of Justice, I was ushered into what is known as the Lawyers Library to go through the file. At the front of the file were police incident reports handwritten on yellow foolscap paper. A cigarette burn through four pages indicated that someone had read them.

One of the points at issue during the appeal was whether Andrei Monov's friends had told police that Jock had intervened in a fight with Gypsies. Three officers who told the investigator that they had heard this from colleagues later withdrew their remarks. When the Court of Appeal found they had in fact made those statements, it dismissed the evidence as hearsay. This raised the question why the officers who had first spoken to Andrei's friends and noted their version of events were never tracked down.

The chief investigating officer on the case, Tanya Alakusheva, had told me she could not find the first police at the scene because attending police that night had come from a handful of stations and no one had taken down their names at the time. Now, here at the top of the case file, I was looking at just the information she needed—a police incident report from an officer who had heard the account firsthand. The report had Alakusheva's name on it and had been signed on her behalf on the day of the incident.

Officer Slaveikov wrote that he had spoken to Blagovest Trifonov, Alexander Donev, Nikolai Rabadzhiev, Vasil Velevski and Mariyan Tsolov, a member of Andrei's group who was never called as a witness. The officer had taken down their identity and contact details, as well as their account of what had just happened. He said that, before the witnesses were taken to Police Station No. 3, they had told him they had 'passed by two Roma people who swore at them'. According to the witnesses, there had been a 'dispute' between the Gypsies and the youths lagging behind. A 'third person' had then intervened who they thought came from the other end of St Nedelya Square. 'This same person pulled out a knife and stabbed two of the boys,' noted Slaveikov, recounting what the witnesses had told him. Alakusheva had this report all along. Her failure—and that of Prosecutor Nikova—to interview Slaveikov is inexplicable. The report lends weight to the defence claim that both Alakusheva and Nikova had excluded the freshest account of events in favour of another, later narrative.

In the bail hearing Judge Mimi Petrova dismissed Jock's argument that he had gone to the defence of someone. She suggested that he had come up with this excuse after hearing talk about an incident report. It is highly likely Petrova was referring to Slaveikov's report. If that is the case, she referred to the officer's notes on what the kiosk worker had said, rather than what Andrei's friends had told him. Trial judge Georgi Kolev also had access to the report and could have called the officer as a witness. Dinko Kanchev told me he had been aware of the report but dismissed it because a court would not accept an incident report as evidence. The Palfreemans knew nothing about it.

Equally bizarre was the paper trail regarding the missing CCTV material. Tanya Alakusheva had requested the traffic-camera recordings on the day of the incident. But she waited five days before filing a request for the recordings from the Ministry of Health CCTV camera, only to be told that those recordings had just been erased. Documents in the court file show that almost six weeks into the investigation, Jock's lawyer asked Tanya Alakusheva to find out if the Ministry of Health recordings could be restored and, if so, to have them examined by an expert. A fortnight later she wrote this reply: 'The hard disk containing the recordings of the security cameras at the Ministry of Health is part of the evidence of this trial and is kept in the Ministry of Health in case we need to do some additional actions on it.' She concluded: 'There's a CCTV recording from the traffic cameras. The forensic report on it is available on paper.'

The Maxtor hard drive was being kept in a Ministry of Health safe as evidence. On the first day of the trial the defence asked the court to have the hard drive tested. Nine months later, Dinko repeated the request. Dismissing protestation from the prosecutor, the court asked the Institute of Computer Technology to appoint an expert for the job. The expert, Dobrinka Dimitrova, was tasked with familiarising herself with the 'trial documents' and producing a report based on the information therein. Her findings make for chilling reading.

Dimitrova explained that she had met with an official from the Ministry of Health, who showed her the hard drive and told her it had been disabled by an electrical failure thirty days after the incident. She wrote in her report that, to ascertain just what condition it was in and whether material could be recovered from it, she would need to test it properly. The paper trail stops here. It appears that the hard drive was never tested.

At the end of September 2009 the defence asked the court to press the Ministry of Health for access to its surveillance computer system. The court was advised that the Ministry of Health had thrown it out when it introduced a new system. However, there was no mention of the hard drive in the Ministry of Health safe. It is possible that it still exists.

. . .

My attention turned to the video recordings that had been recovered—those from the traffic and metro cameras. The defence had been given only two opportunities to watch them, both under difficult conditions. I was given access to a DVD that was said to hold the only copies of this material and spent days watching and re-watching the images. I sat in the same small courtroom where the Palfreemans and Monovs had jostled for space in front of the laptop computer as they struggled to see the last moments of Andrei's life and the last hour of Jock's freedom.

The DVD is kept in a cracked and unlabelled case. Handwritten on the disc is 'DVD 8 178, 04.01.8'. The more I watched this silent recording, the more I could discern from its grainy images, even though faces for the most part were unrecognisable. By combining known details about people's clothing with those parts of the witness accounts that correlate with the actions on the recording, I started to make sense of what had happened.

There are several video clips, each one taken by a different surveillance camera. The camera at the metro shows Andrei and his companions at 1.11 a.m. ascending the stairs to St Nedelya Square. Although the images are far from sharp, it is possible that a family member, for example, might recognise a face and characteristic posture or body movement here. The young people appear to be talking and either singing or chanting. One of the men removes his light-coloured beanie and puts it in his jacket pocket. There is a white stripe marking across the front of his jacket. He is wearing white shoes. Later shots indicate that a figure with a white stripe across the front also has a white stripe marking across the back. In forensic reports, Andrei's jacket is described as having white markings on the front and back but with a black beanie in his pocket. His shoes were described as white sneakers. A grey beanie with gloves inside it was found on the bloodied road but not tested for DNA.

The longest clip was shot from a camera on a high stand on the east side of Maria Louisa which takes in the southern half of the square. Curiously, the time-of-day code on this clip runs at double speed so it cannot serve as a guide. I used the relevant time-of-day codes provided by the CCTV expert Yordan Dalukov and a stopwatch to estimate durations. In his report, Dalukov noted that the time on his copy of the recordings was six minutes ahead of real time.

The poor quality of this recording and the camera's distance from the action make it impossible to identify faces. To estimate the identity of various figures, I relied on evidence in the court file—in particular the witness statements and trial testimony, including Jock's.

It is just possible to make out two figures—one in white clothing—crossing Stamboliyski from the direction of the Happy restaurant and stopping at the kiosk. Presumably they are Anton 'Tony' Doychev and Lindsay Welsh. Dalukov times this move at 1.10.32 a.m. Tony and Lindsay appear to spend about one minute at the kiosk before a figure, who could well be Jock, crosses Stamboliyski to join them. Twelve seconds later yet another figure also crosses the road. He could well be one of Tony's friends warning them to get out of the area. Within the next twelve seconds, Jock and Tony lead Lindsay back to the Happy garden. It is now 1.12.11 a.m. Within about twenty seconds, the first of Andrei's group crosses the square and Stamboliyski, at that point possibly seeing Jock and his friends huddled behind the Happy courtyard wall.

The last members of the group reach the pedestrian crossing lights opposite the Happy restaurant on Stamboliyski Boulevard just over a minute after Jock and his friends left the square. Testimony from group members indicates that those youths include Tony 'the Tall' Yordanov, Andrei Monov, Antoan Zahariev, Kristian Dimov and Alexander Donev. By now, those ahead of them have either crossed the road or are at the kiosk.

Within seconds, a lone figure crosses Stamboliyski and, without stopping, walks past the stragglers still on the square side of the crossing. That figure is likely to be one of 'the strangers' or Gypsies. Two stragglers start following the figure. Judging by the white stripe on his jacket and white shoes, one of them could be the figure who removed the beanie he was wearing in the metro. The other has a lot of white on his jacket. This might have been the scene that Jock's companion Anton 'Tony' Doychev saw when he looked up from his mobile phone and saw a 'quiet' group.

At 1.13.57, another person comes across from the direction of Maria Louisa Boulevard who gestures to the first figure as if to warn him that he is being followed. That person is likely to be the second 'stranger' or Gypsy.

About ten seconds later, the straggler with the white stripe appears to lunge at the second 'stranger', missing him; he then makes a similar lunge at the first one, who promptly runs away. This makes dramatic viewing, in large part because it seems to set the scene for what follows. The question is, who are these two group members, and which of them lunged at the two 'stranger' figures? Alexander Donev told the investigator that Andrei Monov had had an exchange with the unknown people. Martin Stoilov told her that Tony 'the Tall' Yordanov did. Tony told the court that it was him and Andrei.

Even before the second lunge, the rest of the group starts rushing after the remaining stranger. This suggests they are all responding to something shouted. The mass rush starkly contradicts Tony Yordanov's insistence in court that 'none of my friends had come to help'. One group member runs onto Maria Louisa to chase the second of the strangers towards the metro and out of frame. The rest chase the first figure. The man with the white stripe seems to trip in his haste but does not fall.

The surge of youths—from as far away as the Happy restaurant on the other side of Stamboliyski Boulevard—in pursuit of the first man in particular is astonishing. Had Jock been watching from the Happy restaurant, he would have seen this chase. Certainly Mladen, the kiosk worker who had heard the derogatory cry of 'mango', did.

At this point, two stocky figures emerge from behind the Nescafé billboard; they walk arm in arm with their backs to the camera and are seemingly unconnected to the group. They are heading towards the intersection but have to move aside to avoid the rush of youths coming towards them. As the youths fly past, the stocky figures look back briefly but continue on their way without stopping. The last of the group members now disappear behind the billboard.

At 1.14.24, a figure dashes across Stamboliyski, past the kiosk, and along the Ministry of Health building, and disappears behind the billboard. Although nothing about the figure is recognisable, this is almost certainly Jock. If so, he watches what happens between the group members and the two other men for a minute before he runs across the square, thirty seconds of that includes what is happening on the other side of the billboard.

The recording does not show what happens at that point. Although they do not refer to seeing a Gypsy, Viktor Georgiev and Lyubomir Tomov told the court they saw a bashing some ten metres from the metro, after which a man pulled out a knife and waved it around. The car park cabins at the Sheraton hotel face the area behind the billboard, so Viktor Georgiev and Lyubomir Tomov would have had a clear view of what happened. It is likely that when Jock had run across the square, Georgiev had been concentrating on the bashing. He could well have assumed the person he had seen being chased was the same person he heard calling out in English while under attack near the metro.

Emil Aleksiev and Alexander Donev told police there had been an altercation near Bulbank, which is near the metro. Emil later told court he first saw Jock near the ticket booth, which is just on the other side of the billboard. There is an open area south of the metro but between the metro and Bulbank. This area is closer to the billboard and more in line with both the Ministry of Health entrance and one of the two cabins in the Sheraton car park. Possibly this was where the altercation took place.

One minute and twenty seconds pass. During this time the group, Jock and at least one of the 'strangers' are beyond the billboard and so out of camera range. The only movement I can see in frame during this time is a garbage truck going south along Maria Louisa on one of the two lanes closest to the square. It waits for the lights to change at the T-junction. At 1.15.44, two youths run back towards the pedestrian lights. The rest of the group emerges from behind the billboard some thirty-seven seconds later. Also heading to Stamboliyski Boulevard, they are walking, and some are looking over their shoulders. Then the figure with the white stripe runs through the group and onto Maria Louisa Boulevard.

Some fifteen seconds after the majority of the group comes into view, a figure with a large white mark on its back emerges. Jock had an A4-sized 'badge' pinned to the back of his jacket, so this is likely to be him. The figure is walking swiftly. His arms are down. He looks as if he is rounding up other figures who have strayed from the pack. It is possible to construe this as Jock ensuring that nobody broke away and rushed at him from behind. The video is grainy, so it is not possible to see if he is carrying a knife. If he was brandishing the knife at this point, Jock would have appeared threatening to those in the rear, although they are not running away from him.

It is possible that most of the group members were not even aware that Jock was approaching them. Mladen the kiosk worker described a large group of youths returning across the square, laughing and drunkenly bumping into his kiosk. This suggests that many of them were relaxed and had seen nothing near the metro to alarm them.

But the mood changes quickly. Three cars driving south along Maria Louisa pull up at the T-junction lights, several metres away from what happens next. Just as Jock reaches the intersection of Stamboliyski and Maria Louisa, there is a commotion. The recording shows many of the youths bending and throwing things. One of them is the figure with the largely white jacket who was with the youth with the white stripe when he made the initial lunges at the two 'strangers'. This figure is to the left of Jock at the intersection. One of the cars waiting for the lights to change moves into the outside lane but stops just short of the lights and the melee that is now spilling onto Maria Louisa. It is very likely that this is the point when the kiosk worker first noted two groups throwing pavers at each other. It is possible that this is the moment when Tony looked up from his mobile phone again and this time saw Jock running between two lines of boys who then surrounded him, and when Lindsay Welsh saw something happening to Jock. This may also be the point when Nikolai Rabadzhiev turned to see what had been going on. If so, that might explain why the prosecutor placed the melee here rather than closer to the metro, where the independent witnesses had testified it began.

Less than fifteen seconds after emerging from behind the billboard, Jock appears to be hit in the head and then falls to the ground. In his written report, Yordan Dalukov, the expert CCTV analyst at the trial, did not describe this sequence, and the Palfreemans seemingly missed it when they viewed the recording. But Viktor Georgiev testified he had seen it. After one or two seconds on the ground, Jock jumps up and steps backwards onto Maria Louisa. The swirl of movement then continues between a tree, the kiosk, and the two telephone booths at the intersection. Jock appears to be surrounded. There is nothing stopping those around him from running away, contrary to what some of the group claimed in their statements. Instead of running away, they continue moving towards him and throwing objects they have picked up from the ground.

Some fifteen seconds after he fell, Jock takes off between some of the youths and, as if running away, heads towards the Ministry of Health, then disappears out of camera range. The group pursues him. Jock comes into shot again as he walks along the ministry building in the direction of the kiosk. His right arm is stretched out in front of him. It is not possible to see whether he is holding anything, but presumably he has the knife in his hand. The figure with the white stripe once again runs away from the group towards Maria Louisa Boulevard.

Martin Stoilov testified that Andrei Monov ran away like that after he saw Jock attack Antoan Zahariev with the knife. Martin could have been referring to this moment or to the moment when the figure ran just before Jock appeared from behind the billboard. It is not clear at what point in the sequence of events Antoan was injured. In her indictment, the prosecutor located the attack on Antoan and Andrei in the same area, noting that the strikes to Antoan and Andrei had occurred one after another, in 'one continuous action'. If they did, the CCTV recording suggests that Jock would have feared for his life by the time he inflicted them.

Lindsay wrote in her statement that she thought she saw Jock being chased. The video shows that she had already gone after Jock and was at the square in time to have seen this chase and the ensuing melee. Andrei's friends Kristian Dimov and Blagovest Trifonov told the investigator there had been a blonde woman calling out to Jock during the attack. The

Palfreemans failed to detect her presence on the scene in the brief viewing time they were permitted. Nevertheless, this aspect of the recording makes it all the more extraordinary that the prosecutor—who could view the material as closely and for as long as she wished—argued both in her indictment and at trial that it was unnecessary to speak to Lindsay because Grayham, who was not even at the scene, had testified that she did not see a stabbing. Lindsay's subsequent failure to remember seeing the ensuing fight could be explained by a combination of factors: shock, her high level of intoxication, Jock being in the middle of a swirl of movement that blocked her view, and the passage of time.

By now two more cars have pulled up at the lights. The youths keep coming at Jock and appear to surround him. They pick up and throw more objects. The ones closest to the kiosk take turns to run in towards him and then dash away. Then one of them starts walking away from the pack and falls near the corner of Maria Louisa and Stamboliyski boulevards. The expert report says this happened at 1.17.39. Although the picture is so indistinct that no clothing or facial features are recognisable, it is reasonable to assume this was Andrei Monov; we know he did end up on the road. The court file contains photographs of Andrei's jacket and a light-coloured beanie on the road. The straggler with a lot of white on his jacket who was with the youth who lunged at the 'stranger' goes to the fallen figure and then returns to the others, who are still with Jock.

Some twenty seconds after Andrei falls, some friends help him move some thirteen metres further along Stamboliyski Boulevard, closer to where the tribute to him still stands. The fact that none of the witnesses ever mentioned this should simply remind us that memory can inadvertently be selective.

When the camera swings back to the area between the Ministry of Health and the kiosk, the focus sharpens. Jock is prostrate on the ground, largely hidden by a tree, and two men are holding back some of the youths, who are described by witnesses as shouting and spitting at him. Workers from the Sheraton come into vision and go straight to Jock. The woman who was with Nikolai Kotev and had been watching all this with him—possibly the alleged prostitute—comes to see what is going on; her face is identifiable.

The straggler with a lot of white on his jacket takes off his jacket, then a few moments later, puts it on again. He is noticeably tall. At one point Jock starts to move off, but a guard stops him.

The scene now fills with police lights and officers. One officer walks towards a police van with a worker from the Sheraton and one of the guards, who was never identified. As Jock is led towards a police van, a scrum follows the van, then surrounds it, with some figures appearing to be hitting or rocking it.

Images such as these are open to various interpretations. They give a sense of the sequence of events, but they cannot resolve all questions. The CCTV video does strongly suggest that two group members triggered an incident with two 'strangers', which escalated when a large number of youths chased one of the figures out of camera range. The group member with the white stripe seems to have been the prime instigator of the initial action. It is possible he was Andrei Monov. It is possible the man with a lot of white on his jacket was Tony Yordanov. But the indistinctness of the images means that not even Andrei's or Tony's mother could tell for sure. It is also possible that these figures were two of the other group members indentified as lagging behind at the pedestrian crossing. The footage suggests the youths pursuing Jock could have got away from him several times, but chose not to. It suggests that Jock went too far in pushing the youths away from whomever he had run after in the first place—presumably the 'stranger'. What is certain is that moments before Andrei was fatally stabbed, Jock had been struck by something that caused him to fall to the ground; he was then chased as he tried to escape.

It took fewer than five minutes for an incident to go from a group of youths chasing two men to Andrei dying on the road. Five minutes fuelled by snap decisions, alcohol, aggression and a knife.

The slogan on the Nescafé advertisement they had all run past could not be any more eerie: 'An unexpectedly good combination' indeed.

. . .

When I interviewed Tanya Alakusheva, she said the charge of hooliganism had not been her recommendation. According to her, the killing had been an accident, and she felt for both Jock and Andrei. *'Zloto sleze na zemyata,'* she said as we parted: 'Evil came down to Earth that night.'

. . .

Aksenia Monova arranged to meet me in the Lawyers Library at 11 one morning. I had already sent the notary several letters, asking if Aksenia would tell me her side of the story. My interpreter had also had many telephone discussions with her on my behalf. Mrs Monova said she wanted to show me things in the court file. I arrived at 9.30 to review parts of the file, as I hoped she might be able to shed light on them.

Aksenia arrived early, accompanied by a court official. She flicked through the pages until she reached the autopsy reports, then pointed at a photograph of her son's body, the rib cage cut open. 'This is what your man did to my son!' she said. 'It is Mother's Day today, and this is my present,' Aksenia continued, turning to photographs of Andrei's blood-drenched shirt and of his battered face on the autopsy slab. In an angry tone, she added that the man, whose name she never uttered, would still be young when he was released from jail. Then she launched into a tirade against the head of the Bulgarian Helsinki Committee, Dr Krassimir Kanev. 'He's all about human rights,' she said. 'Isn't the greatest human right the right to life?' She turned to the court official and scolded her for allowing me to go through the file and look at her 'naked son'. Tears welled in the court official's eyes. Tears welled in mine. Then, just as suddenly as Aksenia had appeared, she left the room. In a follow-up telephone conversation she said she would consider another meeting if I first provided her with information about the allegation that Jock had been involved in an attack in Sydney. I left it at that. My job was only to get her side of the story.

. . .

The head of the prison told me that, after a long stretch without incident, Jock was now causing trouble again. Jock did not accept the court verdict, he said, and this made him harder to reform. He added that if the prison management team did not believe he had reformed, Jock would have no chance of being granted parole after serving ten years.

Krassimir Kanev has been visiting prisoners across the Balkans and in Russia for most of his career. He told me parole is rarely granted in Bulgaria, so no matter what Jock did, his chances of early release were slim. He described Jock as 'charismatic, strong of character and a natural leader' with a 'unique' determination to help those he felt were being wronged or ill-treated. However, Krassimir said even after ten years in jail, Jock would not be the same person his parents had farewelled at Sydney airport. 'It's like being buried alive,' Kanev said. 'The prison experience will have irrevocably changed him.'

The day I left Bulgaria, Jock became involved in a fight outside the prison canteen. A new prisoner had been pushing into the queue for weeks, and the guards had done nothing to stop him. Jock believed that if this continued, the prisoner would regard him and the other old-timers as his bitches, to use the prison vernacular—people he could step on with impunity. Jock felt he needed to establish boundaries. When the prisoner pushed in again, he hit him.

Since then, Jock has increased pressure on the prison authorities to abide by the legal regulations. At one point he staged a hunger strike in protest over unfair punishment and conditions. The honorary Australian consul, Indiana Trifonova, has her hands full taking up Jock's complaints to the various authorities.

Dinko no longer acts for Jock now that his case has run its course, but he speaks fondly of both him and Simon. He smiles as he recalls their debates and arguments.

During the first two and a half years he was in prison, Jock began quietly drumming up support among foreign and Bulgarian inmates for a prisoners' association or union; if they banded together, he argued, they would have more success in forcing authorities to adhere to the regulations. Jock won immediate support from his friends in the foreigners' section. Convincing the rest of the prison population was harder. Jock had fleeting conversations with Bulgarian prisoners whom he passed on his way to the exercise yard and the visitors room. But guards were always around and words had to be carefully chosen, right down to the name of the group being proposed. Jock could not appear to be organising a revolt of any kind.

His problems went beyond the guards and snitches. Bulgarian prisoners feared that getting involved could destroy their chances of early release and make their time in prison more difficult. Jock paid a new lawyer to help him register the association so that prisoners would have the safeguard of belonging to a non-governmental organisation, but the lawyer took his money and disappeared.

When Jock told Krassimir Kanev what had happened, Kanev offered him the assistance of lawyers from the Helsinki Committee to apply to the Sofia Court for formal recognition of the prisoners' association. Jock was president, Stoyan, the Bulgarian lifer he had met in isolation, was vice-president, Murad was treasurer and a Bulgarian prisoner named Yanko was the secretary. There were some fifteen other founding members. In August 2012, Jock's application was approved, and the Bulgarian Prisoners' Rehabilitation Association was born. Kanev was elated. According to him, this was a first for Bulgaria. Jock and he are now working together on taking some of the problems raised by prisoners to both Bulgarian courts and the European Court of Human Rights.

. . .

In August 2012 Hristo Monov took his two adopted daughters to a weekend of football matches held in memory of his son. Andrei's friends and Levski fans chanted 'Andy is with us, forever with us'. Hristo gently stroked the hair of one daughter who wore a black-and-white scarf bearing Andrei's name and silhouette.

Hristo told a television reporter that football was more than a game for his son. 'He [Andrei] not only understood the game, he got the philosophy behind it. He thought that it's a way people can express themselves as well as the essence of our society—namely to live together, to compete, to enjoy what we are doing, to obey the rules.'

. . .

That summer I returned to Bulgaria for my seventh and final visit. This time I was given permission to interview Jock in his cell, Cell 17. As I had already seen much of the prison, including other parts of the foreigners' section, the general decay and overcrowding did not surprise me. Jock's cell is the biggest on the second floor. In return for that luxury, he is required to serve as a stabilising influence for convicted illegal immigrants. The irony of a murderer looking after men whose only crime is to have broken border control regulations is not lost on Jock. Nevertheless, he takes the role seriously.

The day I visited was swelteringly hot. A guard sat in the corridor outside the cell but never entered. Jock was wearing a singlet, jeans and his trademark Army-style boots. He had stopped smoking. Laughing, he said smoking just feeds the government coffers and ultimately pays the guards. He fidgeted with the rosary beads in his pocket. When I remarked on his watch, Jock said he was one of the only prisoners who had one and got constant requests for the time. Without the watch, he could not estimate how long it was until meals arrived or when he could go to Bible classes, the computer room or the yard. It lets him measure time passing. Bursting with energy, Jock was keen to discuss politics and history. Although I had seldom found him at a loss for words, he was far more relaxed here than in the area where prisoners usually see visitors. He offered me coffee as we sat at a rickety table near the open cell door.

After countless hours of discussions with Jock over four years, I am still struck by his capacity to adapt and survive, as well as by his passion for life. During this visit he seemed eager, jumpy, impatient, like an overgrown teenager. He seemed mature beyond his years and still a boy—a boy in a box, without a future.

Despite the cracked pipes held together with tape, the leaking, crumbling ceiling, and the cockroaches, the cell was tidy. Jock and his cellmates had used a sheet to cover a wall on which former prisoners had glued photos of naked women cut from magazines. A large Eureka flag hung from the ceiling. An Iraqi flag hung on one side of the cell, an Iranian flag on the other side. Prisoners come from everywhere. A map of the world, a Bulgarian icon and photographs of revolutionary leaders decorated the walls: Che Guevara, Fidel Castro and Vasil Levski.

Jock occupies a corner with a barred window that looks out onto another block of cells. Outside, one prisoner was shouting at another: 'I will hit you with this iron pan!' Everything seemed to be made of rusted iron and everything had sharp edges. As I moved around the cell, my trouser leg snagged on the corner of another prisoner's bed and tore.

Jock's two square metres can be divided from the rest of the cell by a sheet 'curtain'. A bookshelf bolted to the wall above his bed is filled with books people have sent him over the years. There is a stamp album his grandmother sent him in which he collects the stamps that come on letters sent by sympathisers around the world. Clothes stuffed into plastic bags hang from the bookshelf. Among them is a Union Jack badge that Anton 'Tony' Doychev gave Jock when he visited him in prison.

At the head of Jock's bed is a small television. Stuck to the side of the screen are two small photographs: one of his parents, the other of Jock and Spencer as young boys with baby Angus. On the section of wall that runs beside the bed is a copy of the order of service for the funeral of Jock's school friend Louis Simpson, who died of cancer. Beside it hangs a crucifix. There is also a photo of Spencer and Jock, taken the first time Spencer came to visit. Arms around each other, they are both grinning. Jock looks like a happy kid, brimming with optimism.

Jock has written the words of Joe Hill's stirring 'Workers of the World, Awaken' on the wall near his pillow: 'If the workers get a notion they can stop all speeding trains . . .' Next to his bedhead is a small bench where prisoners sit and watch TV with him or talk about their problems.

On a small desk next to the foot of Jock's bed is a prison-made fish tank that he bought from a prisoner for cigarettes. In it he is breeding guppies, which he feeds with cockroaches. On the window sill next to the desk he has some chillies growing in pots. In winter, he covers the plants with a plastic bag to hothouse them. Under his iron-framed bed sleep two stray cats that adopted him as kittens. Jock named them Lion and Tiger and feeds them whatever he can spare.

A prisoner with no shirt and a distended belly button pushed a rusty iron trolley along the corridor outside Jock's cell. He was delivering lunch. Jock spoke to him in Bulgarian and brought in the cell's allocation: six cold cooked livers, three cups of tomato sauce with olives, and a loaf and a half of bread. As he bent down to pick up the cats, Jock's knees creaked like those of an old man—the result of a poor diet and immobility. He spends twenty-two and a half hours a day in this cell, seldom moving from his bed.

The formal recognition of the prisoners' association had given Jock a new lease of life. 'I hope that every day someone in the [prison] administration is swearing about Jock Palfreeman,' he said, laughing. When I asked why he was sticking out his neck for others, Jock said it was partly from self-interest: 'What helps other prisoners helps me.' But he was motivated by altruism, too: 'I am in prison because I was helping other people,' he added. 'Why am I doing this? Because I still want to help other people.'

A number of Catholic high schools, including Riverview, are studying Jock's case as part of their syllabus on social justice. Students aged eleven to sixteen discuss whether the individual has a responsibility to help others even when it could be dangerous to do so and was Jock morally bound to intervene when he saw someone being attacked. The students I observed were passionate defenders of his attempt to help and in awe of his courage for doing that on his own, but divided on whether he should have brought out a knife. After the class, one of them showed me a letter Jock had written in response to her questions about what Simon had done for him. 'My dad is awesome,' he had written. In Jock's vocabulary that is high praise indeed. He had seen a whole new side to his father. 'Dad can do anything,' he told me. 'So long as it's on his list!'

Jock's future remains uncertain. His family want him transferred to Australia to serve the rest of his sentence so that they can be nearby to monitor his well-being. Both Australia and Bulgaria are signatories to an international prisoner-transfer agreement, but the Bulgarian Justice Minister has advised the Australian government that transfer cannot be considered until Jock has paid the civil claimants the compensation awarded to them by the courts.

Simon fears that, even if he managed to raise the compensation money, paying it would not guarantee his son's transfer. He also worries that Jock himself might put a spanner in the works. Jock would need to sign off on the payment, and he continues to maintain that Antoan Zahariev was an aggressor, not a victim, and should therefore not receive compensation.

Simon lives with regrets about all that he feels he didn't do right during the trial. Should he have spent more time getting the court file translated? Should he have hired a private detective? Should he have pushed harder to see more of the CCTV recording? Should he have been more assertive generally?

For a long time, Simon slept beside the phone, always ready for a call from Bulgaria. Now he no longer feels so directly responsible for Jock's fate. The task of applying to the European Court of Human Rights is with the Melbourne pro bono lawyers. As for the request for Jock's transfer to an Australian prison, that is in the government's hands.

Yet Simon still sleeps fitfully, unable to shake a lingering sense of dread. For as long as Jock remains in Bulgaria, Simon will carry the fear of a midnight call telling him something has happened to his son in jail, and that he will never see his grin or hear his laugh again.

In the meantime, each night in the Hunter Valley, grandfather Tony's solar-powered lamp still shines, waiting for the day of Jock's return.

LIST OF CHARACTERS

THE AUSTRALIAN FAMILY
Jock Palfreeman
Simon Palfreeman, his father
Helen Palfreeman, Simon's second wife and Jock's stepmother
Mary Jane Palfreeman, Jock's mother and Simon's former wife
Spencer and Angus Palfreeman, Jock's younger brothers
Barbara Palfreeman, Simon's mother
Tony Palfreeman, Simon's father
Geri Palfreeman, Simon's sister
Paul Henaghan, Geri's partner

JOCK'S AUSTRALIAN FRIENDS
Karl Ferguson, school friend
Louis Simpson, school friend
Hugh Simpson, Louis Simpson's brother
Ashleigh (Ash) Hart, friend from school years
Marty Silk, school friend

JOCK'S BRITISH FRIENDS
Grayham Saunders
Lindsay Welsh

JOCK'S BULGARIAN FRIENDS

Anton Doychev (known as Tony)—met Jock at the Rock Bar that night

Iliyan Yordanov, Jock's first close Bulgarian friend

Sonja Nikolova, Iliyan's cousin

Dobri Danchev

Diana Alexandrova (known as Didi)

Tihomir Pashev, former Army captain with whom Jock lived outside Samokov

Simeon Panov (known as Simo), Gypsy, rescued by Jock in a previous incident

THE BULGARIAN FAMILY

Andrei Monov, died from a knife wound

Hristo Monov, father, psychologist

Aksenia Monova, mother, lawyer

AT ANDREI MONOV'S FUNERAL

Lazar Gruev, head of the Court of Cassation, the highest court in Bulgaria

Mihail Mikov, Member of Parliament and eventually the Interior Minister

Chavdar Georgiev, Deputy Environment Minister and lawyer

Zlatin Tepsiev, head of the Levski Fan Club

Sonja Momchilova, family friend

ADDITIONAL FRIENDS OF ANDREI MONOV

Gabriela Videnova

Ivailo Iliev

IN THE GROUP WITH ANDREI MONOV AT ST NEDELYA SQUARE

Antoan Zahariev, victim of non-fatal knife wound

Kristian Dimov, Andrei's close friend

Martin Stoilov

Emil Aleksiev

Tony Yordanov (known as Tony the Tall)

Alexander Donev

Nikolai Rabadzhiev, met Andrei for the first time that night

Blagovest Trifonov

Kaloyan Karlov

Vasil Velevski

INDEPENDENT WITNESSES

Mladen Nikolov, kiosk worker

Viktor Georgiev, security guard at the Sheraton

Nikolai Kotev, Sheraton car park attendant

Asen Stoychev, police officer at scene soon after melee

Lyubomir Tomov, Sheraton car park attendant

Emil Yankov, taxi driver

POLICE STATION NO. 3

Tanya Alakusheva, Chief Investigating Officer

Zlatina Butchkova, Investigating Officer

Nikola Kostov, Investigating Officer

Petar Katsarov, officer at scene soon after melee

Viktor Lyubenov, officer at scene soon after melee

Krassimira Stoyadinova, officer at scene soon after melee

Slaveiko Tsonkov, officer at scene soon after melee

ASSISTING JOCK IN LEGAL PROCEEDINGS

Galina Vodkadzhieva (married name Stoeva), interpreter and translator

Stoiko Barborski, Jock's first lawyer

Dinko Kanchev, Jock's second lawyer

JUDGES

Mimi Petrova, bail judge

Georgi Kolev, trial judge

Petko Kanchev, lay judge (professional juror)

Snezhana Dushkova, chair of panel of three judges hearing the appeal

PROSECUTION

Parvoleta Nikova, prosecutor

Bozhidar Dzhambazov, current deputy Sofia City prosecutor

Nikolai Kokinov, Sofia City prosecutor

EXPERT WITNESSES

Yordan Dalukov, Interior Ministry analyst of CCTV footage

Stanislav Hristov, Director of the Forensic Medicine and Deontology Centre at Alexandrovska Hospital; part of the team of forensic doctors who performed the autopsy

Ivan Ivanov, forensic DNA scientist

Maria Grozeva, forensic medical specialist

Georgi Angelov, Ministry of Health doctor

Nadezhda Peycheva, CCTV camera operator

Boris Shtarbanov, forensic psychiatrist

Elka Stoycheva, forensic psychiatrist

Lilyana Behar, forensic psychologist

Dobrinka Dimitrova, computer hard drive analyst

PRISONERS

Vasia, a Russian who met Jock in remand

Sasha, a Russian who met Jock in remand

Mohammed, a Swede of Iranian background

Murad, a Chechnyan

Glenn, a Dane

Budimir Kujovic, Serbian drug trafficker

Nikolai Arabadzhiev, Bulgarian murderer

Stoyan, Bulgarian prisoner sentenced to life

OTHERS

Krassimir Kanev, head of Bulgarian Helsinki Committee, human rights advocate

Mother Beate and Sister Maria, Benedictine nuns who visit Jock in prison

Petko Valov, Catholic priest who visited Jock in prison

Rumen Petkov, Interior Minister who resigned

Rangel Stanchev, alleged boyfriend of Prosecutor Parvoleta Nikova

Assen Yordanoff, Burgas-based investigative reporter

Milen Dimitrov, Burgas regional head of police

Angel Georgiev, Senior Prosecutor in Burgas and in charge of investigation into Rangel Stanchev

Svetlozar Lolov, 'The Rice Baron'

Magdalina Guenova, blogger

Yonko Grozev, Bulgarian human rights lawyer and commentator

AUSTRALIAN DIPLOMATIC STAFF

David Chaplin, former consul at the embassy in Athens

Indiana Trifonova, honorary consul based in Sofia

PRO BONO AUSTRALIAN LEGAL TEAM ASSISTING SIMON

Julian McMahon, criminal defence barrister

Peter Morrissey, SC

Ruth Shann, junior barrister

ACKNOWLEDGEMENTS

My original aim was to talk to all the key players in this tragic story. Although they were all contacted, some declined the opportunity to take part—in particular, Hristo Monov and, through his lawyer, Antoan Zahariev. Others allowed limited access. Aksenia Monova agreed that I could write in her voice but spent little time talking to either my researcher or myself. Mary Jane Palfreeman also gave me very little time. Although I contacted many of the young men who had been with Andrei when he died, few would say more than that they wanted to put the tragedy behind them.

Initially Jock Palfreeman was against my writing this book. Ultimately he agreed to participate in it, and took part in many interviews about his background, his beliefs, his friendships and fears, as well as about the case and life inside the prison. The wider Palfreeman family overcame initial reservations about entering the public sphere and participated in interviews with me.

I am grateful to Jock and to his family and friends around the world who shared their recollections. I am also grateful to the great many Bulgarians who talked to me about what happened and who provided me with documentation, many of whom wished to remain anonymous. Their generosity of spirit and hospitality enriched my experience of this fascinating country.

Among the people who provided me with invaluable background information were Hamza Acaoglu, Malina Alexandrova, Jessica Chassen, Cvetan Cvetkov, Major (Retd) D.J. Cunningham, Professor Ivaylo Ditchev, Bozhidar Dzhambazov, Mila Georgieva, Markus Inama SJ, Dr Krassimir Kanev, Commissar Petur Krustev, Tanya Raynova, Desislava Simeonova, Joeri Buhrer Tavanier and Associate Professor David Wells, as well as journalists Rossen Bossev, Matthew Brunwasser, Alexenia Dimitrova, Atanas Tchobanov and Assen Yordanoff.

I am indebted to Nadejda Collins and Violeta Dimova-Nikols for their help in translating Bulgarian documents and interviews, to Annie Dutton for transcribing my interviews and to Ron Ekkel and Dobrin Kashavelov for photography.

I am also indebted to the encouragement and assistance provided to me by former Executive Producer of *Foreign Correspondent*, Greg Wilesmith, Supervising Producer of *Australian Story*, Rebecca Latham, and Executive Producer of *Australian Story*, Deb Fleming.

A handful of friends tirelessly waded through early drafts and provided feedback, in particular Dominie Banfield and Bronnie Hattam. I am also grateful to Colleen Coghlan, Claire Forster, Charlie Hawkins, Julian Mather, Richard Payne and my astute mother, Jane Hawkins. Ann McGarvie helped me to piece together details from witness statements early in my research.

Richard Walsh has nursed this project along from the first page with patience, grace and skill. It has been a joy working with editors Rebecca Kaiser, Aziza Kuypers, Jo Lyons and Liz Keenan, as well as designer Lisa White.

But my greatest thanks go to Bulgarian journalist Boryana Dzhambazova who worked closely with me on this project for more than two years. Her investigative skills and tenacity, as well as her commitment to accuracy and balance, have been inspirational. Any discrepancies in accuracy or analysis are mine. Often crosschecking with Nadejda Collins, Boryana also translated the many documents, newspaper articles and television interviews that inform this narrative. Where there was not an obvious equivalent for an expression or word in English, we relied on our best judgement. Others may query that. The court transcripts are often so poorly written that it has been difficult for Bulgarian translators to understand them much less to translate them into English.

A project spanning five years was always going to take a toll on my own family. Dear Ian never flinched in paying the bills and acting as a sounding board, always urging me to continue. Angus and Eliza gave me the reason to do so.